HOLMAN
Old Testament Commentary

HOLMAN *Old* Testament Commentary

Judges, Ruth

GENERAL EDITOR

Max Anders

AUTHOR

W. Gary Phillips

HOLMAN
REFERENCE

NASHVILLE, TENNESSEE

Bible versions used in this book:

Unless otherwise stated all Scripture citation is from the HOLY BIBLE, NEW INTERNATIONAL VERSION®. Copyright © 1973, 1978, 1984 by International Bible Society. Used by permission of Zondervan Publishing House. All Rights Reserved. The "NIV" and "New International Version" trademarks are registered in the United States Patent and Trademark Office by International Bible Society. Use of either trademark requires the permission of International Bible Society.

Scripture passages marked NASB are taken from Scripture taken from the *New American Standard Bible*, © Copyright The Lockman Foundation, 1960, 1962, 1963, 1968, 1971, 1972, 1973, 1975, 1977, 1995. Used by permission.

The King James Version

ISBN: 978-0-8054-9465-5

Dewey Decimal Classification: 222.3
Subject Heading: BIBLE. O.T. JUDGES
BIBLE. O.T. RUTH

Judges, Ruth/W. Gary Phillips
      p.   cm. — (Holman Old Testament commentary)
Includes bibliographical references. (p.).
ISBN
  1. Bible. O.T. Judges—Commentaries. 2. Bible O.T. Ruth—Commentaries I. Title. II. Series.

—dc21

Printed in China

8 9 10 11 12 13   19 18 17 16 15

To Betsy.
"Everyone knows that you are
a woman of excellence"
(Ruth 3:11 NASB),
and that I am the most
blessed among men.
May God grant us another
three decades of joy.

Contents

Contents

Editorial Preface

Today's church hungers for Bible teaching, and Bible teachers hunger for resources to guide them in teaching God's Word. The Holman Old Testament Commentary provides the church with the food to feed the spiritually hungry in an easily digestible format. The result: new spiritual vitality that the church can readily use.

Bible teaching should result in new interest in the Scriptures, expanded Bible knowledge, discovery of specific scriptural principles, relevant applications, and exciting living. The unique format of the Holman Old Testament Commentary includes sections to achieve these results for every Old Testament book.

Opening quotations stimulate thinking and lead to an introductory illustration and discussion that draw individuals and study groups into the Word of God. "In a Nutshell" summarizes the content and teaching of the chapter. Verse-by-verse commentary answers the church's questions rather than raising issues scholars usually admit they cannot adequately solve. Bible principles and specific contemporary applications encourage students to move from Bible to contemporary times. A specific modern illustration then ties application vividly to present life. A brief prayer aids the student to commit his or her daily life to the principles and applications found in the Bible chapter being studied. For those still hungry for more, "Deeper Discoveries" takes the student into a more personal, deeper study of the words, phrases, and themes of God's Word. Finally, a teaching outline provides transitional statements and conclusions along with an outline to assist the teacher in group Bible studies.

It is the editors' prayer that this new resource for local church Bible teaching will enrich the ministry of group, as well as individual, Bible study, and that it will lead God's people truly to be people of the Book, living out what God calls us to be.

Acknowledgments

I would like to express deep appreciation for the encouragement of my family: my wife Betsy, my children David, Rebecca, Beth (and now Bill), and my father Bill Phillips. In addition, there are those whose help and prayers followed this book in its journey: my spiritual family at Signal Mountain Bible Church (particularly the elders), my patient co-pastor Tim Schoap, and my friends Dr. Richard Mayhue (who enlisted me to teach a course on Judges and Ruth at The Master's Seminary), Nick Decosimo (who has been willing to read anything I write), and Phil Carter (who has been willing to fix any equipment I break).

Holman Old Testament Commentary Contributors

Vol. 1 Genesis
ISBN 978-0-8054-9461-7
Kenneth O. Gangel and Stephen Bramer

Vol. 2 Exodus, Leviticus, Numbers
ISBN 978-0-8054-9462-4
Glen Martin

Vol. 3 Deuteronomy
ISBN 978-0-8054-9463-1
Doug McIntosh

Vol. 4 Joshua
ISBN 978-0-8054-9464-8
Kenneth O. Gangel

Vol. 5 Judges, Ruth
ISBN 978-0-8054-9465-5
W. Gary Phillips

Vol. 6 1 & 2 Samuel
ISBN 978-0-8054-9466-2
Stephen Andrews

Vol. 7 1 & 2 Kings
ISBN 978-0-8054-9467-9
Gary Inrig

Vol. 8 1 & 2 Chronicles
ISBN 978-0-8054-9468-6
Winfried Corduan

Vol. 9 Ezra, Nehemiah, Esther
ISBN 978-0-8054-9469-3
Knute Larson and Kathy Dahlen

Vol. 10 Job
ISBN 978-0-8054-9470-9
Stephen J. Lawson

Vol. 11 Psalms 1-72
ISBN 978-0-8054-9471-6
Steve J. Lawson

Vol. 12 Psalms 73-150
ISBN 978-0-8054-9481-5
Steve J. Lawson

Vol. 13 Proverbs
ISBN 978-0-8054-9472-3
Max Anders

Vol. 14 Ecclesiastes, Song of Songs
ISBN 978-0-8054-9482-2
David George Moore and Daniel L. Akin

Vol. 15 Isaiah
ISBN 978-0-8054-9473-0
Trent C. Butler

Vol. 16 Jeremiah, Lamentations
ISBN 978-0-8054-9474-7
Fred C. Wood and Ross McLaren

Vol. 17 Ezekiel
ISBN 978-0-8054-9475-4
Mark F. Rooker

Vol. 18 Daniel
ISBN 978-0-8054-9476-1
Kenneth O. Gangel

Vol. 19 Hosea, Joel, Amos, Obadiah, Jonah, Micah
ISBN 978-0-8054-9477-8
Trent C. Butler

Vol. 20 Nahum, Habakkuk, Zephaniah, Haggai, Zechariah, Malachi
ISBN 978-0-8054-9478-5
Stephen R. Miller

Holman New Testament Commentary Contributors

Holman Old Testament Commentary

Twenty volumes designed for Bible study and teaching to enrich the local church and God's people.

Series Editor	Max Anders
Managing Editor	Steve Bond
Project Editor	Dean Richardson
Product Development Manager	Ricky D. King
Marketing Manager	Stephanie Huffman
Executive Editor	David Shepherd
Page Composition	TF Designs, Greenbrier, TN

Introduction to

Judges and Ruth

This week I went to see two of my heroes. Both of them are dying and both are trusting Christ. One was my wrestling coach at an all-boys military high school, Major Luke Worsham. Under his tutelage, "the Maj" helped many boys to learn the values of hard work, fairness, duty, and integrity (and picked up a few national championships along the way). He taught us that you do your best and leave it there. Next time, win or lose, you do your best again. Life is an adventure; you don't dwell on yesterday, but you enjoy today and you prepare for tomorrow. He marked my life.

The second man was a police captain from New Jersey who retired to the Southeast as a relatively young man, began some businesses in the area, and used his influence in the community for Christ. "Cap" Miller headed the evangelism program at our church and always had a cheerful word of encouragement for everyone. Visiting his home one morning, I noticed that the garbage collectors had stopped and parked at his driveway. When I asked about it, his wife laughed and said that every week they stopped there and waited because Cap served them hot coffee in the winter and sodas in the summer. Then they visited for a few moments as he usually shared a word about Christ with these men who admired him.

Heroes who model truth deeply impact those who admire them. Believers know the value of biblical heroes whom we can periodically revisit within the pages of Scripture. However, simply because a person's story is recorded in Scripture does not mean he is worthy of emulation. It doesn't take long in Judges and Ruth to realize that these are not stories about human heroes. They are about God, the ultimate hero. They are about God's patience, God's persistence, God's pity, and God's provision for God's people.

INTRODUCTION TO THE BOOKS OF JUDGES AND RUTH

The bad news is this: the Book of Judges is a very modern book. Here's the good news: the Book of Ruth is also a very modern book. Both took place during a spiritually schizophrenic period—between Israel's conquest of Canaan under Joshua and the united kingdom beginning with King Saul.

Like a tired television rerun, the Book of Judges exposes the monotonous downward spiral of a culture that had turned its back on God. It unveils cycles of increasing depravity in which the sins of the culture became the sins of God's people—a period that anticipates today's relative ethics (Judg. 17:6; 21:25). Civilizations have been compared to revolving doors rotating on the axis of depravity. Historian James Hitchcock argued this premise from a comparative study of civilizations: cultures follow a predictable "sociology" of moral decline.

First, unthinkable thoughts are expressed (the rationale: "We must hear all points of view"). Second, "respected people" take such ideas seriously (the rationale: "We must not be so rigid"). Third, "respected people" publicly accept the new ideas as viable (the rationale: "*They* have a right to do whatever *they* want"). Finally, "respected people" publicly acknowledge they adopt the ideas as their own (the rationale: "*We* have a right to do whatever *we* want, and *you* must not be so intolerant").

Thus, within an amazingly brief period, the unthinkable becomes the new orthodoxy, and those who disagree are rigid, eccentric, and perhaps even dangerous to society. George Santayana was correct: "Those who will not learn the lessons of history are doomed to repeat its mistakes." Since we are often slow learners, it is not surprising that the average age of the world's greatest civilizations is about two hundred years.

However, while a study of Judges and its neighbor Ruth certainly reveals sins to shun, there are also examples to emulate. There are moments of weakness, but there are also moments of greatness. God has given his people a narration from which we may learn, by means of stories, the ways in which God has remained faithful to his covenant promises and his covenant people as well as the ways in which he has worked in individual lives. One very comforting point rings with clarity: "If we are faithless, he will remain faithful, for he cannot disown himself" (2 Tim. 2:13).

BACKGROUND TO THE BOOKS OF JUDGES AND RUTH

But first, we must be aware that we are entering a story that is already in progress. Anyone who has listened to a serial television or radio show is familiar with the phrase, "in our last episode," which draws the audience back to the context of the story. When we open the pages of Judges, we are immediately confronted with the idea, "in our last episode," or (in this case) "after the death of Joshua" (Judg. 1:1). Ruth likewise reminds us of its historical context: "in the days when the judges ruled" (Ruth 1:1). A brief review of this period of Bible history is in order.

1. Exiting Joshua: "The Way We Were." The Book of Joshua narrates a period of conquest and triumph. At the end of his life, Joshua issued a call to all of God's leaders and all of God's people (Josh. 22–24); he concluded by drawing a spiritual line in the sand with this challenge: "Choose for yourselves this day whom you will serve. . . . But as for me and my household, we will serve the LORD" (Josh. 24:15). They were not to let any*one* or any*thing* displace God as the object of their commitment, devotion, loyalty, or love.

2. Pausing on the Threshold: Looking Forward, Looking Backward. The books of Joshua and Judges invite comparison because they both deal with leadership, corporate identity, and collective obedience and disobedience. Ruth focuses more on individual obedience, loyalty, and servanthood.

When Moses died, Joshua was hand-picked to take over; when Joshua died, he had no "right-hand man," no single prominent successor. Instead, several different individuals—both men and women—emerged as deliverers. Joshua consistently spoke with the moral authority of God; few of the judges were consistently people of high moral integrity. In Joshua Israel was unified in conquest; in Judges Israel was fragmented. In Joshua the people were mostly obedient. In Judges the people chased repeatedly after the gods of the Canaanites. In Joshua there was a clear objective morality in place by which sin was judged. In Judges there was a subjective morality that tolerated sin. In Joshua there was clear commitment to the Lord by God's leaders who challenged Israel to serve God (Josh. 24:15). In Judges even God's leaders at times compromised, and—no surprise—God's people were characterized by moral relativism (Judg. 17:6; 21:25).

Yet within and among these contrasts, the Book of Ruth suggests not only that God has not abandoned his people, but also that there is a remnant of his people who have not abandoned their God. It is possible for godly people to live godly lives in godless times. Consider the following contrasts:

Joshua	Judges	Ruth
Single leader	Many leaders	Family headship
Moral authority	Military authority	Divine authority
Unity	Division	Oneness
Moving outward	Moving downward	Moving upward
Wars	Warriors	Peace
Serve God (24:31)	Serve self (21:25)	Serve others (1:16–17)
Objective morality	Subjective morality	Effective morality
Conquest	Calamity	Calm
Land	Lust	Love
Colonists	Renters	Refugees
Sin regulated	Sin tolerated	Grace illustrated

3. Entering Judges and Ruth: Not Exactly "The Good Old Days." If Christian filmmakers ever produced "The Judges Film," it would be rated "R" (or possibly "NC-17"). The book is definitely "for mature audiences"—although one would be hard-pressed to call it entertainment. Here is a partial list of sins from the catalog of Judges: idolatry, murder, sexual perversion, conspiracy, prostitution, infidelity, gang rape, and kidnapping. And yet, within this period, there are encouraging vignettes of victory, both in Judges and in Ruth.

If the story of Ruth were made into a movie, it would be rated "G" and would serve as a template for family values. It begins with disobedience and tragedy but quickly moves to portray the positive virtues of loyalty, servanthood, self-sacrifice, encouragement, generosity, romantic love, and deep faith in the God of the covenant. Ruth herself has been compared to an exquisite gem set against the dark background of the period of the judges, all the more lustrous because of the contrast between her faithful service to God and her family at a time when "everyone did as he saw fit" (Judg. 21:25). Given the period in which she lived, another comparison may be that the story of Ruth is like the spiritual calm in the midst of the whirling winds of a moral tornado. In Judges we find *extraordinary* people who live *sub-ordinary* lives; in Ruth we find *ordinary* people who live *extraordinary* lives.

AUTHORSHIP AND DATE

Who wrote these books, and when were they written? Both books are anonymous, although external tradition (the Jewish Talmud) says that both were written by Samuel. There is some internal support for this view. First, the perspective from which the author wrote was during the united kingdom, the time when Samuel lived. Note the repeated phrase "in those days [in contrast to *these* days] Israel had no king" (Judg. 17:6; 18:1; 19:1; 21:25). The phrase also suggests the period before the division of the kingdom after Solomon, because then it would read "kings," not "king."

A second internal peg that helps narrow the time of writing is found in the reference to the Jebusites as present "to this day" (Judg. 1:21). David dispossessed the Jebusites in 1004 B.C. (2 Sam. 5:6–7), which means the books were written before this time. Third, the ark of the covenant was removed from Shiloh in Samuel's day (1 Sam. 4:3–11) but was still there during the time of the judges (Judg. 18:31). All of this points to a writer from the time after Saul's coronation as king (1043 B.C.) but before David's capture of Jerusalem (1004 B.C.); this fits well with the tradition that Samuel was the author. The Talmud says, "Samuel wrote the book which bears his name and the book [singular!] of Judges and Ruth" (*Baba Bathra*, 14b). Eugene Merrill comments, "While this tradition cannot be validated, there is nothing inherently improbable about it" (*Bibliotheca Sacra*, April–June, 1985, 139n).

At this point we should note that neither of these books provides a polemic for kingship. First, there were extended periods of peace and prosperity which were unrelated to the absence of a king. Second, the only attempt at kingship during the period (Abimelech, Judg. 9) was a disaster.

As far as the chronological bookends are concerned—that is, the time of the "events" that the books record—we may deduce the end of the period by adding backwards from the division of the kingdom about 931 B.C. through the reigns of Solomon, David, Saul, and the judgeship of Eli (which we believe took place *after* the Samson cycle), a total of about 150 years to about

1043 B.C. (see 1 Sam. 4:18; 13:1; 1 Kgs. 2:11; 11:42). Figuring from the other direction, our beginning point would move forward from the time of the exodus (about 1446 B.C., accounting for the years of Solomon's reign mentioned in 1 Kings 6:1, for the wilderness wanderings, and the death of Joshua at the age of 110 some 72 years after the exodus), and including the generations listed in Judges 2:7–10, we arrive at approximately 1300 B.C. (see also Deut. 29:5; Josh. 14:7,10; 24:29). If these calculations are accurate, then from 1300 to 1043 B.C. there are 257 years for the events of the Book of Judges.

However, if we were to add up the years given in Judges, we arrive at a total of 407 years. So how do these two pieces of information fit together? The answer is that some judgeships were *consecutive* ("after," as in Judg. 12:8,11,13), while others were *concurrent*. There was no central government, and some of the stories (e.g., Ehud and Gideon) were local, not national.

Within this time frame, "in the days when the judges ruled" (Ruth 1:1), the events of the Book of Ruth took place. Since she was the great-grandmother of David (Ruth 4:17), the time of Ruth may well have been during the late twelfth century B.C., the period approximately corresponding to the days of Gideon.

OVERVIEW OF JUDGES

Judges 1:1–3:6: Corrosion (politically, 1:1–36; spiritually, 2:1–3:6)

- Like stadium floodlights (deals with the nation)
- Like a virus (you are host to something external to you)
- Like a documentary film, rated PG (for realistic situations)

Judges 3:7–16:31: Cycles (twelve judges)

- Like spotlights (deals with tribal leaders)
- Like malaria (you contend with a recurring disease)
- Like a *film noir,* rated from PG-13 to R (for sexuality and violence)

Judges 17:1–21:25: Collapse (idolatry, 17:1–18:31; civil war, 19:1–21:25)

- Like laser beam (deals with individuals)
- Like cancer (the disease cannibalizes you; the only cure is to destroy a part of you)

- Like a horror or slasher movie, rated NC-17 (for sexual violence and extreme gore)

OVERVIEW OF RUTH

Ruth 1: Ruth's Decision ("'Til Death Do Us Part")

- Loss of Family (1:1–5)
- Loss of Friend (1:6–18)
- Loss of Face (1:19–22)

Ruth 2: Ruth's Devotion ("Boy Meets Girl")

- Boy Sees Girl (2:1–7)
- Boy Meets Girl (2:8–13)
- Boy Feeds Girl (2:14–17)
- Girl Reports to "Mother" (2:18–23)

Ruth 3: Ruth's Redeemer ("Some Enchanted Evening")

- Naomi Plots: The Mate (3:1–5)
- Ruth Proposes: The Date (3:6–10)
- Boaz Promises: The Wait (3:11–18)

Ruth 4: Ruth's Reward ("Happily [For]Ever After")

- Litigation (4:1–6)
- Negotiation (4:7–12)
- Generations (4:13–22)

DIGGING DEEPER

When entering the period of the judges, five issues merit attention. The first three aid in the exposition of the book (the meaning of "judges," the gods of the Canaanites, and the Bethlehem trilogy). The last two, for those who wish to dig deeper still, are more apologetic in nature (the coherence of Judges, Ruth and ethical issues arising from the Book of Judges).

1. Who Were the "Judges"? There were twelve judges, six major and six minor. One interpreter described them as "charismatic military leaders whom God raised up and empowered for specific tasks of deliverance." While it is true that they were more likely to wear body armor than flowing black robes, it is not always certain that they were "charismatic," nor is it certain that all were involved in military campaigns. What is certain is that they were *not* what one ordinarily associates with the term *judge*.

The Hebrew term for "judge" is the word *shophet*, which had a certain elasticity of meaning. It could refer to civil decision makers, governors, or military deliverers (see Judg. 2:18–19). Within the Book of Judges, careful study yields the following observations.

First, some judges faced and were delivered from local problems while others apparently faced national crises. Second, none of the judges established a royal hereditary dynasty (the tragic story of Gideon's son Abimelech is a case in point). Third, the fact that some judges are mentioned only in passing (Shamgar has only one verse!) indicates that the list of judges included in the book is complete. Fourth, there was a downward spiral among the judges themselves. The story line moves from noble judges (Othniel, Ehud, Deborah, Barak) to a hesitant judge with a questionable legacy (Gideon) to a gangster judge (Jephthah) to a blatantly immoral judge (Samson). Such a downward progression even among God's deliverers prepares us for the dismal conditions reported in Judges 17–21.

2. The Gods of the Canaanites. God prohibited the Canaanites from staying in the promised land and practicing their religion. They could leave voluntarily, or they would be killed; the choice was eviction or execution (see issue 4, "The Coherence of Judges, Ruth"). At other times and other places, God put no such wholesale edict against an entire culture. What was so repulsive about the Canaanites that God insisted they be removed from the land?

The answer to this question is the Canaanite religious system. Their most popular god was Baal, the god of rain and thunder and a son of the god El. The term *Baal* is general ("master, owner, lord") and is used seventy-one times in the Old Testament (fifty-three singular, eighteen plural). Baal was thought to control reproduction—of the earth, of livestock, and of humans! Second, the female deities Asherah and Ashtoreth appeared at one time or another as the female consort of Baal; apparently the Canaanites made little distinction between these goddesses (see Judg. 6:25).

Besides Baal and his consort, the Canaanites also worshiped other "minor" gods. (There were also various localized forms of Baal worship, such as Baal of Peor in Num. 25:3, Baal Gad in Josh. 11:17, Baal-Berith in Judg. 9:4, and Baal-Zebub in 2 Kgs. 1:2.)

The form Baal worship took is called "sympathetic ritual." Worshipers attempted to coax Baal and his consort into copulation (the result of which was rain and the fertility of both the land and the livestock) by showing them how it was to be done. Religious orgies, probably with temple prostitutes, were common. The "sympathetic rituals" usually took place in elevated areas close to the clouds, where Baal could hear and see what the humans were doing (see various references to "the high places," e.g., 1 Kgs. 13:33; 14:23).

This was the essence of man-made religion and the opposite of God's plan: to have his creatures replicate his character and moral attributes. God desires that his will be done on earth as it is in heaven, not the reverse (Matt. 6:10; see comments at Judg. 2:11–13). Sadly, when people turned away from God, it did not take long for the veneer of civilization to wear thin.

3. Bethlehem: A City of Two Tales. The little town of Bethlehem becomes prominent at the end of the Book of Judges, mentioned six times within chapters 17–21 (17:7,8,9; 19:1,2,18 (twice). The final two stories in Judges take place in or near Bethlehem, the center stage for sin. If this were all we knew about Bethlehem, we would place it in the same moral category as we do Sodom and Gomorrah. But God grants one more "Bethlehem story" to show that there is redemption and grace in an unlikely place.

Because the Book of Ruth may have been originally attached to Judges, the three stories together are called by some scholars "the Bethlehem Trilogy" (additional references to Bethlehem are found in Ruth 1:1,19 [twice],22; 2:4; 4:11). The Septuagint (LXX) placed Ruth after Judges, which our English Bible follows. Josephus agreed, as did Origen and Jerome. The Talmud referred to the two books as one book. The earliest extant Hebrew Bible has a different arrangement, however, placing Ruth after Proverbs (some suggest because Ruth and Naomi were exemplars of Prov. 31). Yet another arrangement, favored by Block, places Ruth just before the Book of Psalms.

While there is no absolute certainty of its original place in the Hebrew canon, there are literary reasons for endorsing the view of the Septuagint— these books are entwined as literary antonyms (in this case, opposites that attract!). Although the final illustrations of depravity in Judges are centered in Bethlehem, so is the final deliverance. In Judges God forgives and delivers constantly and consistently. In Ruth Boaz pays debts, gives peace, fulfillment, promise of a future, and a home. From Bethlehem arises the kinsman-redeemer, as God's loyal love embraces both Jew (Naomi) and Gentile (Ruth).

Bethlehem is also "the City of David," whose name is the last word that ends the Book of Ruth (Ruth 4:22). When David's final "son" comes, the Lord Jesus Christ, because of his work on the cross we who know him may live happily eternally after (see further under issue 4, "The Coherence of Judges, Ruth"). Whether Ruth was to be placed after Judges in canonical order, the text places itself there both chronologically (Ruth 1:1) and thematically.

4. The Coherence of Judges, Ruth. A good friend who had been reading through Judges asked me, "How do you make sense of the entire book? It seems chopped up, as though the last section was just tacked on for no good reason." This man is a perceptive reader (actually, he is a judge reading Judges!) who believes in the truth of Scripture and has a deep desire to understand how the book fits together. The purpose of this section is to probe the coherence of these sections at the meta-narrative level. Does the structure of Judges reflect a plan, and does Ruth (which we have suggested is connected to Judges) relate at all to this plan? We will examine the coherence of Judges and Ruth in stages.

The coherence of Judges 1–16. The first segment of Judges (1:1–3:6) introduces the historical setting of the book, introduces the judges (in a symmetry of six major and six minor judges), and in the first of the judges reveals the paradigm to which the major cycles will conform (3:7–11, rebellion, retribution, repentance, restoration, and rest). The theme of decline is introduced; there is decline at the tribal level (1:27–36, moving from having the Canaanites living among the Israelites to the Israelites living among the Canaanites) and at the generational level (2:7–11, apostasy by the third generation). This decline is mirrored at the larger level through the decline with the cycles themselves; they gradually regress both in scope (from the national to the individual level), in ethics (from admirable to questionable to immoral), and in structure (in the last cycles the paradigm of 3:7–11 breaks down). Such clear regression through the cycles toward a gradual crescendo of disobedience and fragmentation demonstrates literary unity and consistent intention through these chapters.

The coherence of Judges 17–21. Common themes from Judges 17–18 and Judges 19–21 make it almost certain that these stories were crafted with a view to their relationship to each other. The first episode deals with spiritual decay, whereas the second deals with the resulting moral decay. Both episodes deal with homelessness of individuals and tribes; both mention a fighting force of specifically six hundred men (18:11,16–17; 20:47); both specifically include Mount Ephraim in the story (17:1; 19:1); both center in Bethlehem (see issue 3, "Bethlehem: A City of Two Tales"); both mention Shiloh in their concluding sections (18:31; 21:19–24); and both may be viewed as case studies in the explicitly stated operating principle of moral relativism, "everyone did as he saw fit" (a statement included in both segments, 17:6; 21:25). It is as though, prior to the story of Ruth, the author was saying, "This is just how bad things could get!"

The coherence of Judges 1–21. Does the entire book hang together? Briefly, the last degenerate judge was Samson, who was from the tribe of Dan. Tribal identity provides the perfect transition into the first of the two Bethlehem stories, which deals with the degeneration of the tribe of Dan. A further display of coherence is found in thematic bookends (the literary term is *inclusio*). That is, the book introduces, prior to the cycles, a statement that there was a three-generation pattern of moral and spiritual degeneration (2:7–11); the book concludes, after the cycles, with two stories, each of which includes grandsons—of Moses (18:30) and Aaron (20:28).

The coherence of Judges and Ruth together. Does Ruth fit with this plan, or is it entirely unrelated to the Book of Judges? The last two stories in Judges are thematically tied to Ruth, both positively (through common themes) and negatively (through contrasts). All three segments (Judges 17–18; 19–21; Ruth 1–4) offer stories of common people and "grass roots" faithfulness—or lack thereof. All three contain a "surprise" visit from someone well-known (in 17–18, the grandson of Moses; in 19–21, the grandson of Aaron; and Ruth is herself the great-grandmother of David). All three are "Bethlehem" stories (see issue 3, "Bethlehem: A City of Two Tales"), and thus provide representative cases from the geographic center of Israel.

The Book of Ruth complements Judges at the meta-narrative level, forming one story—with a different ending! Rather than end with despair due to man's depravity, there is deliverance due to God's grace. Bethlehem is redeemed, manhood and womanhood are redeemed, the family is redeemed, the tribe and the culture are redeemed.

Further, in Judges 19–21 almost everyone is anonymous: as Black suggests, the woman could be every woman, and every woman could commit adultery, every host could commit atrocities against women, every husband could abandon his wife, every man could be callous toward women, every woman was a potential victim of rape and murder, every town was a potential hell-hole, every tribe was a potential gang! But as Ruth begins, anonymity ceases; almost everyone is named, as people have identity and significance. Women who were horribly abused (e.g., the pornographic "snuff film" of Judg. 19–21) are here given hope because after Judges, two vulnerable women are treated with respect, as subjects not as objects—and in Bethlehem! Even the land (which had been in famine) now "obeys"—its produce provides the context for Ruth's redemptive story.

Indeed, the tale that began by reaching back into the Book of Judges for both its context (Ruth 1:1) and its setting in a time of famine (Ruth 1:1,6), ends looking forward within a context of physical, moral, and spiritual prosperity.

Consider one more important aspect of coherence and contrast within these three segments: the Ten Commandments. Every single commandment of the Decalogue is violated in Judges 17–21. The writer of Judges offers a catalogue of depth of depravity. Consider each of the commandments:

- Commandment #1: the priority of God (violated throughout chs. 17–18; 19–21)
- Commandment #2: no idols or images (violated 17:3–4)
- Commandment #3: no taking of God's name in vain (violated 17:2; 18:6)
- Commandment #4: Sabbath worship God's way (violated 17:5)
- Commandment #5: honor parents (violated 17:2)
- Commandment #6: no murder (violated 18:25,27; 19:26–30; 21:10-11)
- Commandment #7: no adultery (violated 19:2,25)
- Commandment #8: no stealing (violated 17:2,4; 18:14–20; 21:20-23)
- Commandment #9: no lying (violated 17:3–4; 18:6)
- Commandment #10: no coveting (violated 17:2; 18:9–10,14).

The point is that Israel has violated her national constitution, and that she is clearly under the justifiable wrath of her covenant Lord. Further, the grandson of the lawgiver is guilty of leading a tribe into false worship!

By contrast, Ruth is a picture of covenant faithfulness, and even aliens who enter the covenant by faith (as did Ruth) partake of "rest." Also by contrast, the great-grandson of Ruth will become the one who will lead Israel into true worship (2 Sam. 7; Ruth 4). The Book of Ruth contains no violations of any covenant stipulations (even the nearer kinsman who is an obstacle is not presented as a bad man). Even so, Ruth is a tract not of law but of grace, of God's kindness. It is difficult to maintain that these brush strokes that paint Ruth as the literary antonym of Judges are merely coincidental; rather, they suggest the master's hand.

5. Ethical Questions in Judges. God is good, but there are some divinely sanctioned practices, especially in Judges, that invite further reflection lest doubts be raised about God's goodness. It's not hard to read through Judges and have nagging questions emerge: Did God's judge really do *this*? Did God really command *that*?

We do a sort of ethical "double take" when we look, for example, at the command to exterminate the Canaanites (chs. 1–2), the assassination of Eglon by Ehud (3:12–30), the deception and murder of Sisera by Jael (chs. 4–5), the "execution" of Jephthah's daughter (ch. 11), and the provocation of the Philistines by Samson's chronic vandalism and vendettas (chs. 13–16; Samson was *not* a good neighbor!).

How are we to think about these things? First, simply because behavior is reported does not mean it is required or sanctioned; that is, there is a difference in Scripture between what is *described* and what is *prescribed*. Second, the fact that the Spirit of God came upon these judges does not mean that everything the judge did was done in the right way (e.g., consider the strange behavior of Gideon, Jephthah, and Samson). Each episode and each issue must be examined individually.

When considering the specific problem of Canaanite extermination, there are three patterns of truth emerging from the larger context of Scripture that help put this particular issue into perspective: the principle of "solidarity," the justice of God, and the patience of God.

The principle of "solidarity" (oneness with a group). Often in God's dealings with man, both judgment and blessing fall upon all in the group, regardless of the merit (or demerit) of all the individuals who comprise the group, because of the merit or demerit of the one. Theologically, in Adam all of humanity sinned, and therefore we bear the consequences for something we didn't directly do (but would have done, given the chance; see Rom. 5:12–21). During the flood, every man, woman, and child (with eight exceptions) were exterminated. I am sure that in the days of Noah there were some individuals who were more guilty and others who were less guilty. During the conquest of the city of Ai, God permitted many of his people to die. He explained the reason: "Israel has sinned" (Josh. 7:11), but eventually Achan confessed, "I have sinned" (7:20).

Positively, the principle of solidarity is to our eternal benefit because in Christ (the "last Adam") we have our redemption, something that we did not and could not achieve individually (Rom. 5:12–21; 1 Cor. 15:45; 2 Cor. 5:21). Of course the question remains, What about the people who were either blameless (or at least less blameworthy) and received collective judgment, or else were guilty and received collective mercy? What about those rare Canaanites who were less guilty of the moral excesses of their group? We believe that God sorts out these issues in his final judgment, which is very individual indeed!

The principle of divine justice. Genesis 18:25 poses a fundamental question that presumes an affirmative response, "Will not the Judge of all the earth do right?" Because of God's omniscience, God knew what *would* happen if the Canaanites were permitted to stay and cohabit with his people. As it turned out, the very worst did take place, and Israel's downward plunge was severe indeed. Had Israel obeyed God's word, the nation would have avoided centuries of judgment and pain; in fact, one could argue that there would have been no attempted genocide in the days of Queen Esther because Haman the Agagite (very likely a descendant of the Amalekites) would never have been born. Faith in God's justice tempers our limited understanding of God's judgment.

The principle of divine patience. Genesis 15:16 states, "For the sin of the Amorites has not yet reached its full measure." God started a slow four-hundred-year countdown for the Amorites (a term sometimes used interchangeably with "Canaanites") either to repent or to remove themselves from the promised land. They knew that the Israelites claimed the land and planned to return to what God had given them. While Israel was in Egypt for over four hundred years of bondage, God's long fuse continued to burn. In fact, there was a forty-year extension added while Israel wandered in the wilderness. The Canaanites knew about God's power and knew what had happened in Egypt. They had multiple opportunities to leave the land.

Further, the sins of the Canaanites were great (see issue 2, "The Gods of the Canaanites"); the Lord said that the land was going to vomit them out (Lev. 18:21–27), a vivid image of heaving under the load of internal poisons. But rather than leave, the Amalekites sent raiding parties to pick off the weak, sick, and elderly at the end of Israel's line of march and to brutally murder all stragglers (Deut. 25:17–18).

In sum, God gave them hundreds of years to change and then gave a forty-year extension (and some, like Rahab, did change; she knew all about the Israelites and trusted the Lord). Then God commanded the Israelites to drive out the Canaanites; displacement trumped extermination. Only if they refused to leave were there to be wars of extermination. Consider this fact: Every other war the Israelites fought was defensive; this was their only offensive war in Scripture.

One final perspective is important. As believers the issue of faith is always before us. We don't know what would have happened in other circumstances, but God does. We don't know the motives of others, but God does. We don't know how others will be judged at the final judgment, but God does. So in light of *our* ignorance, and *his* knowledge, it is both logical and comforting to trust him with our uncertainties.

Judges 1

❧❧❧

The Folly of Editing God

> "*All* that is necessary for the triumph of evil is for
>
> good men to do nothing."
>
> E d m u n d   B u r k e

GEOGRAPHICAL PROFILE: JERUSALEM

- Inhabited by the Jebusites
- Elevation: 2,500 feet (the phrase "go up to Jerusalem" is used 27 times in the Bible)
- Name means "foundation of peace"
- Mentioned more often than any other city in Scripture (752 times)
- Often called "Zion" (162 times; possibly means "stronghold")
- The most significant city in the world, both literally and symbolically (Ps. 87:2–5).
- Neither Judah nor Benjamin was able to take and hold the city during the period of the judges
- From the time of David on, God's "dwelling" (1 Kgs. 8:13)
- Site of Messiah's resurrection, ascension, and second coming (Luke 24; Zech. 14:5)
- Final dwelling place of God's people will be the New Jerusalem (Rev. 21:9–10)

GEOGRAPHICAL PROFILE: HEBRON

- In the past, the home of Abraham (Gen. 13:18)
- About 19 miles south by southwest of Jerusalem
- Name means "confederacy"
- Elevation: 3,040 feet
- Mentioned 67 times in Scripture

- Originally named Kiriath Arba or city of Arba, which may refer to "four" (an ancient confederation of four towns or rulers?) or to an individual named Arba (Josh. 14:15)
- During the period prior to the judges, the home of the fierce Anakim, who frightened all the spies except Joshua and Caleb (Num. 13:22–33)
- In the near future, the centerpiece of Caleb's holdings (Josh. 14:13–14; Judg. 1:10)
- Served as a city of refuge owned by the Levites (Josh. 20:7; 21:11), surrounded and presumably protected by Caleb (Josh. 21:12), who owned all the surrounding towns, fields, suburbs.
- Became the city from which David ruled (2 Sam. 5:5) during the first seven years of his reign

GEOGRAPHICAL PROFILE: BETHEL

- Name means "house of God" (by Jacob, Gen. 28:19; see 12:8)
- Mentioned 64 times in Scripture
- About 12 miles north of Jerusalem
- Situated on a key east-west trade route; strategically important
- Included within Ephraim's territory (Judg. 1:22)
- Called Luz by the Canaanites (Josh. 18:13; Judg. 1:23)
- During the divided kingdom (after 931 B.C.) became prominent as a spiritual center for the Northern Kingdom (1 Kgs. 12:26–33)

I N   A   N U T S H E L L

The Israelites made a wonderful beginning (seeking God's guidance, vv. 1–2) but soon lapsed into disobedience. The first part of the chapter chronicles the adventures and failures of Judah (vv. 3–20), punctuated with the courage of Caleb (vv. 11–15,20). Almost in a verse-by-verse march through the chapter, excuses increase as disobedience increases. The final segment of the chapter plunges us into a downward tribe-by-tribe spiral of defeat (vv. 27–36).

The Folly of Editing God

I. INTRODUCTION

A Walk with No Cause for Pause

*W*hen we begin the Book of Judges, the first chapter can make us wonder if there is anything here worth pondering. It seems little more than a stark retelling of "just the facts," with nothing of human interest or military excitement to raise our interest. However, when we dig deeply into the chapter, we face the fact that facts are not "just facts." The statement "Jamestown was the first British settlement in North America, founded in May of 1607" is factually true. Yet it is almost misleading because of its brevity. Behind that statement there is an immense history of aspirations, faith, dreams, obstacles, death, and devastation.

In a sense, storytelling is the art of knowing what to exclude. A carefully framed story, however, can reveal by its context and repeated themes a much more powerful portrait than the brevity of the canvas on which those words are drawn. Likewise, digging into Judges 1 exposes us to the greater picture of what God was doing for his people. How do we translate their lessons (good and bad) to apply to us?

In most major airports there are long stretches of automated walkway that enable travelers to get from one terminal to the next either with more speed (as they walk "double-time") or more comfort (as they rest while being mobilized). Imagine that you are walking the wrong way on an automated walkway. Its movement is slow enough that you can make progress in the direction you are headed. But if you stop, you don't progress, nor do you stand still; you regress. In some ways the Christian life is like that—it is often described as a "walk" in Scripture. It's not a climb up a hill, not a coast down a hill, but simply an ongoing walk. The bad news is that "the world, the flesh, and the devil" are all flowing against you, and there are times when you are tempted—not to turn away from your Lord—but to take a break and put your spiritual disciplines on pause.

Pretend you have a remote control device that governs your spiritual development. Like most remotes, this device has a pause button. What would happen if you said, "God, I want to take a break from you! I am planning a vacation from virtue, and I want to yield to my temptations. But don't worry, God—it will be just for a week, or at the most a couple of months. I'll catch up later"? But we cannot put God on pause. Further, we cannot fast forward to try to catch up for lost ground.

In Judges 1, God's people promised to walk with God, but instead they tried to ignore him, to put him on pause, and they regressed. There is no such thing as taking a vacation from our walk with God. The good news is this: "The one who is in you is greater than the one who is in the world" (1 John 4:4).

II. COMMENTARY

The Folly of Editing God

> **MAIN IDEA:** *After Joshua's death God's people had a task to complete: finish the occupation of the land God had given them by means of God's guidance and God's power. Although they began well, the Israelites gradually moved from obedience to disobedience, "editing" God's command. Beginning with Judah, the narrative moves geographically from south to north and provides a litany of the successes and failures of each of the tribes.*

Judges 1:1–3:6 comprise a unit. Chapter 1 chronicles the facts like a newspaper article. Chapters 2:1–3:6 are God's editorial page, offering the theological interpretation of those facts. Indeed, Judges 2:1–3:6 record the spiritual "cause" behind the "effect" both of the incomplete military conquest and the subsequent dark ages of the judges.

Total Obedience: Straight and Narrow (1:1–2)

> **SUPPORTING IDEA:** *In a vacuum of leadership, the Israelites acknowledged that God was their leader and sought his guidance. God not only guided but also promised his enabling power for their task.*

1:1. *Guidance Requested.* If the brevity and detail of chapter 1 are more like a newspaper narration, the first half of verse 1 (after Joshua's death) is the newspaper obituary, which will be expanded in 2:6–10. Unlike Moses, Joshua had no successor, or "right-hand man," who would assume leadership. Joshua had apportioned the conquered land among the tribes and had overseen the negotiations and agreements over boundaries (Josh. 13–19).

The **Israelites** began well. Joshua's last exhortation to them was to obey God's word and serve him (Josh. 24). Now with a unified voice they came to **the LORD** for guidance. They **asked** (probably of the priest who used the Urim and Thummim; see "Deeper Discoveries") which tribe should take the lead and **be the first to go up and fight** against **the Canaanites**. It is both tragic and ironic that the book that began with unity (1:1) ended with civil war (chs. 19–21).

1:2. *Guidance Received.* **Judah** was chosen by God to begin what should have been the end of the military operations, and half of the chapter is devoted to Judah's military exploits (vv. 2–20). Long before, Judah had been prophesied to lead the nation (Gen. 49:10) and had taken the "point" position as the nation marched in the wilderness (Num. 2:9). Judah again would take the lead later in Judges (Othniel in 3:7–11; see also 20:18).

Not only did God answer, but the response contained an affirmation that God had already **given** (not "will give") Judah the victory. There could be no more promising beginning to this book and to this era. The expectation of continued victory heightened the contrast when the dream degenerated into a nightmare.

B Partial Obedience: Curve in the Road (1:3–15)

SUPPORTING IDEA: *In the midst of victory (vv. 4–5,8–10), the spiritual resolve of Judah was twice compromised. First, despite God's assurance of solitary victory, Judah made a coalition with the Simeonites (v. 3). Second, Judah dealt with Adoni-Bezek contrary to God's explicit command (vv. 5–7).*

1:3. *Making a Merger.* **The men of Judah** accepted the honor and the responsibility. However, they invited **the Simeonites their brothers** to go with them for reciprocal help. There was a sort of logic to this agreement: first, Judah and Simeon were closer than other tribes, being full brothers of the same mother (they were two of six brothers, all sons of Leah; Gen. 29:33,35). Second, the inheritance of Simeon was embedded within the boundaries of Judah (Josh. 19:1,9). Third, the small number of fighting men from Simeon (less than half the rest, Num. 26:14) would make solitary conquest by Simeon unappealing, whereas joining forces would seem mutually beneficial.

However, one might argue that Judah was guilty of "editing God" here. God did *not* say "Judah *and Simeon* shall go up." One may only speculate that this arrangement could have aborted God's plans for raising the profile of Simeon through miraculous victory when its time came (as with Gideon in 7:2,7). It is one thing to *use* human resources, but quite another thing to *rely* on them (an attitude which we may infer from the context). The very reason for Simeon's smallness was the result of the same kind of sin (religious and moral compromise with the gods of other cultures) that Joshua had warned against (Num. 25:1–14). Later, Simeon virtually ceased to exist as a distinguishable tribe (note its absence even from the tribal list in Judg. 5). God receives the most glory when the victories he provides are unexplainable in human terms but point beyond human abilities to God.

1:4. *Conquest of the Canaanites, I.* This first battle of the Book of Judges was paradigmatic of what *should* have become normative. The source of their victory was unquestionably **the LORD** who **gave the Canaanites and Perizzites into their hands**. The term *Canaanites* often spoke of the inhabitants of the promised land collectively; at other times the individualized enemies were specified, as in verses 5,21,26,34–36.

1:5–7. *Maiming of a Monarch.* The "Ruler of Bezek" (**Adoni-Bezek**, probably a title rather than a name) lost the battle to the invading Israelites, and **fled**. When **they chased him and caught him**, the Israelites **cut off his thumbs and big toes**. There is no editorial comment offered about this mutilation, except that given by the victim himself: **God has paid me back** for similar mutilation of **seventy kings** who **picked up scraps under my table** (while he assumed his ultimate fate would be the same as what he had imposed on his victims, we do not know if this took place).

The practical purpose of such treatment is obvious: the victim could not lead in battle or wield weapons; he could not escape easily; and he served as an object of derision and humiliation. Presumably for years to come he would be a human trophy that Judah could point to with pride (a questionable motive). But shortly after returning **to Jerusalem, he died there**, possibly of infection or loss of blood (although since Jerusalem had not yet been conquered, the timing is open to speculation). What of his words about God's justice? The term for God that he used was generic, and did not necessarily imply repentance or any relationship with the God of Israel.

This story invites evaluation. While Judah's merger with Simeon made at least some sense, Judah's maiming of this ruler made little sense. If we use the interpretation of the ruler himself, Adoni-Bezek understood that God was paying back cruelty for cruelty. However, the "eye for an eye" (*lex talionis*) legislation in the Old Testament was given to avoid vengeance that exceeded the crime and to keep revenge in check. More importantly, God had told his people very clearly to drive the Canaanites out of the land. Those who refused to go were to be put to death (Deut. 7:1–2; 20:16–17), not tortured. Earlier Judah had received God's guidance (Judg. 1:2); here she did not seek it.

Judah "edited" God, ignored his guidance, and embraced the guidance of Canaanite culture in their treatment of prominent prisoners. The distorted message to outside observers would be that the God of the Israelites was no different than the gods of the Canaanites (see the attitude of Samson, Judg. 15:11).

1:8–10. *Conquest of the Canaanites, II.* The Israelites conquered Jerusalem, killing all its inhabitants and burning the city—very likely obliterating the visible expressions of a Canaanite culture. Then they went down to three areas labeled by their topography—**the hill country, the Negev and the western foothills**—where they conquered the Canaanites living there. **Hebron**, within the hill country, was defeated (actually by Caleb, v. 20). Three named enemy leaders were vanquished: **Sheshai, Ahiman and Talmai.**

1:11–15. *Vignette of a Victor.* Hebron and its surrounding territory was a part of Caleb's bequest from Joshua (Josh. 14:6–15), and nearby **Debir** was important to his holdings. This chapter records the first and last time we see this great man in Judges. **Caleb** made a remarkable offer: any man who captured Debir would also capture the hand of his daughter **Acsah** in marriage. Caleb's nephew **Othniel son of Kenaz** was the victor, and they were married.

Later, Acsah registered a concern with her father, although not about her marriage. Rather, the bequest of land was **Negev** (desert-like, dry ground) and had no source for proper irrigation. In recent decades the Israelites had done precious little farming, and Acsah, like the woman in Proverbs 31, planned to provide well for her family. So Caleb gave her what she requested. The phrase **upper and lower** is probably a *merism*, a figure of speech in which beginning and ending points are expressed, meaning "from A to Z" (see Rev. 1:8 where God is the "Alpha and Omega"—a claim that is certainly not restricted to two letters; rather, the Word is the beginning, the end, and everything in between!). The point is that Caleb lavished upon his daughter the upper reservoir, the lower reservoir, and everything in between.

In this episode everyone was seen in a positive light. Caleb was kind and generous, Othniel (whom we will see as the paradigmatic judge in ch. 3) was brave and indulgent, and Acsah was analytical and bold. In retrospect, the city of Debir may have been the "bride-price," and the springs may have been the dowry (see 1 Sam. 18:25). The admirable behavior of everyone in this family at the beginning of this book is set in stark contrast to the familial fragmentation and abuse on display at the end of the book (Judg. 19:24–29; 21:19–23; note that this episode is also recorded in Josh. 15:13–19).

Ⓒ Partial Disobedience: Downhill Slope (1:16–26)

SUPPORTING IDEA: *In this segment the disobedience of the Israelites seems more intentional, as three tribes displayed an unwillingness to follow God's guidance: Judah (vv. 16–20), Benjamin (v. 21), and Ephraim (vv. 22–26). This section also reports excuses the Israelites used to justify their disobedience.*

1:16–20. *Excuse of Technology.* Earlier Moses had invited the Kenites to join the Israelites because of his relationship to them by marriage (apparently the Kenites were a tribe within Midian). Although they joined the Israelites, they did not join in the conquest, but rather chose to **live among** the Canaanites—and eventually they became "Canaanized" and were indistinguishable from those who rejected Moses' God.

True to their promise, **Judah** joined **the Simeonites their brothers** (see v. 3) and completely **destroyed** Zephath, calling it **Hormah**, or "destruction." A further positive development was that Judah conquered three other cities, **Gaza, Ashkelon and Ekron—each city with its territory.** All of this good news was summarized in this assertion: Judah **took possession of the hill country.** Why were they able to remain consistently victorious? The answer is clear: **The LORD was with the men of Judah.**

Victory was to be complete, extending beyond the hill country and encompassing **the plains.** Allowing the Canaanites to remain in the land would yield devastating consequences. However, the armaments of their enemies in the plains included one item that would have been unusable in the hill country: **iron** (plated) **chariots.** A modern comparison would be an army armed with muskets and knives fighting an army equipped with machine guns, rocket launchers, and modern tanks.

The context makes it clear that all of these victories took place because the Lord was with Israel (he gave guidance, v. 2, and he gave victory, vv. 4,19). Technological superiority of the enemy was not an issue when the captain of Israel's army created and owned all the materials! Just as the victory in the highlands (v. 15) was from God, he also would have given them victory in the lowlands if they had called on him. God wanted the conquest and disposition of the land to be unexplainable in human terms; unfortunately, Judah allowed human terms to dictate divine limits! In their view armaments trumped Adonai. Despite the miracles they had heard of (the plagues, the exodus, the Red Sea, etc.) and the miracles they had seen (particularly the conquest of technologically superior Jericho), they adopted the attitude that God was no longer powerful enough for them.

The inclusion of the fact that **Hebron was given to Caleb, who drove from it the three sons of Anak** served as a contrast to Judah's faithlessness (see Josh. 14:9; Deut. 1:36). Caleb's consistent attitude was that God was greater than all obstacles which humans may encounter (Num. 13:30; 14:24). Later, Deborah and Barak led the Israelites against an army that had nine hundred iron chariots, and God received praise for a miraculous victory (see Judg. 4 and 5)!

1:21. *Episode of Tolerance.* However, in contrast to Caleb's total obedience and victory, **the Benjamites** traded the challenge of conquest for the comfort of co-residency, and **failed to dislodge the Jebusites**. This is the first explicit statement we encounter that does not contain any excuse for their disobedience. Here silence speaks. The careful presentation of "just the facts" invites the interpretation that the Benjamites lived in Jerusalem with the Jebusites because this was their choice. At the least, the Benjamites chose to regard these Canaanites as less offensive, less dangerous, and the threat of their gods less serious than God revealed these things to be. It comes as no surprise that later Benjamin served as the geographical context for a final case study in depravity (chs. 19–21).

1:22–26. *End Justifies the Means.* The Ephraimites (**house of Joseph**) went up against **Bethel**, and again the victory was attributed to **the LORD**. Although God apparently did not command them to do so, they mounted a surveillance operation. The **spies** spotted **a man coming out of the city** and found him willing to barter his information for his life. He showed them **how to get into the city** (perhaps a secret entrance, such as the water tunnel in 2 Sam. 5:8). In return, he **and his whole family** were permitted to escape while the Ephraimites took it upon themselves to commute the execution sentence that God had declared upon all the inhabitants of Bethel. God was with them and would have given them victory, regardless of the means used to achieve that end.

However, the Ephraimites chose to conquer the city in their own wisdom apart from God and made a binding treaty with this man and his family (the promise that he would be **treated well** is much less forceful than the covenant terminology of the Hebrew text). The man and his family were indeed displaced, but unlike Rahab (see Josh. 2:12, where covenant terminology is likewise used), they were not integrated within Israelite covenant life. Instead, he was permitted to continue his Canaanite practices, build a city, and in effect transplant Bethel (**Luz**) and its culture. This compromise solved no problem; it merely deferred a problem until later. This is the second time in this chapter that the Israelites have chosen to "edit" God's command.

Total Disobedience: Downward Spiral (1:27–36)

> **SUPPORTING IDEA:** *The author identified twenty-one sites that were not taken. Over and over again, rather than drive out or destroy the Canaanites (Deut. 20:11–17), they let them remain. Their failure was a result of their sin (not believing God), and its result was a boring and predictable litany of failures.*

1:27–28. *Failure of Manasseh.* The tribe of **Manasseh** refused to obey God's command; they **did not drive out the people of Beth Shan or Taanach or Dor or Ibleam or Megiddo and their surrounding settlements**. Thus five cities and all their supporting and surrounding satellite towns were permitted to remain unhindered. The only reason given was that **the Canaanites were determined**—that is, the determination of the Canaanites to stay was greater than the determination of the Israelites to obey God. They **never drove them out completely**. Later when the Israelites did have military ascendancy, they used them for **forced labor**, in order to render the lives of the Israelites less demanding. This is the first of four impressments mentioned in this chapter that were practiced by the Israelites (vv. 30,33,35). Later still, the Israelites would themselves become forced labor for their Canaanite hosts.

1:29. *Failure of Ephraim.* **Ephraim** failed to **drive out the Canaanites living in Gezer**. Rather, they cohabited with the Israelites in a place that would prove to be of strategic military significance (a north/south and east/west crossroad).

1:30. *Failure of Zebulun.* Moving further north, **Zebulun** also failed to obey God but allowed **the Canaanites living in Kitron or Nahalol** to dwell **among them**, again using them for **forced labor**.

1:31–32. *Failure of Asher.* In the other attempts at conquest, the Israelites permitted pockets of Canaanite resistance to live among them, with what would become disastrous results. With **Asher**, not only did the cities of **Acco or Sidon or Ahlab or Aczib or Helbah or Aphek or Rehob** resist Asher, but for the first time the Israelites were portrayed as intruders permitted to live among their **Canaanite** hosts!

1:33. *Failure of Naphtali.* Yet again the Israelites were permitted to live among the Canaanites. Not only did Naphtali not **drive out those living in Beth Shemesh or Beth Anath** (sites specifically devoted to Canaanite worship), but the Israelites also **lived among the Canaanite inhabitants**, again using them as **forced laborers**.

1:34–36. *Failure of Dan.* Still further north, the litany of failure reached a crescendo. The **Danites** were overwhelmed by the **Amorites** (here mentioned for the first time in Judges). They were so dominated that they were unable **to come down into the plain.** Later, **the house of Joseph** (Ephraimites) became stronger and annexed part of the Danite land, pressing some of the Amorites **into forced labor.** In sum, as we scan verses 27–36, it is clear that disobedience to God's command produces boring and repetitive consequences.

> **MAIN IDEA REVIEW:** *After Joshua's death God's people had a task to complete: finish the occupation of the land God had given them by means of God's guidance and God's power. Although they began well, the Israelites gradually moved from obedience to disobedience, "editing" God's command. Beginning with Judah, the narrative moves geographically from south to north and provides a litany of the successes and failures of each of the tribes.*

III. CONCLUSION

When God's People Get "Canaanized"

There has never been a comparable time in history when Christianity has had more competent apologetics information available—and yet people are still not persuaded. Why? Not because of the overwhelming cogency of intellectual objections to Christianity. Rather, people make their moral choices and align their beliefs accordingly. This is also sadly true within the church. When entering a Christian bookstore, one could become overwhelmed by the number of volumes devoted not to biblical studies, or to having an impact on our world, but books designed to help us cope with how the world has impacted us! The sins of the culture have become the sins of the church. It's not surprising that through religious and moral compromise the Israelites became like the people they were supposed to overcome.

Even though Christians are God's people, at times we forget *who* we are, and *whose* we are. Once we are lulled into moral compromise, we grow to enjoy the lower morality and finally adjust our beliefs accordingly. Thankfully God's Word provides exhortations and examples to pull us back, so long as we do not edit God.

PRINCIPLES

- God has given believers three resources for growth: his Word before us, the Holy Spirit within us, and the church around us. We ignore any of these at our spiritual peril.
- Standing on the truth of God's Word without compromise (as Caleb did) provides a visible testimony that brings glory to God.
- Any victories that come our way ultimately come from the Lord (Judg. 1:2,4,19,22; see Jas. 1:17).
- God wants our successes to be so grand that they exceed human explanation but point beyond us to him.

APPLICATIONS

- God says what he means and means what he says. Make sure you do not "edit" God.
- Don't assume that you can put God *on pause* and resume your spiritual walk without having regressed; we do not take "spring break" away from God without excessive tuition payments.
- When you fall into sin, get back up. God promises he will forgive (1 John 1:9), as he repeatedly forgave the Israelites.
- Stay faithful! He who began a good work in you will complete it until the day of Christ (Phil. 1:6).

IV. LIFE APPLICATION

Running with the Bulls

In 1924 Ernest Hemingway participated in a local celebration in Pamplona, Spain, which gained international attention when he immortalized it in *The Sun Also Rises*. It is a part of La Fiesta de San Fermin, named for a cleric who was martyred by being dragged through the streets by bulls. For the last six centuries, participating in "the running of the bulls" through the streets of Pamplona toward and into the local stadium has been taken as a mark of manhood. In fact, many people have been killed since 1924, when Hemingway romanticized it. Possibly running in front of very large, angry bulls is not a wise thing to do! There are some senseless situations you don't voluntarily put yourself in because they are dangerous. We know better, but at times we simply choose to do what we should not do.

Rather than drive the Canaanites out of the land or exterminate them, the Israelites chose to disobey God. They felt that the danger was over, that they had at the very least driven the bulls into holding pens and tranquilized them—surely the people of God wouldn't get hurt! Surely enough had been achieved! And if the bulls were somehow to reawaken, surely they would go after somebody else, not them. The latter is indeed the gamble the bull-runners wage, but the odds are not good. In fact, as a guideline for the spiritual life, it is a lose/lose proposition. The result was that the Canaanites eventually regained their strength, and the Israelites found themselves running ahead of the bulls, desperately seeking refuge and rest, trying not to get trampled. This chapter is dark and dreary. By contrast, God wants us to obey him and to live in his victory over the world (John 16:33).

V. PRAYER

Lord, our visible actions are seen by others, but our motives are laid bare before you. You know when we are honest with you and when we allow our view of our obstacles to distort our view of the greatness of your power and of the truth of your word. At times our circumstances seem more real to us than your promises. Forgive us when we distort your truth to make ourselves comfortable.

We ask that our lives would be unexplainable in terms of us, but point beyond us to the only one who truly gives victory. Through Christ our Lord. Amen.

VI. DEEPER DISCOVERIES

A. Roll Call

Since Judges 1 is very complete and deliberate in recording basic facts, any omissions are significant. If one were to go through the chapter and "call the roll," four tribes would be missing: Reuben, Gad, Levi, and Issachar. It makes sense that Reuben and Gad are missing—they lived outside the promised land (Josh. 22), and their Amorite enemies already had been defeated by Moses (Num. 21). Likewise, Levi had no territorial allotment but lived within and among all the other tribes (Num. 18:20–21; Deut. 14:27,29). Only the absence of Issachar is unexplained, but the presence of Issachar in Judges is represented by Deborah and Barak (Judg. 4–5; see 5:15) and by Tola (Judg. 10:1). Issachar was quite numerous and prominent during the monarchy (1 Chr. 7:5).

B. Urim and Thummim (1:1)

The guidance sought by the Israelites was probably to use the means of inclusion and exclusion (or affirmation and elimination) that were a part of the priests' clothing called the "Urim and Thummim." These were given to Joshua (Num. 27:21) and likely were used to point to Achan in Joshua 7 (for other passages, see Exod. 28:30; Lev. 8:8; Deut. 33:8; 1 Sam. 28:6; Ezra 2:63; Neh. 7:65). It could be that the guidance described in Judges 1:1–2 came about through the Urim and Thummim and also through some prophetic verbal guidance (because of the revealed word of encouragement, "I have given the land into their hands," v. 2).

C. Perizzites (1:4)

The term *Perizzites* referred to a populous subgroup or to a tribe within the land itself. Scholars are not exactly certain where they lived, but they are mentioned often in the Old Testament (from Gen. 13:7 through Neh. 9:8, but only three times in Judges). One general observation should be made:

through the Book of Judges we will encounter people (and sometimes peoples) whom we do not know and geographical locations that have not yet been identified or that are lost to us. Even so, our geographical ignorance does not affect our understanding of the message of this important book.

D. Jerusalem in Judges 1: Defeated (1:8) or Defiant (1:21)?

It seems that Jerusalem was conquered in verse 8, only to show up as an unconquered location in verse 21. How may we understand this conflict? Block suggests, "Jerusalem was a border city, located on the boundary between Judah and Benjamin. The city that was burned in verse 8 probably identified the Jebusite fortress on the southern hill of the city, between the Kidron and Hinnom valleys, and which David eventually captured and made his capital. Accordingly, the unsuccessful Benjamite effort in verse 21 must have been directed against the citadel farther north" (Block, 92).

E. A Match Made in Heaven? (1:11–15)

The customs of other cultures seem strange to us. Arranged marriages make perfect sense to much of the world, whereas the concept of "dating" makes little sense to them. Years ago one of my students was a very articulate Ph.D. in electrical engineering from India, who met his wife for the first time on his wedding day. Today they have a happy home and are deeply in love. When Caleb arranged the match for his daughter's hand, his intent was not to devalue her but to secure a worthy husband and protector for her. Later when she came to Caleb with a request, he took the initiative in asking what *he* could do for *her*, and he valued and honored her request.

What is ironic about Caleb's family is that not one of them was descended from the twelve tribes—all were proselytes (Kenizzites). However, they were such devout believers in the God of Israel that presumably before Acsah was even born Caleb was so well respected within Judah (the tribe of his assimilation) that he was chosen to represent Judah as a leader among the spies of Numbers 13 (see also Num. 32:12; Josh. 14:6,14; Gen. 36:11,15,42).

F. Structure of the Chapter

At times there is more than one way to outline a passage of Scripture, when different criteria are invoked. By using a military criterion, one could divide chapter 1 into success (vv. 1–15) and failure (vv. 16–36). By using the criterion of fulfilling God's command to conquer the land and drive out its inhabitants, one could use the cliché title, "The Good (vv. 1–15), the Bad (vv. 16–26), and the Ugly (vv. 27–36)." By using the criterion of geography, one sees a very deliberate pattern moving from the struggles in the south—Judah (vv. 3–20), Benjamin (v. 21), Joseph (Ephraim, vv. 22–26) to struggles in the north—Manasseh (vv. 27–28), Zebulun (v. 30), Asher (vv. 31–32), Naphtali (v. 33), and the northernmost tribe, Dan (v. 34; Ephraim, v. 29, is a possible exception here). But in light of what follows in the Book of Judges, we chose to outline the chapter using the lens of obedience to God.

VII. TEACHING OUTLINE

A. INTRODUCTION

1. Lead Story: A Walk with No Cause for Pause
2. Context: After the conquest under Joshua, the Israelites began well but soon started compromising God's command. The end of this chapter is a microcosm of the whole book: occasional vignettes of victory embedded within the matrix of malignity. Block observes that the movement of the cycles corresponds with the direction set in this first chapter, from Judah (Othniel), Benjamin (Ehud), Ephraim (Deborah), Manasseh (Gideon), Gilead (Jephthah), to Dan (Samson).
3. Transition: The first chapter of Judges is a chronicle of the basic facts from the time of Joshua to the spiritual causes of the dark days of the judges. In Joshua 22–24 God's leader warned God's people to follow God's guidance in order to claim God's promises. In Judges 1 God's people have no leader, ignore God's guidance, and gradually descend into greater disobedience. Judges 2 will provide a study of the spiritual causes undergirding this disobedience.

B. COMMENTARY

1. Total Obedience: Straight and Narrow (1:1–2)
   a. Guidance requested (1:1)

    b.   Guidance received (1:2)

2. Partial Obedience: Curve in the Road (1:3–15)

    a.   Making a merger (1:3)

    b.   Conquest of the Canaanites, I (1:4)

    c.   Maiming of a monarch (1:5–7)

    d.   Conquest of the Canaanites, II (1:8–10)

    e.   Vignette of a victor (1:11–15)

3. Partial Disobedience: Downhill Slope (1:16–26)

    a.   Excuse of technology (1:16–20)

    b.   Episode of tolerance (1:21)

    c.   End justifies the means (1:22–26)

4. Total Disobedience: Downward Spiral (1:27–36)

    a.   Failure of Manasseh (1:27–28)

    b.   Failure of Ephraim (1:29)

    c.   Failure of Zebulun (1:30)

    d.   Failure of Asher (1:31–32)

    e.   Failure of Naphtali (1:33)

    f.   Failure of Dan (1:34–36)

C. CONCLUSION: WHEN GOD'S PEOPLE GET "CANAANIZED"

VIII. ISSUES FOR DISCUSSION

1. Read Joshua 1:7–8 and then read James 1:23–25. If you were to translate these passages into two commands (imperatives) telling you how to live your life, what would they be?

2. Caleb is a wonderful example of a believer whose testimony is a bright spot in this dark chapter. Study Joshua 14:6–15 and construct a profile of the "Character of a Champion."

3. Discuss this idea: Refusal to obey God will lead to spiritual compromise, and when you compromise, you never win. Remember the old parable of a man who was about to shoot a bear? The bear said, "Wait! What do you want?" The hunter said, "I want a fur coat for the winter." The bear said, "And I want a full stomach. Let's compromise." Later, the bear got up and walked away—alone. He had his full stomach, and the hunter had his fur coat. Spiritual compromise

is always one-sided; you will be eaten (1 Pet. 5:8). Satan is a liar (John 8:44) and simply does not play fair.

4. Think about this: How do you differ from your unbelieving friends in the jokes you tell? The entertainment you choose? The way you spend your time? The way you talk about other people? The way you spend your money? Is there any observable (and winsome) difference that marks you as a follower of Jesus?

5. Let's assume there is a motivational difference between "partial obedience" and "partial disobedience." What do you think it would be?

Judges 2

A Case of Spiritual Insanity

Q u o t e

"*T*he place for the ship is in the sea,

but God help the ship if the sea gets into it."

D .   L .   M o o d y

Judges 2

I N   A   N U T S H E L L

*T*he chapter begins with a divine visitation from the angel of the Lord (vv. 1–5) in which God explains to Israel that, though he has been faithful to them, they have been faithless to him. During the life of Joshua and his immediate followers, Israel stayed true to the Lord, but with only one generation past, they developed spiritual amnesia and became "the prodigal nation" (vv. 6–10). The chocks were removed, and the slippery slope of decline began (vv. 11–23) through what will become the cycles of chapters 3–16.

A Case of
Spiritual Insanity

I. INTRODUCTION

Going Crazy over You

*F*or a moment, enter the world of a loving wife who suspects her husband of being unfaithful. With a broken heart she confronts him, and he begins his confession.

"Yes, even though you have been faithful to me and have loved me unconditionally all these years, I am being unfaithful to you."

"Tell me," the wife asks, "do you love her?"

"Yes, I do love her."

"What about our years together, through the joys and through the sorrows?"

"I guess I just can't help myself."

"Is she pretty?"

"Yes, she is a model."

"Is she younger than me?"

"Well, she was a teenager in 1959 when she was conceived."

Somewhat confused, the wife continues, "Why do you love her? Does she love you? What's her name? What's special about her?"

"Wait a minute. One question at a time! I admit the attraction was only physical at first. Her name is Barbie, and she is gorgeous. She has an astonishing figure and she makes no demands on me. In fact, she doesn't care if I do whatever I want to do, whatever is right in my own eyes. There are only two problems with her: she's only ten inches tall, and she has too large a wardrobe. As far as whether she loves me, she hasn't said anything yet."

The wife looks at him and asks, "Have you lost your mind? Are you insane?"

While this scenario may indeed seem obtuse, the same insanity or lack of perspective on reality is not unlike Israel's choice to pursue the gods of the Canaanites. In fact, idolatry is placing anything before God as having ultimate value (whether money, possessions, a sport, a person, a job, etc.). When we displace God, he looks at our little idols with infinite sadness (because he knows they cannot fulfill our longings) and with infinite jealousy (because God is a passionate God).

Sin is not logical. It is utterly irrational. At the moment we choose to sin, we suppress our logical abilities, and say, "At this point I know better than God does, and further, I don't really believe this will be bad for me, either in the short term or in the long run. Even though the Creator who made me, who also gave me the instruction manual for my life, tells me not to do this, I think I know better, and I will do what I want." So we suppress God's guidance, we suppress our awareness of God, and we choose what can only be described as spiritual insanity.

II. COMMENTARY

A Case of Spiritual Insanity

MAIN IDEA: *Although God is always faithful to his children, when we are faithless, he allows us to make our own choices, including choices that bring self-destructive pain upon us. Even so, he does not abandon us, but like the father of the prodigal son is always waiting to enfold us in repentance within his patient, loving arms.*

Ⓐ Confrontation: Slugged by an Angel (2:1–5)

SUPPORTING IDEA: *God sent his special angel to confront the Israelites with two truths: God had been faithful, and Israel had responded with disobedience. Now judgment would follow.*

2:1. *Cause of the Visitation: God Had Been Faithful.* At special times of crisis, God sent **the angel of the LORD** to convey his message to the recipient. While it is possible that the angel was simply God's messenger (the meaning for "angel") who spoke God's words in the "first person," it is also possible that the angel was the pre-incarnate Christ (see "Deeper Discoveries"). His point of origin was **Gilgal**, which may have served as a "message within the message." Gilgal was mentioned thirty-eight times in the Old Testament and had greater significance theologically than geographically. It was the memorial site after the Israelites crossed the Jordan River (Josh. 4:19–20; 5:9–10) where the Israelites set up camp, erected the memorial of twelve stones, circumcised all the men of the second generation, and celebrated the Passover (Block, 110).

More significantly, it was at Gilgal that the battle plan was revealed to Joshua by "the commander of the LORD's army" (Josh. 5:15). "Army" or "host" (NASB) refers to angelic forces (see Rev. 19:11–21). If this was the same divine person, then God's challenge was clear: "When you obeyed my word at Jericho you were victorious; obey me now. You made commitments of faithfulness at Gilgal; keep them now." Two pegs of God's faithfulness were mentioned: the exodus and the conquest. These examples of God's faithfulness were followed by the promise, **I will never break my** (not "our") **covenant with you** (see Lev. 26:12).

2:2. *Cause of the Visitation: Israel Had Been Faithless.* God gave two mandates to his people, both of which they **disobeyed**. He told the Israelites not to **make a covenant with the people of this land**. However, not only did they make covenants with God's enemies, they also failed to **break down their altars** (see Exod. 23:20–33; 34:11–15, especially vv. 12–13, and Judg. 6:25–28; God's commands had not been rescinded). God asked rhetorically, **Why have you done this?** God's point highlighted the fact that sin is never a logical choice. The Canaanite altars represented gods that did not speak and did not feel. By contrast, God speaks (indeed, demands a response!), and God feels deeply, as his children saw. He is a jealous (passionate) God who is slow to anger, but when his wrath is kindled, he acts—or, in this case, withdraws his active protection. Over a millennium later, the very one who was grieved by sin was the one who would die for those sins (Isa. 53:6,11; 2 Cor. 5:21).

2:3. *Effect of the Visitation: God Withdrew.* The cause of God's action was Israel's faithlessness despite God's faithfulness. The effect was twofold. First, God withdrew his protection and his presence from the nation. Not only did he **not drive** the Canaanites **out**, but the Canaanites would oppress the Israelites as **thorns in your sides** (an external burden; note the image in Num. 33:55 and Josh. 23:13) while their idols would serve as an ongoing temptation (an internal burden; the root for the Hebrew term **snare** means "to lay out bait") allowing God's people to further self-destruct. This was precisely what God had promised he would do (Josh. 23:13). Disobedience to God's commandments does not result in freedom but in bondage.

2:4–5. *Effect of the Visitation: Israel Wept.* The second result was manifested in a threefold response from **the Israelites**: first, they **wept aloud** (see Num. 14:1–2). Second, they commemorated their effusive emotional eruption by naming the place "weeping" (**Bokim**). And third, **they offered sacri-**

fices to the LORD but it was too little, too late. Samuel later observed, "To obey is better than sacrifice" (1 Sam. 15:22; see Ps. 51:16). If their slobbering spectacle had reflected genuine repentance, the Book of Judges would have been very different from this point. Over and over again, Israel forgot her Lord. Like an infant with a narrow attention span, she would soil herself, cry loudly until cared for, and then (giving no thought to the caregiver) lapse into self-absorption until the next self-induced crisis. What is understandable for an infant is unthinkable for those who have covenant commitment.

B Commemoration: Heritage of a Hero (2:6–10)

SUPPORTING IDEA: *As long as Joshua and his immediate followers lived, Israel did not reject God. Israel's defection was not the product of a single decision or event, but the accumulation of innumerable decisions over a three-generation span of time.*

2:6–9. *People Served God All the Days of Joshua and the Elders.* A little review is in order, which our author provides. We are reminded that the root cause of Israel's apostasy had nothing to do with geography, politics, or economics. In a nutshell, it was this: Israel forgot God. It took only three generations for the encroachment of spiritual amnesia to become complete. This was not a case of absent-mindedness, but a deliberate rejection of the significance of God's work in the past on behalf of Israel. It was the answer to the rhetorical question God asked in verse 2, "Why have you done this?" The explanation reaches backward into history, and the text now provides a flashback (see Josh. 24:28–30).

After **Joshua had dismissed the Israelites**, he **died at the age of a hundred and ten** and was **buried in the land of his inheritance, at Timnath Heres in the hill country of Ephraim, north of Mount Gaash**. We are reminded that he was **the servant of the LORD**, a term explicitly said of only three people in the Old Testament (the other two are Moses and David; see also Isa. 42:19 for the messianic servant). After Joshua (and Caleb), none of the leaders among the judges seemed to be able to lead the nation in collective obedience.

Until the end of Joshua's **lifetime**, that generation followed their leader and **served the LORD**. It made sense: as children they had observed firsthand the Egyptian plagues, the parting of the Red Sea, the giving of the law, the preservation in the wilderness; as adults they had taken part in the stunning victory at Jericho and the conquest of the promised land. They had experienced the direct guidance of God on numerous occasions. They knew God and had seen his work in their lives. They had often observed both God's grace and his judgment. The next generation knew God and knew the stories *about* what God had done, but they had not experienced him for themselves.

2:10. *People Snubbed God and Did What Was Right in Their Own Eyes.* The third **generation . . . knew neither the LORD nor what he had done for Israel**. At some point there was a breakdown in the process of transferring God's truth to the next generation. The priests failed because they were to "teach the Israelites all the decrees the LORD has given to them through Moses" (Lev. 10:11). The fathers failed, since according to Deuteronomy 6:1–9 they were to teach God's truth both formally and informally, using the world as a classroom and life as a laboratory to communicate God's truth in a vital way.

The result was that before long God's people developed spiritual amnesia (see Isa. 1:14; Hos. 4:1–6; Jer. 8:4–12; 9:23–24 on the importance of remembering!). Within the span of just a few words in the text, a generation came and went, until the reader now faces an Israel that looks no different from the Canaanites among whom they chose to live (see Judg. 17:6; 21:25).

Ⓒ Calamity: Diagram of Decline (2:11–23)

SUPPORTING IDEA: *The litany of willful rebellion and moral decline unfolded tragically time and again. The dark side of God's love permits judgment upon his beloved people. At the same time, God will not let Israel go, even amidst its continued rejection of him and its pursuit of other gods.*

2:11–13. *Israel's Rejection of God, I.* This entire segment could easily take as its title the introductory words, **the Israelites did evil in the eyes of the LORD**. These words condense the rest of the chapter. The phrase "did evil in the eyes of the LORD" occurs about sixty times in the Old Testament, and eight times in the Book of Judges (2:11; 3:7,12[two times]; 4:1; 6:1; 10:6; 13:1). The statement will introduce the judgeships of Othniel, Ehud, Deborah/Barak, Gideon, Jephthah, and Samson. The phrase is particularly interesting as it is twisted in Malachi 2:17, where the prophet indicts a group of "second generation" so-called believers with these words: "You have wearied the LORD with your words. 'How have we wearied him?' you ask. By saying, 'All who do evil are good in the eyes of the LORD.'" Those removed from direct experience with God have little hesitation (as we said in the last chapter) about editing God's command.

The term *evil* here refers to intentional violation of God's revealed command in a covenant context. This is not the evil of someone who transgresses a regulation imposed from the outside about which they were unaware; rather, this is the deliberate violation of a law that one has specifically promised not to violate.

Their evil was twofold: first, **they forsook the LORD, the God of their fathers**, abandoning whatever teaching they had received (Deut. 6:1–9). They had been taught about what God had done for them, that he **had brought them out of Egypt**, preserved them, and fought for them. They knew about the wilderness, about Jericho, but they had no firsthand experience of a relationship with the Lord themselves; they had never seen him, nor had they seen his works.

By contrast, they could visually see the local Canaanite gods. Walking by sight and not by faith, **they followed and worshiped various gods of the peoples around them**. Ironically, the gods of the Canaanites were nothing more than metal, stone, and wood, whereas the Lord was the creator of all the materials from which humans fashioned idols. They worshiped a component part of the creation rather than the Creator (Rom. 1:25), and this **provoked the LORD to anger because they forsook him**.

The objects of their religious affections were **Baal and the Ashtoreths**. The term *Baal* is a general title ("master, owner, lord") and occurs seventy-one times in the Old Testament (fifty-three singular, eighteen plural). It was used to refer to many gods but was most often identified with the god of weather. The female companion of **Baal** was Astarte, whose plural form occurs in our text as **Ashtoreths**. Again, this term represented many localized forms of the goddess but was most often identified with fertility.

The Canaanites combined "worship" of these two gods in religious orgies where they attempted to coax the gods, by example, into having copulation. The worship of these gods usually took place in elevated areas close to the clouds, where the gods could hear and see the humans better (note the commands to destroy and tear down the "high places," a term that occurs seventy-four times in the Old Testament; see 5:18). This was the reason why their worship was described in these terms: they "prostituted themselves" (v. 17; see Hos. 4:12–14). The worship of the gods of the Canaanites was the very essence of man-made religion and spiritual adultery. Canaanite worship was exactly the opposite of the true worship of God.

Isaiah charged the Israelites: "Seek the LORD while he may be found; call on him while he is near. Let the wicked forsake his way and the evil man his thoughts. Let him turn to the LORD, and he will have mercy on him, and to our God, for he will freely pardon. 'For my thoughts are not your thoughts, neither are your ways my ways,' declares the LORD. 'As the heavens are higher than the earth, so are my ways higher than your ways and my thoughts than your thoughts'" (Isa. 55:6–9).

God's people are to think God's thoughts and to walk in God's ways; the focus is to be the glory of the Creator, not the creature. In Canaanite worship the object was to entreat the gods to do in heaven what was being done on earth. In Israelite worship true worshipers demythologize the creation (the weather is not animate or a person), understand that God is transcendent and omnipotent, understand that God has revealed himself and done so for their good, and therefore conform their lives to his revealed will. In other words, God entreats his people in New Testament terms to pray, "Your will be done on earth as it is in heaven" (Matt. 6:10), not that God be coaxed into replicating in heaven what his worshipers do on earth. Their rejection of the LORD could not have been more devastating. Their view of God was wrong. Simply put, they "violated the covenant" (Judg. 2:20).

2:14–16. *God's Reckoning with Israel, I.* The result came as no surprise and is quite clear: **In his anger against Israel the LORD handed them over to raiders who plundered them.** Not only that, he **sold them;** even further, **the LORD was against them to defeat them.** This passage demonstrates first that God is absolutely sovereign over the movements of nations that are merely pawns (or secondary causes) as history fulfills God's primary purposes (see Dan. 2; 4:17,25; 9). Second, it demonstrates that even though the idols made of stone, wood, and metal were impassive and unfeeling, God was not. His emotions ranged from anger to pity. When Israel was **in great distress,** God's response was to raise up a judge who "saved them out of the hands of their enemies as long as the judge lived" (Judg. 2:18).

God loves his children, and as human parents hate to see their children suffer when they can intervene, God also is compassionate; at the appropriate time, he steps in.

2:17. *Israel's Rejection of God, II.* Tragically, the Israelites again **prostituted themselves to other gods and worshiped them.** Time and again this cycle would be repeated: "rebellion, retribution, repentance, restoration, and rest." While there was occasional relief (rest) when the judge delivered, the "rest" did not last long.

2:18. *God's Reckoning with Israel, II.* However, **the LORD had compassion on them as they groaned under** her oppression ("groaned" is a word used to describe the inarticulate moanings made by a man whose arms are broken, Ezek. 30:24). God is a passionate God, deeply in love with his people on whom he has lavished extravagant grace. When his people were **oppressed** ("squeezed, pressured," e.g., Num. 22:25) **and afflicted,** God was affected (the word translated "afflicted" occurs only twice in the Old Testament, here and Joel 2:8, "where it describes a crowd jostling for space," Block, 130).

2:19. *Israel's Rejection of God, III.* Rebellion quickly resurfaced **when the judge died.** Not only did the cycle begin again, but each cycle sank toward a deeper level of depravity. Thus, the proper image of the cycles does not take place on a level plane but rather on a descending slope, a slippery slope to slavery. They committed acts **even more corrupt than those of their fathers.** Tragically, **they refused to give up their evil practices and stubborn ways** and spiraled deeper into a vortex of violence and vice. "Instead of effecting fundamental repairs on this deteriorating dike, they plugged the holes with their fingers. As soon as the finger was removed, the water gushed through with increasing force" (Block, 132).

2:20–23. *God's Reckoning with Israel, III.* God's final reckoning is described in these verses. The cause is that **this nation has violated the covenant** God made with **their forefathers** (cp. v. 1), which to God means that they have **not listened to me.** Israel is described as "this nation," a term usually reserved for Gentile nations (the same term, *goyim,* is used to describe pagan Canaanites in vv. 21,23).

The point is that there was little difference between the behavior of the Israelites and that of the Canaanites. The effect was that God would **no longer drive out before them any of the nations Joshua left.** Rather, the Canaanites would remain as an ongoing **test** that Israel could take and retake until they succeeded, perhaps like a hurdle whose bar is fixed at a particular level to serve as an ongoing challenge. God did not raise the bar. He simply wanted them to learn to **keep the way of the LORD and walk in it.**

The epilogue to the chapter is found in the last verse: God **allowed those nations to remain; he did not drive them out.** One question remains: Since the Israelites were indistinguishable from the Canaanites, why did God continue to wait for his people, to love them, to protect them, and to care for them? The reason certainly had nothing to do with the obedience or loveliness of the faithless Israelites. God's faithfulness is anchored in his character, not ours. He is the loving father awaiting the return of "the prodigal nation."

MAIN IDEA REVIEW: *Although God is always faithful to his children, when we are faithless, he allows us to make our own choices, including choices that bring self-destructive pain upon us. Even so, he does not abandon us but like the father of the prodigal son, is always waiting to enfold us in repentance within his patient, loving arms.*

III. CONCLUSION

In the Middle of the Night

It was the middle of the night. A man crept into a room where a beloved child slept. After a few moments he laid his hands on the child, who cried out in pain. The man quickly threw blankets over the still-asleep child, rushed out of the house, and into a waiting car where his accomplice was expecting him and eager to be down the road. He restrained the child on the drive, careful to avoid looking suspicious so that the police wouldn't stop them, until they got to an industrial-looking building that was frightening to the boy. The man handed the child over to other people—*and all of them wore masks.* They took the boy to a room where they restrained him and tortured him with sharp objects. Finally the man who had taken him from the home entered the room. He also was wearing a mask. He looked at the boy, took a knife, and plunged it into him, slicing him open.

Have I just described a brutal kidnap-murder or a surgeon who is performing an emergency appendectomy on his own son at the hospital? One can shoe-horn the details to fit either scenario. The first scenario is sinister; the second is saving (but still painful). It depends on the motives of the perpetrators and on their relationship to the victim. God allowed the Canaanites to remain in the land. His purpose was not to destroy his people but to preserve them (see Gen. 50:20). Sometimes it is necessary for the Great Physician to perform surgery on his children in order to save their souls.

PRINCIPLES

- God is the Lord of history who uses human beings—including kings and rulers—to accomplish his purposes (Dan. 4:17).
- It is possible to lose our dependency on God and to forget that in him "we live and move and have our being" (Acts 17:28). Like most second-generation and third-generation believers, we tend to take God for granted.
- Sin has a way of desensitizing its victims; as we return to the same sins over and over, they don't seem so bad or quite as "sinful" as they once did.
- God's character does not change. He is faithful to his promises, not because of who we are but because of who he is. "If we are faithless, he will remain faithful, for he cannot disown himself" (2 Tim. 2:13).

APPLICATIONS

- Give thanks that nothing on the planet takes God by surprise. All of us—collectively and individually—are in his hands.
- Take spiritual inventory. Check to make sure you have made the transition from faith in someone else's faith to your own first-generation experience with Christ.
- Confess your sins; don't ignore this spiritual discipline and allow sins to accumulate.
- Enjoy God's blessings but avoid allowing them to make you more blessing-centered than God-centered.

IV. LIFE APPLICATION

God Is Not a Grandfather

My story is not dramatic or unique. On the other hand, it is not uncommon within Christian circles. I was raised in a Christian home led by a devout father and mother. They loved each other dearly, lived consistently, and tried to raise me and my sister to love the Lord. Our happy home was filled with friends and laughter. My sister seemed not to waver but embraced the Lord and walked with him from a young age. She endured paths of suffering, but those made her stronger; she walks with the Lord to this day.

My path was more of a meandering trek. While I made a verbal profession of faith at the age of seven, the truth of the matter is that several of the other boys in my Sunday school class were being baptized, and I didn't want to be left out. In my growing years I acknowledged the truth of the doctrines of Christianity, but I had no relationship with Jesus Christ. In retrospect, because I believed my parents and they did not lie to me, I therefore believed them when they told me about Jesus. I had placed my faith in *their* faith; I was, in a manner of speaking, God's grandchild, not his child. My walk and the choices I made over the next several years gave little evidence of regeneration.

I arrived at the broad gates of a very liberal university where I invested four years of my life, and it did not take long for me to be exposed to significant challenges to the truth of Christianity. One night as I walked through newly fallen snow toward my dormitory, I realized that faith in my parent's faith wasn't enough; it was not saving faith. I realized that God doesn't have grandchildren, only children, and I placed my personal faith in Jesus Christ. Later I majored in philosophy, and while I knew nothing at that time of Christian apologetics or the towering intellectual heritage of our faith, I knew deep within me that Christianity was true, even though I had no answers at that time for the doubts that plagued me. The reason I knew it was true was because of Christ within me and because of the genuineness of "long obedience" I had observed within the home in which I was raised.

Israel had a godly heritage. They had the examples of the life of Joshua, the lives of the elders who survived Joshua, as well as the experiences of other godly men like Caleb. Still, they chose to turn their backs on God. The allure and excitement of the surrounding pagan culture was more enticing than a life of obedience and inner spiritual peace.

Each person who has a godly heritage faces similar choices. Clearly, God doesn't have grandchildren. Clearly, he wants a first-generation relationship with each of us. Clearly, he doesn't force himself on us. He stands at the door and knocks; if we admit him, he will take what little we have to offer him, but will give to his "children" every conceivable spiritual blessing (Eph. 1:3; Rev. 3:20).

V. PRAYER

Father, we look at the seen, not at the unseen, yet you are the Lord over both realms. There are times when we are tempted to regard you more as a grandfather whose eyes are dim and whose hearing is failing than as the Almighty Father of the universe. We are tempted to believe that sin is not so sinful and that your grace is not so rare. May we not forget the long obedience of those who have gone before us. May we demonstrate faithful service and loyal love before our generation. Through Christ our Lord. Amen.

VI. DEEPER DISCOVERIES

A. Confronting the Creator

This chapter records the first of three confrontations in Judges between God and Israel (see also 6:7–10; 10:10–16). Block notes that in a comparison of the three confrontations, "one observes a progression of the communicators of the divine response . . . an envoy of Yahweh (2:1–5); a prophet of Yahweh (6:7–10); Yahweh himself (10:10–16)" (Block, 110).

B. Touched by an Angel

The angel of the Lord is very likely the pre-incarnate Christ, he who would become flesh for us. Here is some biblical evidence that this being was more than a man: he was distinct from the Lord, yet was called the Lord (Gen. 16:7–13, 18:1–21; 19:1–28; 22:11–12; Exod. 3:2–6; Judg. 13:3–22); Manoah said that the angel of the Lord was God (Judg. 13:3,9,18,19–22); the angel of the Lord claimed that he was God; note the shift in Exodus 3:2–6 from "angel of the LORD" (v. 2) to "I am the God of your father" (v. 6).

C. Chronology of the Chapter (2:6–10)

The Book of Judges is largely chronological, but there are occasional topical flashbacks, as we see particularly in verses 6–10. Although chapter 2 sets the stage for the rest of the book with basic information, some of the events of this chapter reach back into episodes that took place in the Book of Joshua, placed here for sake of completeness (prior to the period of the cycles in 3:7–16:31). Like flashbacks in a good story, we learn that much tribal occupation had already begun (Josh. 15:13–19).

D. The Write Stuff

The literary structure of the last segment (vv. 11–22) demonstrates unity of purpose within what some would see as a rambling indictment. The first part (vv. 11–13) is chiastic, an ABC/CBA structure: Israel served the Baals (vv. 11b,13b); Israel abandoned the Lord (vv. 12a,13a); Israel pursued other gods (vv. 12b,c). The last part (vv. 16–22) occurs in an AB/AB/AB (rebellion/reckoning) pattern.

VII. TEACHING OUTLINE

A. INTRODUCTION

1. Lead Story: Going Crazy over You
2. Context: The first chapter of Judges gave the facts behind the decline of Israel during the "dark ages" of the judges—the history of what happened. Judges 2 is theological and tells "why" it happened. In a sense, Judges 2 is a condensed version of the Book of Judges and prepares us for the first cycle and its judge Othniel (Judg. 3).
3. Transition: It is one thing to find out the facts about any major catastrophe. It is quite another to ask "why did this happen?" When the event is a spiritual calamity brought about by human choices, the question "why" forces us to look at deeper issues, the kinds of issues that strip bare not only our sin but also our motives. As we enter Judges 3, we enter the raw landscape of man's sin contrasted with the glory of God's salvation.

B. COMMENTARY

1. Confrontation: Slugged by an Angel (2:1–5)
   a. Cause of the visitation: God had been faithful (2:1)

    b. Cause of the visitation: Israel had been faithless (2:2)

    c. Effect of the visitation: God withdrew (2:3)

    d. Effect of the visitation: Israel wept (2:4–5)

2. Commemoration: Heritage of a Hero (2:6–10)

    a. People served God all the days of Joshua and the elders (2:6–9)

    b. People snubbed God and did what was right in their own eyes (2:10)

3. Calamity: Diagram of Decline (2:11–23)

    a. Israel's rejection of God, I (2:11–13)

    b. God's reckoning with Israel, I (2:14–16)

    c. Israel's rejection of God, II (2:17)

    d. God's reckoning with Israel, II (2:18)

    e. Israel's rejection of God, III (2:19)

    f. God's reckoning with Israel, III (2:20–23)

C. CONCLUSION: IN THE MIDDLE OF THE NIGHT

VIII. ISSUES FOR DISCUSSION

1. Why does God "give people over"? Compare the actions of God in Judges 2:1–5 with those in Romans 1:18–32. Note in particular the repeated phrase found in Romans 1:24,26,28. Why does God permit people whom he loves to choose to self-destruct?

2. The Israelites were content to rest upon their collective history with the Lord. There are times when people raised in Christian homes (particularly with Christian parents who lived in spiritual integrity) have a tendency to place their faith in their parents' faith. But God has children, not grandchildren. God's children have a relationship with him and do not rest in a false security arising from a godly heritage. What do you think a person can do to make sure his faith is real and not borrowed from his parents?

3. Here are some possible steps in a downward spiral toward sin. First, you tolerate sin in your life as "no big deal." Second, you begin to accept the sin as normal. Third, you begin to forget the way God once worked in your life. Fourth, you begin to ignore God's Word (Josh. 1:7–8; 22–24). Fifth, you stop seeing things as God sees them. Sixth, you begin to think that all the victories in your life are

explainable in terms of you. Would you add or delete anything from this list?

4. God has made us emotional, rational, and volitional beings (and in some of us one dominates over the others!). Emotions are also a part of our worship. The emotions of Israel were deep and effusive when God confronted them in Judges 2. But did the emotional reaction of Israel indicate repentance? Compare similar situations in Numbers 14:1–2 and Malachi 2:13–15.

5. Consider the pattern of discipleship through family generations found in Deuteronomy 6:1–9. See if you can identify various ways of teaching God's truth. How do we avoid the inoculation of the next generation of believers with lukewarm Christianity?

Judges 3

Same Old Same Old

I. INTRODUCTION
Boring and Predictable

II. COMMENTARY
A verse-by-verse explanation of the chapter.

III. CONCLUSION
The Person God Uses

An overview of the principles and applications from the chapter.

IV. LIFE APPLICATION
A Trio of Talent

Melding the chapter to life.

V. PRAYER
Tying the chapter to life with God.

VI. DEEPER DISCOVERIES
Historical, geographical, and grammatical enrichment of the commentary.

VII. TEACHING OUTLINE
Suggested step-by-step group study of the chapter.

VIII. ISSUES FOR DISCUSSION
Zeroing the chapter in on daily life.

"*Y*ou're gonna have to serve somebody. Well, it may be the devil or it may be the Lord, but you're gonna have to serve somebody."

B o b   D y l a n

BIOGRAPHICAL PROFILE: OTHNIEL

- Caleb's nephew, who became Caleb's son-in-law
- Champion of the conquest of Debir (Judg. 1:11–15)
- Family, not Israelites by birth but by conversion
- Assimilated into the tribe of Judah
- Cycle is paradigmatic of all subsequent cycles
- No moral flaw recorded

BIOGRAPHICAL PROFILE: EHUD

- Family was from the tribe of Benjamin
- Held in high respect among Israelite peers
- Courageous and clever
- Considerate of his men
- Trained to be an ambidextrous warrior

BIOGRAPHICAL PROFILE: SHAMGAR

- First of the "minor" judges
- Shortest story of all the judges
- Father named after Canaanite goddess of war
- Not a Hebrew name
- Far more we don't know about him than we do

Judges 3

I N   A   N U T S H E L L

Judges 3 introduces a pattern that will be repeated throughout the time of the judges. Israel does evil in the Lord's sight. God disciplines his people by giving them into the hands of an enemy. The people cry out to God. God hears and raises up a leader or leaders to deliver his people.

Same Old Same Old

I. INTRODUCTION

Boring and Predictable

The young woman sat across my desk, annihilating tissues. Her tears were torrential, her sobs racked her soul. Her story was, quite tragically, predictable. I had heard it before, and I knew I would hear it again—she loved her boyfriend, and together they yielded to impatience and sexual sin. Soon she became pregnant, and her boyfriend discreetly vanished from her life. Here's where the tragedy was compounded: her father, a deacon at a large church, simply could not stand for "his good name" to be besmirched, so he guided his daughter to get an abortion. That way, nobody knew. Except for God. And, some five years later, except for me. And now, some ten years later still, except for you as readers.

How often is this cycle repeated with monotonous regularity? Only the names and a few details vary. Let's face it: sin is boring and predictable. This is clear even from the most shallow reading of the Book of Judges. Director Billy Wilder was asked how he liked a new film. "To give you an idea," he said, "the film started at eight o'clock. I looked at my watch at midnight—and it was only 8:15." The unfolding plot of sin in the life of God's people is so predictable that we are given few details of how it was manifested. In Judges it's the "same old same old." By contrast, however, God's deliverance reflects variety and is unpredictable. Othniel, Ehud, and Shamgar form an odd trio of deliverers indeed, and the cycles they represent remind us first of all that sin reeks, and it stinks dreadfully; second, that God redeems, and he redeems fully—and sometimes almost playfully!

II. COMMENTARY

Same Old Same Old

> **MAIN IDEA:** *God's people descend into predictable patterns of sin. As the cycles of rebellion, restitution, repentance, restoration, and rest progress, three very different judges were raised up by God to accomplish his purposes for his people. God did not leave his covenant people without hope; even when they regressed to wallowing in the mire of sin, he remained true to his promises.*

A The Descent of Israel (3:1–6)

> **SUPPORTING IDEA:** *The first segment provides us with the "wide-angle lens" overview of the landscape of Israel's enemies. The "roll call" details the topography of pockets of resistance within the promised land. These enemies were a test for Israel to demonstrate its faithfulness to the Lord; unfortunately, it failed the test miserably.*

3:1–3. *Roll Call: Four Groups (and Groups of Groups).* The LORD did not drive out the Canaanites but left them in the land to **test** his people—not for him to gain knowledge of their disposition of the **wars in Canaan** but rather as an ongoing opportunity for Israel to choose whether she would "accept her status as his covenant people, with all the privileges and obligations attached thereto" (Block, 137). This generation **had not had previous battle experience**; in order to reside in the land they must first rely on the Lord. God commanded the extermination of the Canaanites; Israel said "no."

The result was that these enemies of God remained: **five rulers of the Philistines, all the Canaanites, the Sidonians, and the Hivites** (see "Deeper Discoveries"). The list is not political, economic, chronological, or even exhaustive; it is geographical. It represents the completeness of the challenge by pointing in all four directions: southeast (Canaanites), northeast (Hivites), northwest (Sidonians), and southwest (Philistines).

3:4. *Reason: Israel's Examination.* The rationale for the presence of the Canaanites was theological: **they were left to test the Israelites** (see 2:22; 3:1). God's children were given an examination. The results were not to be posted in heaven (as though God were uncertain about their progress) but rather would be visible for all the world to see. The bottom line was this: Would they, or would they not, **obey the LORD's commands?** God's word came **through Moses** (note the presumption of a written Pentateuch), had been given to **their forefathers**, and now stood as the template by which their performance would be measured.

3:5–6. *Result—the "C.I.A."* The examination results were dismal. They failed every category: Cohabitation, Intermarriage, and Apostasy.

First, not only did they permit the Canaanites to live among them; they also **lived among the Canaanites**. Six Canaanite peoples are mentioned, indicating that this practice was the rule, not the exception. Each time the Israelites had the opportunity to obey God, but over and over again they settled among the Canaanites. They were content to adopt Canaanite culture and adapt Canaanite ways, as the next two points make clear.

Second, **they took their daughters in marriage and gave their own daughters to their sons**, in direct violation of God's command (Deut. 7:1–5; see Josh. 23:12). It is one thing to bring unbelievers into one's home by marriage where at least they may live in an environment governed by God's law. It is quite another to allow one's daughters to live within the structures of Canaanite religion and culture, where they may or may not survive as victims of pagan whims. The point was that Israelite fathers placed higher value on their own comfort than on the protection (much less the godly instruction!) of their own daughters.

Third, and most unspeakable, they **served their gods**. The ways of worshiping Canaanite deities have already been discussed and need not be mentioned here. They failed *culturally, domestically,* and *spiritually.*

Ⓑ The Deliverance Through Othniel (3:7–11)

> **SUPPORTING IDEA:** *The Othniel cycle provides a "normal lens" through which to view a standard portrait of a good judge, almost a template of the cycle of rebellion, retribution, repentance, restoration, and rest. It is skeletal, but helpful. Othniel was a traditional hero; we are to admire his character.*

3:7. *Rebellion.* **The Israelites did evil in the eyes of the LORD** (see Commentary comments on 2:11–13). Despite all that God had done for them, they chose what they could see and hear ("walking by sight") over faith; they could literally see the local gods, whereas the omnipresent Lord seemed remote.

Two complementary aspects of their rebellion are mentioned. First, **they forgot the LORD** who is specifically known not only as "the God" or "a God" but **their God**. Second, they **served the Baals and the Asherahs**. In other words, they worshiped and served the creature rather than the Creator (Rom. 1:25). In Greek mythology the Sirens were daughters of Phorkys and Acheloos (the river god), nymphs who were half woman, half fish. They inhabited the cliffs of the islands between Sicily and Italy. By the sweetness of their singing, they lured unwary travelers to land on the islands, where the Sirens would then tear them apart and eat them.

The Israelites were lured into moral compromise, and they became like the people they were supposed to displace. Unfortunately, Satan is a roaring lion seeking whom he may devour, and God's children are high on his menu; sin cannibalizes its victims.

3:8. *Retribution.* God's **anger . . . burned against Israel**, although we are not told against which tribes. Possibly because of the vastness of the enemy, the oppression encompassed much of the nation. In reaction, God **sold them** to their enemies. This term refers to transfer of property (they belonged to God, and only he could choose to "rent" them out). Their subjugation lasted **eight years**.

The identity of **Cushan-Rishathaim king of Aram Naharaim** is unknown. If Aram is the same as Syria (as in the Septuagint), then the implications are significant. Aram "extended from northeast of the Sea of Galilee to the Taurus mountains in the north and eastward beyond the Habur tributary of the upper Euphrates River" (Block, 152). Naharaim means "of the two rivers," probably the Tigris and the Euphrates. Therefore this king was not merely the leader of a Canaanite city but possibly the most powerful military enemy named in the entire Book of Judges! His name means "Cushan of Double Wickedness," possibly a term meant to instill dread within the hearts of intended victims. (If one wanted to instill terror, it would be less effective to squeak, "My name is Thundar the Thespian!" than to declare, "My name is Thundar the Terminator!")

3:9a. *Repentance.* Israel **cried out**. Their cry was not generic or non-specific; it was directional. It was a cry **to the LORD**. Scripture does not tell us whether their supplication included submission or whether their request was accompanied by repentance.

3:9b–10. *Restoration.* Two aspects of God's reaction are noteworthy. First, the initiative for this judgeship came from God, who **raised up . . . a deliverer**. Just as there had been directionality to Israel's cry, there was directionality to God's initiative: the action was performed **for** them, that is, for his covenant people. Second, **Othniel** (whom we met in 1:11–15) was one of the few judges about whom nothing negative is ever recorded. Earlier we noted that Othniel was Caleb's nephew. He was from a proselyte family that had been assimilated into the tribe of Judah.

Othniel **saved them**. In truth, this was an astonishing victory, presented to readers as "mere facts." The text explains how: **The Spirit of the Lord came upon him,** and he led the people in **war**. We are given no details to satisfy our curiosity—how, when, where? That may be what we "want" to know. But what we "need" to know is who: the Lord enabled the victory that broke the yoke of Aramean oppression (Zech. 4:6).

3:11. *Rest.* The result was that **the land had peace for forty years**, the remainder of the lifespan of **Othniel**. The main character in this segment is not Israel and not Othniel; the main character is God. He heard Israel's desperate plea, he raised up the deliverer, he empowered the deliverance and conquered the dictator; he gave his people rest.

ⓒ The Deliverance Through Ehud (3:12–30)

> **SUPPORTING IDEA:** *The Ehud cycle is not a wide-angle lens nor a normal lens; it is a zoom lens providing us with significant detail of a cycle. Ehud was a unique hero; we are to admire his courage.*

3:12a. *Rebellion.* We are told that **again the Israelites did evil in the eyes of the Lord** (see 2:11), repeating the boring paradigm that initiates the cycles of sin and judgment. Again, this was a case of spiritual adultery, of intense pain for Israel's loving husband, the Lord.

3:12b–14. *Retribution.* As before, God's response was to give the Israelites over to chastisement at the hands of their enemies, in this case **Eglon king of Moab**, who was unaware that he was being used for God's purposes (Dan. 4:17). Historically the Moabites, descendants of one of Lot's daughters (Gen. 19:36–37), had been hostile to Israel (see Num. 22–24). Forging an alliance with **the Ammonites and Amalekites**, Eglon's combined force **attacked Israel** and **took possession** of Jericho, the **City of Palms**, which became his base of operations in Israel. In order to get to Jericho, Eglon first had to subjugate the Transjordanian tribes (Reuben, Gad, half of Manasseh) before his armies could cross the Jordan to attack the rest of Israel. This subjugation lasted **for eighteen years**.

3:15a. *Repentance.* **Again the Israelites cried out to the LORD** (as they had done before and will do again). Israel had run after other gods, only to find that when it was in trouble, the only place to run was to the Lord, its covenant husband (see John 6:68).

3:15b–29. *Restoration.* God raised up as **a deliverer**, a combat ace named **Ehud**. The author unfolds a tale of conspiracy, of courage, and of cleverness. The main character of this intrigue was identified by his family, his tribe, and his uniqueness: he was **the son of Gera** (see 1 Chr. 7:10; 8:3,5,7) of the tribe of Benjamin (which means "son of my right hand"), and he was ironically **a left-handed man**. Literally, the term *left-handed* means "hindered in the right hand."

The idea apparently is not that his right hand was handicapped and thus his left-handedness was due to compensation. Instead, the term probably refers to the practice of binding ("hindering") the right hand of boys and thus forcing them to become ambidextrous. An ambidextrous warrior was a much more formidable opponent because most warriors were used to defending against right-handed opponents, sword against shield. An ambidextrous warrior could fight left-handed, and if combat circumstances permitted, throw the enemy off by switching. (This seems to fit well with the training that other Benjamites received later in the book; see Judg. 20:16 and 1 Chr. 12:2.)

Ehud was particularly resourceful. He had a specific plan, which we discover only as we progress through the story. Apparently his military objectives were clear (to assassinate Eglon and overthrow the Moabite yoke), and his methods of accomplishing them were in place (high court intrigue, daring escape through an unusual route, and a decisive ambush). Ehud's resourcefulness was further seen in that he made a unique **double-edged sword about a foot and a half long, which he strapped to his right thigh under his clothing**. The sword was apparently without a hilt, and he attached it where distracted bodyguards might not think to look.

Ehud was chosen as the agent who **presented the tribute to the king**. We are not told why, although apparently from his ability to raise troops who were willing to follow him in battle (vv. 27–28), he was held in high regard among the Israelites. After the "mission of tribute" was completed, he and his companions took leave of the king, but Ehud then left them **near Gilgal**, where **he himself turned back** to complete his mission of intrigue. Ehud (with his hidden dagger still in place) was granted an immediate audience with Eglon, having told him, **I have a secret message for you, O king**. The term for message is unclear—it may also mean "object"—and its ambiguity may be intentional!

The king (anticipating a bribe, or at the least something to his advantage) foolishly dismissed his bodyguard and received Ehud into the room next to his throne room, where he seated himself. This time Ehud told him that he had **a message from God.** Because of the use of the more general term for "god," it is likely that Eglon was anticipating a word from his Moabite god Chemosh. In any case he arose (perhaps slowly and with difficulty) exposing his vast bulk to Ehud, who **reached with his left hand, drew the sword from his right thigh and plunged it into the king's belly.**

Gruesome details are given which authenticate the realism of the episode: **The handle sank in after the blade,** and **the fat closed in over** the sword. This caused Ehud to leave it in place, and Eglon's bowels loosed with the result that excrement soiled the floor (the NIV reading implying it was the sword itself **which came out his back** is misleading; the verbal descriptions of the entire episode invite an awareness to the observer that most of the senses were involved). Ehud probably anticipated the possibility that he would fight his way out of the palace, but it was more important that his hands and clothes be free from bloodstains than to retrieve a weapon that he might not need.

What follows is high suspense. Time passed. The bodyguard had not seen Ehud leave, but the fact that the doors were locked from the inside coupled with an unmistakable smell led to their conclusion that the king **must be relieving himself** (literally, "covering his feet"—a euphemism describing the condition of one's clothing during elimination) **in the inner room of the house.** While they **waited to the point of embarrassment,** Ehud got away!

Not only was Eglon portrayed as thick of brawn; his elite troops were portrayed as thick of brain. They left their master alone with an assassin without raising any objections, and they allowed Ehud to escape, all the while wondering how he left the room, clueless and dawdling over whether to interrupt their king and see about his safety. The fierce Moabite elite guards were akin to bumbling and inept Keystone Cops. They finally **took a key and unlocked** the chambers, discovering **their lord fallen to the floor, dead.**

When he arrived at Seirah, Ehud **blew a trumpet in the hill country of Ephraim,** apparently a pre-arranged signal, and was joined by **the Israelites . . . from the hills, with him leading them.** Ehud shifted roles from commando to commander and encouraged his men with the use of God's covenant name: **The LORD has given Moab, your enemy, into your hands**. This is the first time in Judges that a man speaks the Lord's name. A strategic decision was made: the troops took **possession of the fords of the Jordan that led to Moab**. The purpose was not just to discourage traffic, but to stop the Moabites from retreating back to their land. They engaged the enemy, and the subsequent battlefield report was that **they struck down about ten thousand Moabites, all vigorous and strong; not a man escaped**.

3:30. *Rest*. **Moab was made subject to Israel** on that day, although we are not told how long Moab's subjugation lasted. Thankfully, **the land had peace for eighty years**—thus two generations were enabled to learn their lesson and to be removed from God's judgment. Sin is certainly not inevitable! As with Israel, our choices are always individual and unique. One fact is clear: God raised up Ehud as his instrument, and God ultimately gave Israel the victory. Without God, there is bondage. With God, there is freedom.

Ⓓ The Deliverance Through Shamgar (3:31)

SUPPORTING IDEA: *The Shamgar cycle is not a wide-angle lens or a normal lens; neither is it a zoom lens. It is a microscopic lens offering us a small snapshot of a cycle. Shamgar was largely an unknown hero, but his audacity is admirable.*

3:31. We know next to nothing about **Shamgar**. He didn't continue and lead or "judge" God's people. We know nothing of his relationship with other believers, if such a relationship existed. In fact, we know nothing of his relationship with the Lord. We know nothing about the duration of peace or of his subsequent career. We do know his name, that he was **son of Anath**, and that his weapon of choice was **an oxgoad**, but these bare facts raise further questions.

First, his name does not seem to be a Hebrew name or to have any standard Hebrew meaning (although it is possible it is remotely related to a word meaning "submission").

Second, Anath was the Canaanite goddess of war, one of the consorts of Baal. It was also a military troop, and "son of Anath" was a common designation identifying soldiers under the command of the Egyptian pharoah. In either case, Shamgar was not a typical child of Israel. If he was indeed Hebrew, nothing about him indicates any spiritual awareness within his family of origin.

Third, the oxgoad was a long pole (eight to ten feet) made of wood, tipped with metal at both ends; one end was a spike for prodding the oxen, the other a kind of chisel for cleaning the plows that the oxen were pulling. His victory over **six hundred Philistines** is unexplained. We wonder if this took place over a period of time, or all at once perhaps in a narrow pass, or in some other scenario. He is categorized as being against the enemies of God's people, so that **he too** (alongside Othniel and Ehud) **saved Israel**.

One point is clear from the context of Judges: God was with Shamgar, enabling his victory. Again, God accomplished his purposes while using strange tools. Sometimes he uses a laser beam; sometimes he uses a sledge hammer!

> **MAIN IDEA REVIEW:** *God's people descend into predictable patterns of sin. As the cycles of rebellion, restitution, repentance, restoration, and rest progress, three very different judges were raised up by God to accomplish his purposes for his people. God did not leave his covenant people without hope. Even when they regressed to wallowing in the mire of sin, he remained true to his promises.*

III. CONCLUSION

The Person God Uses

God used Othniel, Ehud, and Shamgar. God used Paul, a scholar, and God used Peter, a fisherman. What is the profile of the person God uses?

One scholar described his father-in-law, a Nova Scotia fisherman, in this way:

> He lacks my years of university training. I could talk more impressively than he on world events, philosophy, the limitations of the scientific method, and on and on. My vocabulary is vastly greater than his. But let us put out to sea in a sailing boat off the rocky coast of Cape Breton and he seems by instinct to know the depth of the water everywhere. In an uncanny way he can find any port within two hundred miles in a fog without navigational aids. I become a stupid landlubber, helplessly inept and out-classed by this sea-taught marvel of a man. Moreover when he visits my home he wanders around noting what needs to be fixed. I am clumsy with tools, bewildered in the face of

practical jobs. He fixes my lopsided garden gate. What to me was a formidable difficulty is to him an afternoon's recreation.

Am I a better man than he? By what scale are the two of us to be measured? Who can say which of us is morally superior? I can quote the Bible more helpfully and people are often moved when I preach in public. Through my own prayers and ministry he recently came back to God after years of wandering. Yet now his joy in Christ and in the Scriptures makes me ashamed. He seems to have progressed more in a few months than I in years. I stand rebuked before him.

Who will assess us and tell which of us is the better man before God? If I go into the presence of God, the question hangs in the air like an obscenity. I know I have done wrong even to ask it. As the majesty of God fills my vision, all questions of human greatness become pointless. I bend my knees. I fall on my face. I tremble and weep in marvel that such a God calls me his child. I am ashamed by my pettiness, my meannesses, my silly deceits, and my ugly greeds—yet simultaneously aware that I am forgiven, wanted, loved. How can I go from God's presence asserting my superiority over my brethren? I count myself happy to be the least of them all (John White, *The Fight*, IVP, 1976, pp. 146–147).

PRINCIPLES

- God calls all of his children to bring all that they are, in obedience, to all that he is.

- God works in a variety of ways through a variety of people; while he does not deviate from his truth, neither does he always comply with our expectations.

- God allows circumstances in our lives to test our spiritual resilience—when we surrender to sin, we ignore God at our peril; when we endure, by his grace we grow stronger!

- Surrender to sin may begin a downward spiral into a selfish, self-justifying, self-pitying, self-absorbed self-centeredness!

- Whenever we repent, God shows up.

APPLICATIONS

- God will use you if you let him. Don't think your abilities are unusable by the God who made you to be who you are! Let him use you!
- Look around you; rather than being jealous, thank God for the abilities he has given other Christians who are being used by God.
- Remember: walk by faith and not by sight (see 2 Cor. 4:16–18).
- Choose your master! If you become a "slave" to Jesus (Rom. 6:15–23), you will experience the greatest freedom you have ever known.

IV. LIFE APPLICATION

A Trio of Talent

This chapter offers us a triad of talent, a trio of very different people. Think about these three men. Othniel's main qualification was that he had a great godly heritage. Ehud's main qualification was that he was a southpaw. Shamgar's main qualification was, perhaps, well . . . that he owned a stick! They were very different from one another. Othniel had ties to the greatest people in the history of Israel. He didn't coast on that heritage, as is often the temptation, but built upon it.

The bulk of the chapter is taken with Ehud, who was an assassin and warrior of mythic proportions—a Robin Hood or a Rambo. He displayed several admirable qualities. First, he was *careful*. He laid the plan, made the sword, and apparently organized the resistance to await his signal. The entire plan had been meticulously crafted and timed down to the minute. Second, he was *courageous*. He risked his life to carry out his plan; he didn't know if he would come out alive—so many things could have gone wrong. Third, he was *considerate* of his companions. Rather than risk their lives, he got them to safety and then returned prepared to sacrifice his own life on a risky scheme. And Ehud did trust the Lord—he called upon him for his victory. He was an imperfect servant who trusted in a perfect savior.

If the story of Ehud is almost a humorous (adult!) short story, the episode of Shamgar is a one-liner. Oxgoads were to be used on oxen—possibly a visual picture (like Samson's jawbone of a donkey) of derision over one's enemies. Apparently Shamgar delivered Israel for a short period of time, possibly in one decisive battle. It's not that the details are sketchy; the details are non-existent! He was a man who, as far as we know, had a single hour of greatness canonized in Scripture. I imagine he was a Jew, but his father's name is the Canaanite goddess of sex and war, and his own name is not Jewish. He was definitely not prepared at home to be a spiritual leader. He was a peasant from a family that practiced paganism.

Very likely these men would have had little in common; they had very different backgrounds and very different gifts. God used each of them to accomplish his purposes. Do we ever look at other believers and think because they don't look like us, don't talk like us, and don't dress like us, they don't have "the right stuff" and therefore cannot be used by God? Or do we have fixed in our mind the kind of person God can use, and because we don't match our own ideal of what that should be, assume that somehow we are exempt from God's call on our lives?

Some people have impressive minds, others have impressive leadership abilities, others have musical gifts, others have extraordinary compassion, others have athletic prowess. Some are simply plain and ordinary, but maybe like Shamgar they own a stick! When God uses those of us whose talents are limited, he receives even greater glory because clearly any eternal impact is not explainable in terms of us! Besides, as Jesus said, "Apart from me you can do nothing" (John 15:5). God is the one who trashed the tyrants and destroyed the dictators. The greatness of any human enemy is not to be compared with the greatness of God, who is greater than "the one who is in the world" (1 John 4:4).

V. PRAYER

O Lord, you are unlimited in how you empower people to be used for your glory. There are many times when we look at other Christians whose gifts exceed ours, and we are envious, or whose abilities are less than ours, and we feel pride. We confess that we compare and we keep score. Forgive us, Lord, and help us to take our eyes off of ourselves and off of others, and look only to Jesus, the centerpiece of our faith (Heb. 12:1–2). Through Christ our Lord. Amen.

VI. DEEPER DISCOVERIES

A. Four Groups (and Groups of Groups) (3:1–3)

The "five rulers of the Philistines" were not native Canaanites, but they became an overpowering presence in the land. The confederacy of five cities (pentapolis) included Ekron, Gath, Ashkelon, Ashdod, and Gaza (see Josh. 13:3; Judg. 1:18). The next group was "all the Canaanites," a generic term for all the people living in Canaan, including others in overlapping lists. The Sidonians (Phoenicians, whose main city was Sidon; see 1:31) were included, as were also the Hivites (mentioned twenty-five times in the Old Testament; there were several Hivite cities in northern and central Palestine).

B. The Overactive Ego of the Overblown Eglon: An Inkling of an Implication

Eglon provides an interesting caricature of a petty king who thinks himself more powerful than the Lord. His name is a diminutive form of "bull" and is phonetically related to the word "rotund." He is presented as a man who was greedy, undisciplined, foolish, naïve, and whose ego was subject to flattery. Every time his name occurs in verses 12–17, it is accompanied by the title "king of Moab." After verse 20 his name is no longer mentioned and the description of his demise (a heap of blubber mixed with refuse) is grotesque. One scholar suggests that in presenting Eglon almost as a "cartoon character," God is demonstrating by use of contrast how far Israel may fall, almost taunting her back to obedience. In essence God was saying, "Look at the pathetic conquerors whom I can strengthen to enslave you when you reject me! Is this the reputation you desire?" (After all, who wants it known that they were beaten up by Caspar Milquetoast?) Fat chance.

C. Ehud and the Water Closet

In an article which combines speculation with solid research, Baruch Halpern makes an interesting case for the enigmatic escape of Ehud (Halpern, "The Assassination of Eglon," *Bible Review*, December 1988, 33–41,44). In the classic movie "The Shawshank Redemption" (nominated for seven Academy Awards) the main character escaped from an inescapable prison through the sewage system. This is not far removed from the way Ehud escaped the

Moabite palace. There was apparently a toilet off the throne room through which Ehud made his escape after locking all other doors.

D. The Strategy of Assassination

Our text does not invite an evaluation of the ethics of assassination. The point is to demonstrate that if Israel continually rebels against God, she will be permitted to suffer even at the hands of "cartoon characters" like Eglon. However, we may speculate on the question, Does God sanction selective assassination? (see Judg. 4:17–21; 1 Kgs. 2:5–8). Of course, we may say that this story is descriptive, not prescriptive, and that it describes one person's methods. Still, we must ask ourselves, If I could have assassinated Hitler in 1939, would I have done it? And then we would have to ask a follow-up question, Would it be right? It is worth noting that this is one of those rare times in Judges where it is *not* said that the Lord either guided or that the Spirit of the Lord "came upon" a judge to do this. Is this a significant omission? There are times when God picks blunt instruments from his tool shed.

VII. TEACHING OUTLINE

A. INTRODUCTION

1. Lead Story: Boring and Predictable
2. Context: This chapter elaborates on the test (vv. 1–6) which we have already been informed about in 2:22. After viewing God's deliverance through three unique judges, we are prepared and not surprised to see the continuing story of God's deliverance through yet another unlikely pair, Deborah and Barak (chs. 4–5).
3. Transition: When God's people turn their backs on him, the consequences they suffer are at times devastating; self-destruction is never enjoyable to observe. Still, God is alert to our needs and awaits our repentance when we turn to him (although his methods of deliverance are at times unique).

B. COMMENTARY

1. The Descent of Israel (3:1–6)
   a. Roll Call: Four Groups (and Groups of Groups) (3:1–3)

b. Reason: Israel's Examination (3:4)

c. Result—the "C.I.A." (3:5–6)

2. The Deliverance Through Othniel (3:7–11)

   a. Rebellion (3:7)

   b. Retribution (3:8)

   c. Repentance (3:9a)

   d. Restoration (3:9b–10)

   e. Rest (3:11)

3. The Deliverance Through Ehud (3:12–30)

   a. Rebellion (3:12a)

   b. Retribution (3:12b–14)

   c. Repentance (3:15a)

   d. Restoration (3:15b–29)

   e. Rest (3:30)

4. The Deliverance Through Shamgar (3:31)

C. CONCLUSION: THE PERSON GOD USES

VIII. ISSUES FOR DISCUSSION

1. This chapter is straightforward: God's people sinned, and consequences followed. What is unusual is the notion of God's keeping a "test" in place (vv. 1,4) by which they might measure themselves. This is certainly a gauge of the patience of God. Three verses in the New Testament speak of God's patience in the context of judgment, and these merit meditation. Study 1 Peter 3:20 and 2 Peter 3:9,15 to see what you learn about God's character.

2. This chapter also reinforces our understanding of the blend of God's justice with his mercy. Study these passages to see how they inform the Christian about God's justice: Romans 6:23; 1 Corinthians 3:10–4:5; 2 Corinthians 5:10; 2 Thessalonians 1:8–9; and Hebrews 11:6.

3. Finally, consider what Scripture says about the kind of person God uses. Read 1 Corinthians 12:12–26, a passage that exhorts believers not to compare themselves with one another.

Judges 4–5

The Awed Couple

I. INTRODUCTION
Israel's Queen Mum

II. COMMENTARY
A verse-by-verse explanation of these chapters.

III. CONCLUSION
I Am the Path

An overview of the principles and applications from these chapters.

IV. LIFE APPLICATION
Hebrew, Hassles, and Hymns

Melding these chapters to life.

V. PRAYER
Tying these chapters to life with God.

VI. DEEPER DISCOVERIES
Historical, geographical, and grammatical enrichment of the commentary.

VII. TEACHING OUTLINE
Suggested step-by-step group study of these chapters.

VIII. ISSUES FOR DISCUSSION
Zeroing these chapters in on daily life.

"*L*eadership is the ability to get men to do what they

don't want to do and to like it."

H a r r y   T r u m a n

LITERARY PROFILE: JUDGES 4–5, A STORY IN STEREO

Judges 4 and 5 comprise a two-chapter unit that we will study together. Biblical scholars are fascinated by the juxtaposition of these twin chapters, which (along with Exod. 14–15) are unique in the Bible and in most ancient literature. Both chapters tell the same story but in two different ways. They are not identical twins but fraternal twins. Judges 4 is a factual telling of the events; Judges 5 is a poetical recitation of the same events. Judges 4 is for the history class; Judges 5 for the music class (it is, after all, a song; 5:1). Judges 4 educates; Judges 5 entertains. Judges 4 is like a photograph; Judges 5 more like an impressionistic painting. They do not contradict each other; they complement each other and together inform and move us toward the praise of God, who always keeps his covenant. Neither tells the whole story, although chapter 4 gives a chronological plot without which chapter 5 by itself would require much speculation. The careful reader will note the following specific points in which the chapters inform each other:

Judges 4 Prose Omits:	. . . Which Judges 5 Adds:
The Lord's specific help	5:4–5
Roll call of tribal participation	5:13–18
God's heavenly battle	5:20–21
Story of Sisera's mother	5:28–30

Judges 5 Poetry Omits:	Judges 4 Adds:
Initiating role of King Jabin	4:2
Backgrounds for Deborah and Barak	4:4–9
Information about Heber, Jael's husband	4:11
Barak's disappointing pursuit of Sisera	4:16–22

 I N   A   N U T S H E L L

espite the plans of earthly rulers, God's plan for his people is unavoidable; he overcomes all obstacles for those who belong to him, using the unlikely to accomplish the unthinkable in ways that are unpredictable.

The Awed Couple

I. INTRODUCTION

Israel's Queen Mum

On April 9, 2002, Empress Dowager Elizabeth Angela Marguerite, the queen mother of England, was laid to rest beside her husband who had died in 1952. When she married George, she never entertained the possibility that she would become queen, since the line of succession passed laterally by her and her royal husband. However, an unexpected abdication of the throne radically changed her life permanently. Her shy and stammering husband suddenly became King George VI, and she became the queen of a nation. During World War II, Prime Minister Winston Churchill advised her to leave England for her safety. Instead, she insisted on tramping through bomb-ravaged London, talking with ordinary people who were suffering and whose lives had been displaced. She always insisted on wearing her best clothes for these forays because she felt that a dignified appearance conveyed an encouraging sense of stability to people whose lives daily (and nightly, from German firebomb raids) were in turmoil.

At her death at 101 years of age, the queen mother had seen the empire through the entire span of the twentieth century, from the development of the airplane to the widespread use of the internal combustion engine through two world wars and well into the space age and then the cyber-space age! Few women have earned the respect of her subjects as did the "Queen Mum." Her life was one of long faithfulness to her role, of courage, and of moral authority.

When one opens the Book of Judges to read about the next man to serve God as a leader, one is surprised to discover that it's not a man but a woman. Deborah was the "Queen Mum" to Israel (5:7), an amalgam of the qualities of many visible women of history: Golda Meir, Indira Ghandi, Margaret Thatcher, Sandra Day O'Connor, maybe a bit of Annie Oakley, and perhaps some Maria von Trapp—as "The Sound of Music" swells from chapter 5.

But whatever flaws any of these heroines may have had, we are exposed to none in the life of this godly woman. As a prophetess Deborah spoke for God. As a judge she earned the respect of the nation, and to her wisdom the

Israelites willingly submitted. Yet she still functioned as a wife and a mother. God placed her in a particular place and time for a specific purpose. The strongest of the males at that time, Barak, would not go into battle unless she went with him. Chapter 4 tells the story of Deborah and Barak, "The Odd Couple." Chapter 5 offers a paean of praise from "The Awed Couple."

II. COMMENTARY

The Awed Couple

MAIN IDEA: *God's plan for his people is not bound by the plans of earthly rulers (like Jabin and Sisera); he overcomes all obstacles to bring about his purposes for those who belong to him, using those who are willing to be used (like Deborah and Jael) to restore his people to freedom and faithfulness.*

A The Odd Couple (4:1–24)

SUPPORTING IDEA: *Despite our frailty and fear, God turns our trepidation into triumph by his patience and power.*

4:1–3. *Prologue: The Despot and the Vicious General.* Again the cycle of rebellion (4:1), retribution (4:2), repentance (4:3), restoration (4:4–24), and rest (5:31) is present, but the repetition serves less in this cycle as an interpretative grid than as a "given." We are now familiar with the boring pattern of sin: after the death of a prominent leader, in this case **Ehud, the Israelites once again did evil in the eyes of the LORD.** God's response was consonant with his promise to his people: If they gave themselves over to sin, he would in turn give them over to chastisement (see Rom. 1:24,26,28). **So the LORD sold them into the hands of** their enemy. This is not because God is malevolent, but because he is benevolent. It is better to experience some hell on earth (with resulting repentance, restoration, and rest) than to experience hell in hell.

In this cycle the king whom God permitted to oppress his people was **Jabin** (possibly a dynastic name), **a king of Canaan, who reigned in Hazor. The commander of his army was Sisera,** who played a crucial role in this unfolding drama. Sisera terrorized the northern tribes of Israel with his army that included **nine hundred iron chariots** for a span of **twenty years** until finally God's people **cried** out **to the Lord for help.**

4:4–10. *Confrontation.* While the last section introduced two of the main characters among the Canaanites, this section introduces two of the three main characters among the Israelites (we will meet Jael in 4:17). **Deborah** ("honeybee") was **a prophetess**, along with other women in the Old Testament (Miriam, Exod. 15:20, and Huldah, 2 Kgs. 22:14). Her husband **Lappidoth** is mentioned, although he plays no role in what follows. She seems to have functioned as a civil authority when **leading Israel** as a judicial authority when **the Israelites came to her to have their disputes decided** and as a spiritual authority when God spoke through her. The location **under the Palm of Deborah between Ramah and Bethel in the hill country of Ephraim** was central for easier access by the majority of the Israelites.

When God spoke, Deborah obeyed and conveyed a message to our second character, **Barak son of Abinoam from Kedesh in Naphtali.** We must assume a prior relationship that Deborah had with Barak (whose name means "lightning"); he was known as both a leader and a warrior. He was God's choice to set his people free from oppression.

God's message confronting Barak through Deborah was this: **Go, take with you ten thousand men of Naphtali and Zebulun and lead the way to Mount Tabor.** This cone-shaped mountain rises to about 2,000 feet above sea level, 1,300 feet above the Jezreel Valley. God also promised that he would **lure Sisera, the commander of Jabin's army, with his chariots and his troops to the Kishon River and give him into your hands.** God is sovereign over the plans of enemy generals, and his purposes will not be thwarted (Prov. 21:1, "The king's heart is in the hand of the Lord; he directs it like a watercourse wherever he pleases").

However, Barak made one condition for Deborah: **If you go with me, I will go; but if you don't go with me, I won't go.** Although Barak had clear faith (Heb. 11:32), his was a hesitant faith, at least at first. It may be that he felt the universal respect accorded Deborah would assure ease in raising an army on short notice; it may also be that he regarded the presence of a prophet (or prophetess) of God as representing the visible presence of God with the army. Deborah accepted his terms but warned him that because of the way he was going about this, **the honor will not be yours, for the LORD will hand Sisera over to a woman** (presumably Barak thought she meant herself; sharing honor with Deborah was, to Barak, itself an honor).

Thus Barak **summoned Zebulun and Naphtali** (where Barak was from) and quickly raised the army of ten thousand men. The text reminds us that **Deborah also went with him.**

4:11–13. *Corruption.* The next verse does not move us into the battle but introduces a corrupt traitor named **Heber the Kenite.** Related to Israel through Moses, the nomadic Kenites had friendly relations with God's people (1:16). Heber, however, **had left the other Kenites** (not only was he removed geographically, he was also removed from having any family loyalty) **and pitched his tent by the great tree in Zaanannim near Kedesh.** Since this was the region in which Barak was raising an army, it is likely that the reason for the insertion of Heber at this point in the story is because Heber was the traitor who had his people inform **Sisera that Barak son of Abinoam had gone up to Mount Tabor.**

Sisera knew and trusted Heber (see 4:17), so in order to quell this rebellion immediately, **Sisera gathered . . . nine hundred iron chariots and all the men with him, from Harosheth Haggoyim to the Kishon River.** The Kishon River (about ten miles west of Mount Tabor) was dry for much of the year and presented no problem for the mobility of Sisera's war chariots.

4:14–16. *Annihilation.* The story now resumes from verse 10. This is the last speech we hear from Deborah until the song of chapter 5 (unlike Joan of Arc, she was not a part of the battle). She encouraged Barak with two major points. First, the declarative promise was given that this very **day the LORD has given Sisera into your hands**; second, the rhetorical question is put forth, **Has not the LORD gone ahead of you?** There is no question about who was in charge of this battle (kings would "go ahead" of their loyal troops into battle, 1 Sam. 8:20; here instead the Lord would go before them).

Obedient, Barak advanced, and **the LORD routed Sisera and all his chariots and army.** The verb "rout" brings to mind mob confusion and panic (see Exod. 14:24; we learn the cause from chapter 5: the chariots were mired in mud and became liabilities rather than assets). When **the sword** is wielded by God, no human army or human general (Sisera) can withstand him, and no human army or human general (Barak) can claim personal glory. **All the troops of Sisera fell** and were annihilated. One very important person escaped: **Sisera** abandoned his chariot and **fled on foot**, apparently in a direction away from the flight of his floundering soldiers.

4:17–21. *Assassination.* A massive manhunt was mounted to ensnare Sisera with an encircling web that gradually tightened. Since Deborah disappears from the story, we are left to wonder how her prophecy of victory through the agency of a woman (v. 9) could possibly come true. Meanwhile, since Heber (v. 11) was probably the informant who sold Israel into Sisera's hands, it would be logical for Sisera to think that Heber's home would be a safe haven.

The text now introduces us to the **wife of Heber**, a woman named **Jael** who **went out to meet Sisera** and invited him into her tents. Jael ("mountain goat") gave him verbal assurance (**don't be afraid**) and physical comfort (a thick warm **covering** and **milk**). The covering would muffle noise and generate warmth; the milk would help induce sleep. **Exhausted**, Sisera fell into a deep sleep (the same word used of the comatose sleep of Adam in Gen. 2:21 and of Jonah's sleep in the midst of a storm in Jonah 1:5). Then she **picked up a tent peg and a hammer** and did what nomadic wives often did as a regular part of their roles. **She drove** down a tent **peg** but this time **through his temple into the ground, and he died.** Abimelech's fear (Judg. 9:54) became Sisera's reality. One scholar refers to this as "an unusual breach of Near-Eastern hospitality!"

4:22–24. *Epilogue: The Damsel and the Victorious General.* **Barak came** hot on the heels of Sisera, but he arrived at Jael's tent too late, no doubt hoping that at least "some" honor would still be his because he intended to kill Sisera in hand-to-hand combat. Just as she had met Sisera before, **Jael went out to meet him.** One can almost imagine the anticipation of Barak, sword in hand, as Jael told him, **I will show you the man you're looking for.** What Barak found, however, was **Sisera with the tent peg through his temple—dead.** God's word through Deborah was fulfilled but in a way not expected by Barak. What Deborah started, Jael finished.

This victory was not minor but major; it was the beginning of the end for Jabin. As the Lord had done with Sisera, **God subdued Jabin, the Canaanite king, before the Israelites.** The battle was won, and so was the war, "'not by might nor by power, but by my Spirit,' says the LORD Almighty" (Zech. 4:6b).

The text ascribes no condemnation for Jael's action; in the next chapter she is praised as a heroine (Judg. 5:24–27, set in contrast to Sisera's mother, 5:28–31). Those critical of Jael should remember that Sisera "had cruelly oppressed the Israelites for twenty years" (4:3) and that he lay under God's death sentence (Deut. 7:2).

B The Awed Couple (5:1–31)

SUPPORTING IDEA: *When God grants victory, despite numerous difficulties, we are to pause and praise God "from whom all blessings flow." This chapter is a song that celebrates God's works in the prelude (anthem of deliverance, vv. 1–8), the symphony (agents of deliverance, vv. 9–18), and the postlude (acts of deliverance, vv. 19–31).*

5:1–3. *Proclamation.* At this point one expects the cycle to close with a statement of "rest"; after all, the story is complete, and the cycles have run their course—rebellion (4:1), retribution (4:2), repentance (4:3), restoration (4:4–24). However, that closure will await the end of chapter 5, because there is a celebratory song of praise to the Lord, a remembrance in rhyme and rhythm that must be sung! The song "leans on" chapter 4, and without it many of its allusions would make no sense to an uninformed reader. (See the chart at the beginning of this chapter.)

Although chapter 4 introduced us to Deborah and Barak, the "odd couple," in chapter 5 they are the "awed couple"—amazed at God's grace, and offering a paean of praise to the God from whom all blessings flow! The song begins by inviting **kings** and **rulers** to **listen**, as the duo sings a dramatic duet of deliverance. The song is directed **to the LORD, the God of Israel**. Interwoven within the fabric of this poem is a threefold theme: First, God is not localized or territorial, like the gods of the Canaanites; he is the *creator* of all the cosmos. Second, God's purposes will not be thwarted; he is the *commander* of all creatures. Third, God uses his followers to accomplish his will; through Deborah he is the *commender* who honors those who honor him.

5:4–5. *Exaltation.* God is directly addressed and exalted for going before the Israelites into an uncertain war zone. Even though the Canaanites worshiped Baal as the god of the storm, it's clear that the Lord is the creator who controls all of his creation—including the elements! Under his hand **the earth shook, the heavens poured, the clouds poured down water. The mountains quaked before the LORD.**

5:6–8. *Desolation.* Deborah describes the horror of the pre-deliverance living conditions in these three verses: she fixes the events chronologically **in the days of Shamgar son of Anath, in the days of Jael**, shunning the spotlight for herself. During those days, **the roads were abandoned**, because righteous people were afraid of attacks and harassment at the hands of their oppressors. Whenever they had no choice but to travel, **travelers took to winding paths** and stayed out of sight. Farming and trade (**village life**) ceased. However, God chose to use **Deborah . . . a mother in Israel**.

Although the Hebrew is difficult, the phrasing in verse 8 should probably not read **when they chose new gods** but "God chose new ones" (referring to "leaders"; see vv. 1,9). Their courage (which will be lauded in vv. 12–18) is set in relief to the obstacles they must overcome: not only was the enemy well-equipped, but among the Israelites **not a shield or spear was seen among forty thousand in Israel**. It is better to rely on God's *orders* than on a king's *ordnance*.

5:9–11. *Commendation.* Like a proud mother, Deborah's **heart** was **with Israel's princes, with the willing volunteers among the people**. Both believers and profiteers who have turned their backs on God are to **praise the LORD**. Deborah invites those who have grown rich at Israel's expense, **who ride on white donkeys, sitting on your saddle blankets**, and who because of their collaboration with the enemy are not afraid to **walk along the road**, to join in the public praise of the Lord at the public watering places. There **they recite the righteous acts of the LORD and of his warriors in Israel**.

5:12–18. *Evaluation.* The reader is placed in the midst of God's urgent call of Deborah to **wake up**, and to **break out in song**! Likewise, **Barak** is exhorted to **take captive your captives**, as though the battle were already over (which, from God's perspective, was true). Then a "roll call" of those faithful to the Lord is submitted, tribe by tribe. Those who receive praise are from the tribes of Ephraim (Deborah's tribe), Benjamin, Manasseh (Makir), Zebulun, and Issachar (Barak's tribe). However, others were not so forthcoming.

The tribe of Reuben (who had suffered at the hands of King Jabin) engaged in **much searching of heart** while being entertained (**among the campfires . . . the whistling for the flocks**) as though nothing momentous had occurred. Like some believers today, they decided to listen to God's command, take it under advisement, form a committee and study it for a few years, and then issue a strongly worded report. They were stirred to sentiment but not to sacrifice—like those who may have great intentions and who may assume an area of responsibility, but then never follow through.

Without posturing like Reuben, the tribe of Gad (**Gilead**, Josh. 13:24–28) simply did not show up. Neither did the tribes of **Dan** and **Asher** want to go inland to fight a battle for any reason (both had become busy with maritime pursuits); God's call was less important than their financial routine. "Being involved in your struggle doesn't meet my personal needs, thank you very much." By contrast, two tribes merit special mention: **The people of Zebulun risked their very lives; so did Naphtali on the heights of the field.**

It has been suggested that Judges 5 contains both a "Hall of Fame" and a "Hall of Infamy." Within the hall of infamy, there are those who merit "dishonorable discharge" (Gad, Dan, Asher), those guilty of "desertion" (Reuben), and those guilty of "treason" (Meroz). Within the hall of fame there are those who merit bronze stars (Ephraim, Benjamin, Manasseh, and Issachar), those who merit purple hearts (Zebulun, Naphtali), and those who deserve the medal of honor (Jael).

5:19–23. *Confrontation.* The entirety of the battle is condensed into five verses. Not only did the **kings of Canaan** not carry off **silver** or **plunder** (as they had done every other time), they were destroyed by the might of the Creator, who enlisted **the stars** (contra Canaanite astrological superstitions), **the river**, and the **steeds** (horses) in his army! Briefly, **the river Kishon swept them away!** God brought a storm, the rain caused the river to overflow its banks, the chariots became mired in the mud, the horses became frantic, and Sisera's greatest advantage became his greatest liability.

The segment concludes with an unexpected malediction (v. 23) followed by a strong benediction (v. 24). The **curse** was for **Meroz, . . . because they did not come to help the LORD.** Although the location of Meroz is unknown, the meaning is clear: A cluster of Israelites "sold out" their own people to the Canaanites, and therefore fell under God's wrath (this malediction stands as more severe than the rebuke of Reuben, Gad, Dan, and Asher—vv. 15–17).

5:24–27. *Commendation.* In contrast to the Israelites who did not help, **most blessed of women be Jael**, a woman who may not have been an Israelite yet rendered unexpected help. This segment portrays her actions against Sisera with enthusiasm: **she crushed his head, she shattered and pierced his temple . . . where he sank, there he fell—dead.** This point is made: The enemies of God are destroyed—from foot soldier to general—totally, thoroughly, absolutely.

5:28–30. *Anticipation.* In contrast to Jael, there now unfolds what could be a very poignant story of **Sisera's mother** as she peered **through the window,** awaiting the return of her son from battle. Anyone considering the two stories set in juxtaposition to each other would be evaluating these bare facts: a brutal young woman deceived a man who had taken refuge in her tent and viciously murdered him, while his mother faithfully awaited the return of her son from battle, hoping that his delay did not mean he had been hurt. While she worries and wonders from her palace (**Why is his chariot so long in coming?**), we know he will not return. Her ladies-in-waiting wisely (presumably to avoid reprisal) reassure her that he's simply overseeing the division of the spoils of war.

But things are not always as they appear. We have already seen that Jael received the blessing of the Lord for her part in providing closure to the oppression of God's people. What are we to think of Sisera's mother? It may well be that over a twenty-year oppression the appetites of Sisera's mother were well-known among the Israelites, so that the scene before us would not be a surprise to them. The text paints a portrait of her with two bold brush strokes, in which the **spoils** are described: **a girl or two for each man**, and **colorful garments** for her.

Her excitement grew as she envisioned the plunder that would come to her; she moved from garments of color to garments that were **embroidered**, to those that were **highly embroidered** (on both sides, two panels stitched together). It didn't matter that other women were raped and killed to get this material. She is portrayed as a pure utilitarian—"people are valuable only as they gratify me and my desires." One searches Scripture in vain for a more calloused, cold-hearted, and cruel attitude toward other women than this.

5:31. *Conclusion.* The section concludes with the imprecation that all the enemies of the LORD would likewise perish, but that those who love him would **be like the sun when it rises in its strength**. In the Ancient Near East the sun was worshiped as deity or associated with deity as a manifestation of a god. Here, the sun is a picture of triumph over adversity (darkness) for those who belong to the Lord.

Finally, after reframing the elements of rebellion (4:1), retribution (4:2), repentance (4:3), and restoration (4:4–24) in song (5:1–30), the cycle is completed with the "rest" formula: **The land had peace forty years.**

MAIN IDEA REVIEW: *God's plan for his people is not bound by the plans of earthly rulers (like Jabin and Sisera); he overcomes all obstacles to bring about his purposes for those who belong to him, using those who are willing to be used (like Deborah and Jael) to restore his people to freedom and faithfulness.*

III. CONCLUSION

I Am the Path

An old woodsman once gave advice about how to catch a porcupine: "First, you drop a large washtub over him." When he was asked, "Why do that?" he said, "Well, the washtub will give you something to sit on while you ponder your next move." Sometimes we're just not sure what to do next.

Missionary statesman E. Stanley Jones told of a missionary who lost his way in an African jungle. He could find no landmarks and the trail vanished. Eventually, stumbling on a small hut, he asked the native living there if he could lead him out. The native nodded. Rising to his feet, he walked directly into the bush. The missionary followed on his heels. For more than an hour they hacked their way through a dense wall of vines and grasses. The missionary became worried: "Are you sure this is the way? I don't see any path." The African chuckled and said over his shoulder, "Bwana, in this place there is no path. I am the path."

There are times in our lives when we can't see five inches in front of our face. "Lord, I don't know what to do, what to think! Where should I go? How do I deal with this?" The Lord says, "My child, I am the path—the way, the truth, the life. Trust me. I'm with you always, to the end of the age."

But despite these promises there are times when he seems remote, and trusting him seems terribly hard. It means walking by faith, not by sight—and the things we "do see" are very compelling. Here Israel was out-gunned (iron chariots vs. nothing, 5:8), out-positioned (valley vs. hills), and out-manned (40,000 vs. 10,000, 4:10). Three very human responses would be first to build iron smelters to produce weaponry, to institute a draft in order to assemble more soldiers, and to fight in the hills only so that those chariots would be unusable. But God had a different strategy, and as God's people discovered, he was there all along. "The task ahead of you is never greater than the power behind you." We have the power of God's promise: "The one who is in you is greater than the one who is in the world" (1 John 4:4).

PRINCIPLES

- God incorporates the free actions of human beings to accomplish his purposes; he is not a puppet master, but we are clay in his hands (Gen. 50:20).
- Our gain is less important than God's glory!
- Despite our uncertainties, God will remain true to his promise. His plans will not be thwarted.
- Spiritual inertia is a sin that God will judge (Judg. 5:12–18).

APPLICATIONS

- If you have God's promise and know God's will, then move forward by faith.
- Don't dwell on your inadequacies (your outdated equipment, or lack of "weapons") or be overwhelmed by your obstacles (the "iron chariots" arrayed against you). Remember that God is greater than your difficulties.
- Strive to be a spiritual "medal of honor" winner (Matt. 25:21; 2 Cor. 5:10).
- Sing the Doxology each morning this week; reflect on and revel in its words.

IV. LIFE APPLICATION

Hebrew, Hassles, and Hymns

I grew up in church and frankly gave little thought to the words of the hymns that I sang. I snapped out of this lethargy when in seminary, but not in the usual way. It was a Friday, and my Hebrew professor assigned an unexpected and lengthy paper to be due on Monday. Then we sang a hymn prior to beginning the day's exegesis. During the song I looked over to my good friend Bill to grouse about the assignment. I saw that his eyes were closed as he sang. In fact, he wasn't singing. He was praying the words to God as a way of submitting himself and committing his schedule to God. I sang syllables; he worshiped.

In worship, our focus is to be on the attributes of God, not on the abilities of people. The beauty of a soloist's voice or skill in playing an instrument are not to point to the human being (although we appreciate the stewardship of that gift); rather, they point beyond the person to the God who grants such gifts, who loves creativity, and who created music.

In worship, my focus is to be on heaven more than on earth, on giving more than receiving. The focus is *not* to be on how comfortable the pews are, how annoyed I am with the person three pews in front of me, or whether I like the pastor's tie. In fact, I cannot worship in God's presence and stay satisfied with my pettiness. My worship is rendered to an audience of One, and therefore I am less likely to say, "I didn't enjoy the singing" or "The sermon didn't do anything for me." The purpose of the service is to glorify God. God is no better off for my worship of him—I am the one better off! In worship I join the heavenly hosts in praising the eternal God (Dan. 7:10; Rev. 4:4–8; 5:11).

How often do we ignore the words of the precious songs we sing? Consider a song most churches sing weekly, invoking the praise of God: "The Doxology." The Greek word for "glory" is *doxa*. "The Doxology" is a simple song ascribing glory to God, using these words:

> Praise God from whom all blessings flow.
> Praise him all creatures here below,
> Praise Him above ye heavenly hosts,
> Praise Father, Son and Holy Ghost.

Reflect on the words of each line. First, praise is ascribed to God as the source of all blessings. Then the second and third lines identify those who are invited to praise God—all human and animal creatures ("here below"), and all angelic creatures ("heavenly host"). The last line ascribes praise to God more specifically: to the individual members of the Trinity ("Father, Son and Holy Ghost"). After a study of Judges 4 and the song of Judges 5, we agree with the psalmist: "Great is the LORD and most worthy of praise" (Pss. 48:1; 96:4; 145:3).

V. PRAYER

O Lord, you are worthy of our praise and our awe. We confess that we are limited in our faith and lax in our faithfulness. We praise you for your steadfast love that is patient with our spiritual inertia. We ask that our worship would give you pleasure and that we would be involved in accomplishing your will "on earth as it is in heaven." Through Christ, our Lord. Amen.

VI. DEEPER DISCOVERIES

A. Deborah the Deliverer?

We conclude that Deborah was not one of the traditional judges of Israel from the following points: (1) the term *judge* ("deliverer") is not applied to her; (2) the traditional claim that God "raised up" a judge is not applied to her; (3) God said he would give Sisera into Barak's hands, not Deborah's hands; (4) there is no statement claiming that she was empowered by God's Spirit (in contrast to other judges); and (5) it is Barak who appears in Hebrews 11:32 (along with Gideon, Samson, and Jephthah), not Deborah. She relays God's answer to God's people, but "she" is not God's answer (Block, 195).

B. The Jael House

No doubt Heber, the husband of Jael, would not have sanctioned his wife's activity, had he been present. He was a traitor to Israel, whereas she was sympathetic to God's children. One worthy speculation would ask (because of prolific intermarriage during this disobedient period) whether Jael was herself an Israelite, so that Sisera was indeed her enemy.

C. Mother Inferior

The crassness with which Sisera's mother comforts herself is horrific (5:28–30). The term *girl* (NIV) is literally "womb"; that is, this mother viewed other women as nothing more than organs to be used and abused by the soldiers. It would be more cruel than saying "a couple of wenches for each man to rape" (note that the Hebrew language contains respectful words for "girl" and for "maiden" which are *not* used in this passage).

VII. TEACHING OUTLINE

A. INTRODUCTION

1. Lead Story: Israel's Queen Mum
2. Context: In Judges 3, God worked through three unique men. In Judges 4 and 5, he works through two ordinary women (Deborah and Jael) and one hesitant general (Barak). In Judges 6, we will be introduced to a man whose character is very questionable. No matter who the vessel, it is God who is the victor. His vigilance preserves his people.
3. Transition: After the swashbuckling stories of Ehud and Shamgar (Judg. 3), this hero was not a Gideon or a Samson; in fact, it was a woman named Deborah. She combined with Barak to form a team that God used to rid the land of a twenty-year oppression; the result was an ensuing peace that lasted forty years.

B. COMMENTARY

1. The Odd Couple (4:1–24)
   a. Prologue: The despot and the vicious general (4:1–3)
   b. Confrontation (4:4–10)
   c. Corruption (4:11–13)
   d. Annihilation (4:14–16)
   e. Assassination (4:17–21)
   f. Epilogue: The damsel and the victorious general (4:22–24)
2. The Awed Couple (5:1–31)
   a. Proclamation (5:1–3)
   b. Exaltation (5:4–5)
   c. Desolation (5:6–8)
   d. Commendation (5:9–11)
   e. Evaluation (5:12–18)
   f. Confrontation (5:19–23)
   g. Commendation (5:24–27)
   h. Anticipation (5:28–30)
   i. Conclusion (5:31)

C. CONCLUSION: I AM THE PATH

VIII. ISSUES FOR DISCUSSION

1. The tribes of Israel were called to arms to support their brethren; some did, others did not. Review 5:13–18,23, and divide all the tribes mentioned into two categories: those who helped, and those who hindered.

2. As with the Israelites, at times God places a ministry of some sort in front of us. Like them, at times we excuse ourselves from "active duty." Think of three excuses we might use to rationalize our lack of involvement before God. Do you think he is persuaded by our excuses?

3. Three women appear in significant roles in Judges 4–5. Make three columns (one for each woman), find all the verses where each is mentioned, and list everything—good and bad—about them. What positive and negative lessons do you think we might learn from studying their lives?

4. Reflect on this proposition: "God uses free human choices to accomplish his eternal purposes." Now look at the following segments of Scripture to "inform" the proposition: Genesis 50:20; Job 1–2; Habakkuk 1–3; Acts 2:23.

Judges 6

The Timid Hero

I. INTRODUCTION
The Foolishness of God

II. COMMENTARY
A verse-by-verse explanation of the chapter.

III. CONCLUSION
Ninety-five Percent Obedient

An overview of the principles and applications from the chapter.

IV. LIFE APPLICATION
Kermit and Sting

Melding the chapter to life.

V. PRAYER
Tying the chapter to life with God.

VI. DEEPER DISCOVERIES
Historical, geographical, and grammatical enrichment of the commentary.

VII. TEACHING OUTLINE
Suggested step-by-step group study of the chapter.

VIII. ISSUES FOR DISCUSSION
Zeroing the chapter in on daily life.

"One step forward in obedience is worth years of study

about it."

Oswald Chambers

Judges 6

IN A NUTSHELL

God picked a timid deliverer to accomplish his deliverance and display his glory; when we are weak, then we are strong—in him (2 Cor. 12:10).

The Timid Hero

I. INTRODUCTION

The Foolishness of God

God doesn't always do things the right way—or at least the way *we* would do them! His strategies are sometimes odd. We would have sent Paul (the Pharisee, Hebrew scholar, and prize pupil of Gamaliel) to be the apostle to the Jews, and we would have sent Peter (the relatively unsophisticated fisherman) to be the apostle to the barbarian Gentiles. But like spiritual babies in a divine nursery, God switched them at birth—Paul to the Gentiles, Peter to the Jews. In fact, if we were charged to select a group of men to turn the first-century world upside down, we would probably pick C.E.O.'s from the business community, generals from the military community, Roman senators from the political community, and priests from the Jewish temple community. Jesus, however, had a different plan and picked from among those whose lives would, humanly speaking, never make a difference. Consider:

- Peter—the impetuous pendulum, known for his instability.
- James and John—the "Sons of Thunder," apparently in trouble with Galilean police, juvenile division.
- Thomas—the incarnation of Eeyore (of Winnie the Pooh fame), always the last to believe any good news.
- Philip—not the brightest crayon in the box (John 6:5–7; 14:8), who said amazingly imperceptive things.
- James the Less—or "Shorty" (less in stature), about whom we have no information anywhere.
- Simon the Zealot—a former member of the gang that carried daggers to kill pro-Roman Jews.
- Matthew—a pro-Roman Jewish tax collector, who never uttered a word in any of the Gospels.

It is ironic that the only person who did not seem to have disadvantages was a man named Judas, who became the respected C.F.O. of the disciples (John 12:6). Judas apparently was the only one among the disciples who would be a candidate for leadership.

It is clear that God does not act based on "focus groups." He takes the weak things of the world to turn the world upside down (1 Cor. 1:26–31). Although I grew up with reverence for the name Gideon, we first meet him cowering in a winepress—which should be called a "whine press" because he blamed God for his troubles rather than look in his own backyard (literally—there were idols there!). God picked a most unlikely hero so that it would be very clear who was in charge. God uses ordinary people to accomplish amazing things for his glory.

II. COMMENTARY

The Timid Hero

MAIN IDEA: *Despite the unfaithfulness of Israel and the initial timidity of Gideon, God called and encouraged Gideon to deliver his people. God's longsuffering with Israel was illustrated in his longsuffering with Gideon.*

A The Need for Deliverance (6:1–10)

SUPPORTING IDEA: *The persistent sin of Israel resulted in a demoralizing oppression by the Midianites; the Lord indicted Israel, who brought this judgment upon herself.*

6:1. *Transgression.* We are not surprised as the formula for the cycles of sin and judgment again unfolds. And again the **evil** that they did was **in the eyes of the LORD**. No further detail is given; no further detail is needed. This cause produced the predictable effect: the Lord **gave them** over to **the Midianites** (who were assisted by other oppressors, v. 3), this time for a span of **seven years**. The Midianites were descendants of Abraham through Keturah (Gen. 25:2–4) and were not always hostile to God's people (Jethro, Exod. 2). But as Israel's strength grew, so did the Midianite aggression, to the point of direct oppression.

6:2–5. *Oppression.* The Israelites had few places of safety from the marauding Midianites. They used three geological features for refuge: **mountain clefts**, **caves**, and defensible hills (**strongholds**). The pattern of oppression was so strong that the Israelites were disheartened. Every year it was the same thing: they would plant their crops, and every year at harvest time they were **invaded** by **the Midianites, Amalekites** (old enemies, originally allied with Eglon, 3:13) **and other eastern peoples** (probably nomadic groups from the Arabian desert). These enemies pillaged every village, scavenged **the land**, and **ruined** all **the crops**—the grapes, olives, wheat, barley, etc., so necessary for survival. In addition, they rustled all the livestock. The description of the oppressors is formidable.

First, they brought **their** own **livestock** and **their tents**, demonstrating to us that this was not just a hit-and-run raiding party. They brought their livestock to live off the newly sprouting fields, and when they left, nothing remained for the Israelites' livestock. Second, they were so numerous that they resembled **swarms of locusts**; it was a number **impossible to count**. Third, they brought with them a new "technology"—**camels**, who can travel up to four days without water. Thus the Midiantes had the capability of locating in one area within Israel's territory but functioning as a long-range mobile strike force. In sum, **they invaded the land to ravage it**. A more depressing scenario could hardly be imagined for an agricultural society.

6:6–7. *Petition.* The result was that **Midian so impoverished the Israelites** (Heb., Israel "became small") that finally they turned **to the Lord** for help. Their economy, their egos, their emotions were destroyed and their agony was great. They **cried to the** LORD **because of Midian**—not, however, because of their sins. Their reluctance to turn to God is typical of their lack of obedience chronicled in this book; only when they could do nothing themselves, and even then a long time afterward, would they consider calling upon their covenant Lord.

6:8–10. *Accusation.* For the first time, however, God did not respond with immediate deliverance. Instead **he sent them a prophet**, whose mission was not to comfort them but to charge them. They were not crying out to the Lord in penance; they were just crying out in pain. The message from God may be condensed to three points: I delivered you repeatedly; I dispossessed your enemies; and you disobeyed me—yet again!

An unnamed prophet told them: **This is what the** LORD, **the God of Israel, says**. They were reminded that God had been faithful to them in the past—first, **I brought you up out of Egypt, out of the land of slavery** (a poignant reminder that their current existence was little better than slavery). Second, he reminded them that against God **the power of Egypt** and **of all your oppressors** (including the current Midianites) was nothing. Indeed, God originally **drove them from before you and gave you their land**. But like the single prohibition ignored by Adam and Eve in Eden, God told them, **Do not worship the gods of the Amorites**. Also like Adam and Eve, they ignored God's mandate, hence the indictment: **But you have not listened to me**.

There is no record of corporate repentance following this speech. Readers would not necessarily expect God to rescue Israel; he seemed to be giving reasons why he would *not* act in their behalf. They are simply left to ponder their rebellion without any expectation of redemption. Thus the next segment is unexpected and serves to reinforce the unmerited nature of God's provision for his covenant people; when they were faithless, he remained faithful to them.

B The Choice of the Deliverer (6:11–24)

SUPPORTING IDEA: *God called a timid young man named Gideon and commissioned him as Israel's deliverer.*

6:11–12. *Confrontation.* The scene shifts to one apparently insignificant member of that nation who was tucked away from harm, hiding his **wheat . . . from the Midianites**. He was attempting the almost impossible task of **threshing** the grain in a partially enclosed **winepress**. Ordinarily, threshing was done on hilltops so the mixture of chaff and grain could be tossed into the air, allowing the wind to scatter the husks while the grain fell straight down and gathered into a mound. The oppression of the Midianites reduced Israel to such pathetic activities.

It is to this unlikely young man that the angel of the Lord came. His name was **Gideon** ("one who cuts down" in an agricultural context; Block renders the name "hacker" or "hewer"), and he was the son of **Joash the Abiezrite**. The greeting that the angel of the Lord gave him was startling: **The LORD is with you, mighty warrior**. Gideon's present circumstances (and undoubtedly his appearance!) did not evoke an image anything close to what a "mighty warrior" would project. Since Gideon did not react to the title, it is likely that he did not take the introduction seriously.

6:13. *Complaint.* Gideon probably did not discern anything supernatural in this being's demeanor or appearance. He certainly did not respond in awe, but he brought up the age-old theological complaint about the problem of evil: If God is all-powerful and all-good, why does he allow evil to exist, especially against his chosen people? Two points are significant here.

First, Gideon regarded Israel's bondage to be entirely God's fault, with no thought given to the role Israel played in bringing judgment upon herself.

Second, Gideon had not listened carefully to the angels' address that the Lord was with him ("you" is singular) and responded with the complaint, **If the Lord is with us (pl.), why has all this happened to us (pl.)?**

Further, Gideon asked where the age of miracles had gone: **Where are all his wonders that our fathers told us about?** Entirely unaware of what was to come, Gideon backed himself into a difficult theological corner. To him it certainly did seem that the Lord had abandoned them, but, as he would discover, it is awkward to argue with God about miracles!

6:14. *Charge.* Rather than engage in theological dispute about the ways of God, the angel, whom we now understand to be the Lord, commissioned Gideon to **go in the strength you have and save Israel out of Midian's hand.** The rationale was not, of course, that Gideon's strength in itself was adequate to the task; Gideon's strength was to be found in the Lord who declared, **Am I not sending you?**

6:15. *Complaint.* After hearing this startling statement, Gideon backed away from his righteous indignation and began to make excuses why he should not get involved: **My clan is the weakest in Manasseh, and I am the least in my family.** While the second statement may be true (Gideon being the youngest son), the first statement could hardly be taken seriously, not when—during a time of oppression—Gideon himself was master of ten servants (v. 27), and Joash his father sponsored a Baal worship site for the community (vv. 25–26).

6:16. *Commitment.* Again the Lord promised his presence with Gideon (**I will be with you**) and renewed his commission with a promise of overwhelming victory (**you will strike down all the Midianites together**). Gideon was using the wrong criterion; God has never been limited to social status or human resources, or the lack thereof. Simply put, there is power in God's presence (Matt. 28:20). The effectiveness of the Lord's deliverance does not depend upon the ability of the human deliverer.

6:17–24. *Confirmation.* Gideon was concerned about miracles (v. 13), so he decided not to budge until he saw one. His position was that he needed divine confirmation (**give me a sign**) before he would commit himself to action. He also dictated the nature of the sign. The segment unfolds in this way: first, Gideon prepared an offering; second, God provided a consuming flame; and finally, Gideon reacted with fear.

Gideon prepared an **offering** (not a meal), consisting of **a young goat**, a large amount of unleavened bread, and **broth**. Then **the angel of God** told him to put the meat and bread on a nearby **rock**, saturating both with the broth; Gideon obeyed. **With the tip of** his **staff, he touched** the offering on the rock, which blazed with flame, **consuming** all. The divine being then **disappeared**.

Strangely, Gideon's reaction was the opposite of what should have occurred. God had reassured him of his presence and his protection, yet Gideon was terrified, thinking that he had seen God **face to face** and would therefore soon die. Again in grace the Lord communicated in some way to Gideon, **Peace! Do not be afraid. You are not going to die.** In response Gideon built an altar and called it **The LORD is Peace**. Like any scholar concerned with historical accuracy, the writer adds a parenthetical note mentioning that, at the time he was writing, the altar was available for verification: **To this day it stands in Ophrah of the Abiezrites.**

C Deliverance from Idolatry (6:25–32)

SUPPORTING IDEA: *Before Gideon delivered Israel, God gave him a "dress rehearsal": he was to destroy idol worship in his own community.*

6:25–27. *Action.* At this point in the flow of the story, we would expect to progress to the kind of action found in verses 33–35, and then skip from there to the action in chapter 7. However, hard on the heels of God's divine commission (**that same night**), God told Gideon that he had to begin his work of deliverance at home. Before one deals with the sins of others, one must deal with one's own sins (Matt. 7:1–5). Further, the divine power behind any subsequent victory might be questionable if Gideon's own home were still given over to Baal worship.

Thus Gideon took his father's prize bull, **seven years old**, and tore down the altar to Baal and Asherah. Probably on the ruins of these altars (and perhaps from their materials), he built an **altar to the Lord**, on which he then sacrificed the bull. It may well be that the age of the bull has this significance: it was born the year the oppression began, so that each of its years was a year spent under the terror of the Midianites.

The operation was complicated, however. Gideon did not go to his father and make his intentions known. His timidity (he was **afraid of his family and** the men of the town) reduced him to an incursion under cover of darkness. Unable to accomplish this alone, however, Gideon required the services of **ten of his servants**—but as we soon discover, top secret information shared among eleven people is really no secret at all! In addition, it turned out that Gideon actually had good reason to fear. His townsmen were entirely given over to the worship of Baal.

6:28–32. *Reactions.* When Gideon's townsmen awoke the next morning and discovered the destruction of their center of Baal worship, they were incensed. They demanded, **Who did this?** Immediately the "secret" was exposed and the answer was given: **Gideon son of Joash did it**. Powerful family or not, the townsmen collectively **demanded of Joash** to bring out his son for immediate execution. Their reaction is remarkable—God's chosen people displaying moral indignation over the loss of accoutrements of idol worship, the violation of God's first commandment (Exod. 20:3), which ironically carried with it the death penalty (Deut. 13:6–15).

The reaction of Joash, Gideon's father, is curious in light of Gideon's fear of his family (v. 27). Joash ignored the loss of his prime bull and his pagan sanctuary and defended his son. Why? Possibly his son's actions stirred his heart against such pagan worship, or he was himself struck by Baal's impotence (the reason he mentioned to his fellow townsmen), or he was simply a stubborn man who refused to yield his son to the whims of his hostile townsmen. Ultimately we do not know his motives.

His reasoning was clear, however. He became confrontational in reaction to them: Why save a God who needs saving? To this he added a challenge: **Whoever fights for him shall be put to death by morning!** The meaning may be that if anyone killed his son, he would retaliate immediately. Further, it was only good theology to maintain that **if Baal really is a god, he can defend himself**. The God of Israel was certainly able to vindicate himself through miraculous means, in contrast to idols (see Isa. 41:21–24). Does it make sense, Joash asked them, that a true "God" needs human protection? (cp. Elijah's sarcasm in 1 Kgs. 18:27).

Apparently the townsmen backed off from their threats. One result of this encounter was that Gideon was given the name **Jerub-Baal**, meaning "**Let Baal contend with him**" (see Judg. 7:1; 8:29,35; 9:1, etc.; those who assume that Gideon served the Lord with a whole heart from this point on should be aware of his legacy, Judg. 8:27,33).

D Delivering the Deliverer (6:33–40)

SUPPORTING IDEA: *The Lord assured Gideon of success first by enabling him to gather an army and second by confirming his will through the means of the fleece.*

6:33–35. *Gathering the Army.* At this point the story resumes where one would have expected from verse 24. The unsuspecting **Midianites, Amalekites and other eastern peoples** resumed their annual "harvest" of Israel's crops and goods. They located in the Valley of Jezreel. At this point God's **Spirit . . . came upon** (Heb., "clothed") **Gideon and he blew a** ram's horn (**trumpet**) in summons of his own people, **the Abiezrites**. The call to arms was also extended throughout **Manasseh**, and included **Asher, Zebulun, and Naphtali**. Surprisingly, they responded and **went up to meet them**. We know that this response was due more to the propelling work of God's Spirit than to any charismatic magnetism exuded by the hesitant Gideon. In fact, such an overwhelming response did not encourage Gideon but brought about a fresh wave of fear and doubt.

6:36–40. *Fleecing God.* For the original readers, this episode is entirely unexpected. Even though Gideon was now empowered by the Spirit and encircled by thousands of soldiers, he reverted to being "doubting Gideon." The language of Gideon's doubts indict him (**as you have promised . . . as you said**; see v. 16, "I will be with you"). God did not stutter; Gideon understood him clearly. He simply had a hard time taking God at his word. Gideon's problem was a low view of God's revelation and of God's power, perhaps in tandem with an exaggerated view of the enemy's power.

Gideon requested yet another miraculous sign for confirmation. He asked God to control the **dew** overnight so that the dew remained only on a **wool fleece** but none on the dry ground. In his grace God condescended to Gideon's doubtful heart. However, in setting the conditions of the miracle, Gideon may have realized that he did so unwisely. Perhaps any fleece would retain water more so than dirt, which would absorb moisture and then appear to be dry. In other words, was it *really* a miracle?

Although he realized he was on very thin ice here, Gideon again asked God to repeat the sign—only in reverse (dry fleece, wet ground)—something that could never be explained away as a coincidence. Again, **that night God**

did so. God's concern to deliver the Israelites trumped Gideon's need to learn of God's ways—for the moment (see "Deeper Discoveries").

> **MAIN IDEA REVIEW:** *Despite the unfaithfulness of Israel and the initial timidity of Gideon, God called and encouraged Gideon to deliver his people. God's longsuffering with Israel was illustrated in his longsuffering with Gideon.*

III. CONCLUSION

Ninety-five Percent Obedient

Gideon committed to obey God—mostly. As we will see in the next chapters, his commitment was partial, not total. What if 95 percent obedience were our goal? What if we were even *proud* of that? Think about other areas: what would 95 percent efficiency look like? If the telephone company were 95 percent efficient, you would have no telephone service for 1 hour and 12 minutes every day. This page would have 16 misspelled words. Over 28,000,000 pieces of first class mail would be lost—every day. Likewise, you would have no electricity for cooking, refrigeration, or computers for 1 hour and 12 minutes every day. Your automobile would be in the shop 18 days every year. Doctors and nurses would drop 175,000 newborn babies every year. You would have unsafe drinking water for 18 days every year. Hospital life-support systems would be unable to function 18 days out of every year.

There is no joy in a partial walk with God. James warned against being a "double-minded" person, characterized by instability (Jas. 1:8). A person with divided commitments has enough of the world in him that he cannot fully enjoy the things of the Lord and enough of the Lord in him that he cannot fully enjoy the things of the world to which he has given himself. Consequently, he is miserable and "unstable." That is why Joshua challenged, on the brink of the Canaanite battles, that people pick either the Lord or the world (Josh. 24:15).

PRINCIPLES

- God is glorified when our weaknesses reveal his strength.
- God has given us guidance in his training manual for living—the Bible. We do not need to wonder how we are to live, but rather

we are to learn how to live by following the principles found in his Word.

- When we do God's work in God's way, he goes before us and makes our paths straight (Prov. 3:5–6).
- At times God stoops to our weaknesses, but it is unwise to presume on God's longsuffering.

APPLICATIONS

- Deal with the sin in your own backyard, and then turn it into an altar that glorifies God.
- Don't blame God when things go wrong; look for other causes.
- Follow God's guidance, step by step; he will mold you into the person he wants you to be.
- Rely on God's Word and live by it! It is your blueprint for constructing a life that makes a difference.

IV. LIFE APPLICATION

Kermit and Sting

One day a scorpion was walking along the riverbank trying to find a way to get across the river when he came across a frog. The scorpion asked the frog if he would take him across the river by giving him a ride on his back. The frog replied, "No, I would never give a scorpion a ride on my back!" When the scorpion asked him why, the frog replied, "Because if I were to give you a ride on my back, we would only get halfway across and you would sting me; then I would drown!" Quickly the scorpion replied, "But frog, if I stung you, then I would drown also." The frog considered this and then agreed, "I guess you're right. I will give you a ride." The scorpion jumped on the frog's back, and they started across the river. Halfway there, the scorpion drilled the frog with his stinger. As the frog felt the venom race through his body, he looked at the scorpion and asked "Why?" The reply: "Because I'm a scorpion. That is my nature."

To extend the fable, the frog knew he should stay away from the scorpion. Ever since he was a tadpole he had been told to avoid scorpions. Innately he felt he should avoid scorpions. And most importantly, the Frog Maker actually commanded, "Thou shalt avoid scorpions, nor shall you listen to their lies." No matter what promises a personable and friendly scorpion made, a scorpion was still a scorpion.

Whenever the Israelites worshiped idols, they always got stung. Yet they almost willfully refused to learn the lesson that obedience to God was the best way to live their lives.

V. PRAYER

O Lord, forgive us when we listen more to the world than to your command. Thank you for your guidance, your protection, your patience, and your power. We rejoice to know that our lives can make an eternal difference, because when we are weak, then—empowered by your Spirit—we are strong. Through Christ our Lord. Amen.

VI. DEEPER DISCOVERIES

A. The Oppressors

Three oppressors are identified in this cycle. The Midianites were primary; verse 1 indicates the Israelites were given into the hands of Midian for seven years, without mentioning the other oppressors. The Midianites were descendants of Abraham by Keturah (Gen. 25:2–4) and so were related remotely to the Israelites (see the interchange with "Ishmaelites" in Judg. 8:24). Block places them as semi-nomads from the Sinai Peninsula and western Arabia. Moses' wife was the daughter of Jethro the Midianite, a man portrayed in positive contexts (Exod. 2:15–22; 18). The Amalekites were descendants of Esau and had a history of hostility with Israel. They were allied with the Moabites in the very first cycle of oppression (Judg. 3:13). We do not know who the "sons of the east" were, but they may have been an ethnically unidentified (or unidentifiable?) amalgam of Bedouin raiders from across the desert.

B. Camels (6:5)

The reference here is probably not to the two-humped (Bactrian) camel but to the single-humped Arabian dromedary (see Job 1:3). These animals were used very early (see Gen. 12:16; 24:10), primarily around the periphery of desert regions. The use of camels was mostly found farther south and east in the Arabian regions, where the Midianites were from. Camels were able to carry a load of four hundred pounds, plus rider. They could go three or four days without water and could travel about twenty-eight miles per day.

C. A Bull Market (6:25–26,28)

The grammar and meaning of the details of these verses is in question, but the simplest reading is that there was one "prime" seven-year-old bull used to tear down the altar and the Asherah totem. The Hebrew word translated *second* may also mean "exalted, of high rank" (Block, 266). Then when the altar to the Lord was built, that bull was sacrificed unto the Lord (against the consistent NIV rendering, "the second bull").

D. "Fleecing" God

Those who take Gideon's request for a "fleece" as a model for divine guidance are ill-advised. Gideon's request was not an expression of faith but a questioning of God's promises and power. This is far different from asking God to guide by his providential control of circumstances. Furthermore, Gideon was aware that he was acting in disbelief and partial rebellion (v. 39, "Do not be angry with me") even in making such a request.

Those who tend to apply this as a model for guidance often do not apply it fully or faithfully. Gideon was not asking God for a coincidence ("If I sell my car by 5:00 on Friday, I will know God wants me to move to Seattle"); Gideon was asking God for a miracle ("If my car develops organs of speech and utters 'Seattle,' I will know God wants me to move there"). Those who desire guidance by using a fleece should probably get a sheep's fleece and ask God literally to reverse turf wetness and dryness, as Gideon did. And then repent.

VII. TEACHING OUTLINE

A. INTRODUCTION

1. Lead Story: The Foolishness of God

2. Context: Chapters 4 and 5 gave the story of Deborah and Barak, ending with a paean of praise to God for his faithfulness in spite of Israel's unfaithfulness. The next story takes us into one of the most extended cycles in the book, dealing with Gideon's call (ch. 6), his victory (ch. 7), his life (ch. 8), and his legacy (ch. 9).

3. Transition: We would expect after the victory of Deborah and Barak that Israel would have learned its lesson. However, the next generation turned its back on the Lord, resulting in an utterly demoralizing oppression. Rather than work through already recognized leaders, God for the first time chose an ordinary man and empowered him to do an extraordinary job.

B. COMMENTARY

1. The Need for Deliverance (6:1–10)
   a. Transgression (6:1)
   b. Oppression (6:2–5)
   c. Petition (6:6–7)
   d. Accusation (6:8–10)

2. The Choice of the Deliverer (6:11–24)
   a. Confrontation (6:11–12)
   b. Complaint (6:13)
   c. Charge (6:14)
   d. Complaint (6:15)
   e. Commitment (6:16)
   f. Confirmation (6:17–24)

3. Deliverance from Idolatry (6:25–32)
   a. Action (6:25–27)
   b. Reactions (6:28–32)

4. Delivering the Deliverer (6:33–40)
   a. Gathering the army (6:33–35)
   b. Fleecing God (6:36–40)

C. CONCLUSION: NINETY-FIVE PERCENT OBEDIENT

VIII. ISSUES FOR DISCUSSION

1. Read and meditate on 1 Corinthians 1:26–29. Why does God call the weak to do work we think should only be entrusted to the strong?

2. Gideon had two problems: discouragement and inadequacy. Reflect on the significance of Jesus' promises to be with believers always (Matt. 28:18–20) and the Holy Spirit's role as "comforter" (John 14:16–17; literally, "one who is called alongside"). How does God want you to view your inadequacies? Should inadequacies lead to inaction or to faith in the God who provides and strengthens?

3. Why do you think Gideon had to deal with sin in his own backyard first, before God enlarged the boundaries of his influence? What would this mean in your life?

Judges 7

The Hesitant Hero

I. INTRODUCTION
One Huge Identity Crisis

II. COMMENTARY
A verse-by-verse explanation of the chapter.

III. CONCLUSION
It Couldn't Be Done

An overview of the principles and applications from the chapter.

IV. LIFE APPLICATION
Encouraging the Discouraged

Melding the chapter to life.

V. PRAYER
Tying the chapter to life with God.

VI. DEEPER DISCOVERIES
Historical, geographical, and grammatical enrichment of the commentary.

VII. TEACHING OUTLINE
Suggested step-by-step group study of the chapter.

VIII. ISSUES FOR DISCUSSION
Zeroing the chapter in on daily life.

"*The task ahead of you is never greater than*

the power behind you."

U n k n o w n

Judges 7

 IN A NUTSHELL

Against overwhelming odds God granted Gideon and his men a miraculous victory.

The Hesitant Hero

I. INTRODUCTION

One Huge Identity Crisis

*D*o you ever wonder who you are? I mean who you *really* are, what you're made of? Not the image you project, but the identity you possess? It seems reasonable that only those who have suffered deeply, where every layer of façade is stripped away, have the clearest sense of who they are, of what they are really like. The point I am making is that in some ways we do not know ourselves.

In 1964 Alan Redpath, former pastor of Moody Church in Chicago, suffered a near-fatal stroke and sank into depression. He was angry at God and at one point prayed, "Lord, deliver me from this attack of the devil. Take me right home!" He wrote later about his bouts with depression and said that it was then that he sensed the Lord saying, "It is I, your Savior, who has brought this experience into your life to show you [that] this is the kind of person— with all your sinful thoughts and temptations, which you thought were things of the past—that you always will be, but for My grace."

Truly, only God knows us. Scripture says: "Now we see but a poor reflection as in a mirror; then we shall see face to face. Now I know in part; then I shall know fully, even as I am fully known" (1 Cor. 13:12). God alone knows us immediately, intimately, and infinitely. And our identity in Christ is not who we think we are.

I love the comment by comedienne Lily Tomlin: "I've always wanted to be somebody, but I see now I should have been more specific." The search for identity is also the search for significance. Am I the kind of person whose life will make a difference? God appeared to Gideon, who had an image of his identity: he was the least in the family from the least of the tribes. Yet God greeted him, "Hello, valiant warrior." All that we are, we *are* by God's grace. That's all that matters. This was the lesson Gideon had to learn. In New Testament terms, "I have been crucified with Christ and I no longer live, but Christ lives in me. The life I live in the body, I live by faith in the Son of God, who loved me and gave himself for me" (Gal. 2:20).

II. COMMENTARY

The Hesitant Hero

> **MAIN IDEA:** *God took Gideon—and his men—through a systematic reduction in military power in order that a powerful truth might be proclaimed: "'Not by might nor by power, but by my Spirit,' says the LORD Almighty" (Zech. 4:6b). God alone provides victory, and God alone is due glory.*

A Condensing the Army (7:1–8)

> **SUPPORTING IDEA:** *God systematically obliterated any reasonable chance of normal victory by reducing the odds in battle from one-to-four down to one-to-four hundred and fifty!*

7:1–3. *Test #1: Public.* As the story resumes, Gideon and his men were camped at **the spring of Harod** (Heb., "trembling"!), just south of where **Midian** was encamped **in the valley near the hill of Moreh**. In any ordinary historical record of warfare, the next scene (flowing from chapter 6) would take place on the battlefield. But spiritual history also reveals the hand of God "behind the seen." God was about to drastically reduce the army and dispense a most unique battle plan. As things stood at this point, the army of the Lord was to fight against overwhelming four-to-one odds. (The number is derived from two verses: in 7:3 Israel had thirty-two thousand men, and in 8:10 the enemy numbered about one hundred and thirty-five thousand men.)

While it is not impossible for such victories to take place, given certain advantages (superior arms, positioning, etc.), Gideon possessed none of these advantages. The Midianites had superior arms and superior numbers, while the Israelites had few arms and no defined strategy.

Gideon's expectation no doubt was that the next command from the Lord would be to begin the military campaign in earnest. If so, he was to be surprised. Instead, the Lord told Gideon, **You have too many men**. Gideon may have thought his ears were not working correctly. Didn't God *mean* to say that he had "too few" men or that the *enemy* had "too many" men? However, the Lord then explained his reason for such an astonishing assertion: he planned to pare down Israel's army so **that Israel may not boast against me that her own strength has saved her**. What God was about to do must not be explainable in any possible way by human agency. So the man whom God called while winnowing grain was about to winnow his army! And the nation of Israel was to learn the lesson later affirmed by Jonathan, that "nothing can hinder the LORD from saving, whether by many or by few" (1 Sam. 14:6).

God told Gideon to make the men in his "army" an offer that many of them felt they could not refuse (see "Deeper Discoveries"). Humanly speaking, every man in Gideon's militia knew that Israel would lose this battle and that most of them would die. God offered Gideon's men a way out (prescribed by Deut. 20:1–8). If any of the men were afraid to go to battle, they were to be granted an immediate "honorable discharge" (**anyone who trembles with fear may turn back**). The result was that of thirty-two thousand men available to do battle, **twenty-two thousand men left, while ten thousand remained**.

Now the odds were no longer four-to-one but were increased to fourteen-to-one! This was a known and public test; but God was not done! The next method of winnowing the army would be private and would be applied unbeknownst to the men who would yet be discharged from God's attack force.

7:4–8. *Test #2: Private.* Gideon was probably alarmed to see two-thirds of his army leave. His alarm likely became dismay when God again spoke: **There are still too many men**. This time, there was no public announcement, but a private test that only God would administer. As far as the men knew, they were the attack force that would rise up against the Midianites. This time Gideon himself was not informed about the manner of the test but was told simply to **take** the men **down to the water**, where, God said, **I will sift them for you there**.

To his credit Gideon obeyed. When the men were at the spring the Lord told him, **Separate those who lap the water with their tongues like a dog from those who kneel down to drink**. Apparently this "test" separated those who knelt down to put their faces in the water as opposed to those who bent down and used their hands to bring water to their mouths, with the back-and-forth motion of the hand resembling the tongue of a dog. **Three hundred men lapped with their hands to their mouths. All the rest got down on their knees to drink.** (Gideon would have preferred to keep the nine thousand, seven hundred men and send the three hundred packing, but such was not God's plan!)

Some interpreters insist that God's test was to select only those men who maintained a greater overall sense of military preparedness or vigilance, but this does not seem to be the case. The criterion for the test may have been entirely arbitrary, simply designed to diminish the army in drastic ways. Regardless, God made a promise to Gideon: **With the three hundred men that lapped I will save you and give the Midianites into your hands.** The rest of the men did not return home but apparently stayed at their encampment. Meanwhile the select three hundred took **the provisions and trumpets** from their comrades, which will figure into the story shortly.

🅱 Calming the General (7:9–15)

SUPPORTING IDEA: *By eavesdropping on an enemy nightmare and its interpretation, Gideon was finally encouraged that God would provide the victory—just as God had promised (and promised, and promised).*

7:9–12. Entering the Enemy Encampment. The time finally arrived to strike the Midianites—or so one would think. Although the Lord told Gideon to **get up** and **go down against the camp** and assured him that he was **going to give it into** his **hands**, God also knew that the nearby spring was not the only thing that was "trembling." Gideon was deeply afraid, and the Lord gave yet one more sign that would serve as a dose of encouragement. He told him that if he was **afraid to attack**, then he should **go down to the** Midianite **camp** and **listen to what they** were **saying.** Among the unfolding truths of Scripture is the New Testament revelation that God's Spirit (who had already "clothed" Gideon) is the encourager or comforter (John 14:16). It is God's nature to desire that his servant be comforted before engaging in battle.

So Gideon **and Purah his servant went down to the outposts** (the secured perimeter) **of the** enemy's valley **camp. The Midianites, the Amalekites and all the other eastern peoples** appeared so numerous that they seemed **thick as locusts** and the number of their camels was like **the sand on the seashore.** The sheer size of the opposing force and their military preparedness served to remind Gideon of the hopelessness of his venture. However, in the end this foray under the cover of darkness was not about fear but about faith.

7:13–14. Eavesdropping on the Enemy Nightmare. The surreptitious visit did not require searching for a needle in a haystack. God's purpose was immediately accomplished: they **arrived just as a man was telling a friend his dream** within Gideon's hearing. The story of the dream was puzzling, almost cartoonish in content. Here it is in full: **A round loaf of barley bread came tumbling into the Midianite camp. It struck the tent with such force that the tent overturned and collapsed.** Impoverished people ate bread made from barley grain. It was often the food of animals, but lately it was all the Israelites had left when the Midianites finished with them. The barley bread represented Israel at its lowest point. The tent in the dream obviously referred to the nomadic Midianites and their allies.

The interpretation of the man's dream by his comrade was just as odd as the dream itself: **This can be nothing other than the sword of Gideon**, and consequently he concluded that **God has given the Midianites and the whole camp into his hands.** Somehow the listener knew that the bun signified a Jewish victory!

Catch the humor here. What destroys the tent? Not a hurricane, a cyclone, an earthquake, a tornado, a brush fire, a plague, a rockslide, a bolt of lightning, a tidal wave, or an avalanche. No, it was a barley bun. Not a big, oversized bun, either. If you want to get the idea here, think of a bagel (*kosher*, of course). From Gideon's perspective, God showed him (again) that a small, insignificant, almost silly object can attack and overcome the most prodigious of foes.

Imagine you go bowling and bring your own ball. When it's your turn to bowl, out from your pocket you dredge up a tiny BB you have taken from an air rifle. You stand at the end of your lane and line up your tiny orb (you don't try to find finger holes) and then you let it roll! As it rotates its pathetic little way down the alley, nearby bowlers are looking at you like you are insane. But then the BB collides with the pins. The impact causes such a ferocious strike that all ten pins explode, and their fragments fly laterally in an astonishing chain-reaction that disintegrates every pin in the alley!

It is important to pause and consider that this encouragement on Gideon's behalf was another clear demonstration of the sovereignty of God, who placed significant dreams within the minds of his enemies. These dreams were expressed verbally to another person, at just the right time and the right place to be uttered within Gideon's hearing, and whose comrade interpreted the dream (contrary to any expectations) as an indication of Israelite victory. God was disposing of Gideon's fears.

7:15. *Encouraging Israel's Band.* Gideon's response was (finally!) what it should have been in weeks prior: **he worshiped God** and he claimed victory before his troops, believing God's revelation to him. **Get up!** he told them. **The LORD has given the Midianite camp into your hands.** We may correctly complain that God's promise (v. 9) *should* have been more convincing to Gideon than an enemy's dream. However, God condescends to our weaknesses and deals with his children with grace and patience.

> Many years ago a young Midwestern lawyer suffered from such deep depression that his friends thought it best to keep all knives and razors out of his reach. He questioned his life's calling and the prudence of even attempting to follow it through. During this time he wrote, "I am now the most miserable man living. Whether I shall ever be better, I cannot tell. I awfully forebode I shall not." But somehow, from somewhere, Abraham Lincoln received the encouragement he needed, and the achievements of his life thoroughly vindicated his bout with discouragement (*Today in the Word*, December 1989, p. 20)

ⓒ Crushing the Enemy (7:16–25)

SUPPORTING IDEA: *By creating the impression of a huge attack force and causing confusion among the Midianites, God miraculously granted Israel a decisive victory.*

7:16–20. *The Strategy.* The plan of attack was as unconventional as anyone could imagine: "divide and do!" Divide the army into three groups, and then do as Gideon did. The **three hundred men** were divided **into three companies**, probably with one hundred each. Each man was equipped with four "deadly" weapons: a trumpet, a pitcher, a torch, and a voice. There is no mention of any other armament. How these supplies (some of which had been harvested from their vacated comrades, v. 8) were to be employed would shortly be explained.

Each man had a trumpet, or a ram's horn, used to summon troops. They also had **empty** clay **jars**, within which **torches** were concealed. Gideon's battle plan was vague at best (**watch me . . . follow my lead . . . do exactly as I do**). The details were explained only partially: when Gideon gave the signal (**I and all who are with me blow our trumpets**), then all the troops were to follow suit (**blow yours**) **and shout** the prescribed battle cry: **For the LORD and for Gideon** (see "Deeper Discoveries"). Of course, this took great faith from the Israelite warriors. Was it wise, they would surely ask, to enter a battle without sword and shield should things turn against them?

Any offensive attack would be unexpected by the Midianite leaders. After all, they had dominated the Israelites with no opposition for the past seven years. While they were probably aware of the presence of Gideon's militia, it is unlikely they considered such a tiny army to be a serious threat. Carefully, **Gideon** and his **hundred men** crept up to **the edge** of the Midianite encampment. The time was shortly after midnight, after the changing of the guard. There were three traditional watches: from about eight to twelve p.m., from twelve to four a.m., and from four to eight a.m. The surprise attack took place **at the beginning of the middle watch,** or about 12:15 a.m. The replacement sentries had perhaps two or three hours of sleep, while the guards that they just relieved were on their way to bed but were still milling about the camp.

On signal from Gideon **the three companies blew the trumpets and smashed the jars. Grasping the torches in their left hands and holding in their right hands the trumpets they were to blow, they shouted** the battle cry. In ordinary battle formation, only leaders gave signals with ram's horns, a system that avoided confusion. One ram's horn was used to gather Gideon's army (Judg. 6:34); seven were used to conquer Jericho (Josh. 6:6). The point is that three hundred horns would signify to the Midianites a huge attack force immediately upon them. Despite the battle cry (**A sword for the LORD and for Gideon!**), no swords were included in their "armament."

7:21–25. *The Success.* It is not difficult to imagine the confusion. Enemy soldiers were startled from the deepest sleep of the night. Suddenly from three sides **three hundred trumpets sounded** (each of which, they would expect, represented several hundred men), three hundred pitchers shattered in a sound like a thunderstorm, three hundred torches bathed the camp in just enough dim light so that, awake but bleary, everything around them looked like the enemy, and three hundred voices were screaming the Israelite battle cry as loudly as they could.

They got up, half asleep, confused, camels everywhere, and started battling against what they took for the nearest enemy (the confusion was perhaps intensified because the Amalekites and Midianites spoke different languages, plus presumably they were a coalition army without identifying uniforms). Block describes the scene as "psychological warfare at its best" (Block, 283).

Instead of sending the army against the Midianites, God sent, in effect, a "drum and bugle" corps. Normal strategy to conquer the Midianites would be to try to raise a bigger army. God's strategy was to get rid of most of the army, then remove what weapons they had, and then tell them to stand still (**each man held his position around the camp**). While one can try to explain this victory *naturally*, why bother? The text makes it clear—**the LORD caused the men throughout the camp to turn on each other with their swords** (v. 22). God did this *supernaturally*. The likelihood of this victory was like having this year's superbowl champions being soundly thrashed 85–0 by a team of kindergarteners.

The result was that the enemies were routed and fled back toward their own territories (**to Beth Shittah toward Zererah as far as the border of Abel Meholah near Tabbath**). The aftermath to the battle consisted of two "mop-up" operations. The first apparently included those nine thousand, seven hundred soldiers who were back in their encampment (**Israelites from Naphtali, Asher and all Manasseh**), but who were rallied to pursue the fleeing Midianites. Second, **Gideon sent messengers throughout the hill country of Ephraim** and rallied those forces to cut off the Midianite escape route across the Jordan River. The Ephraimites also captured two key **Midianite** generals, **Oreb** ("Raven") **and Zeeb** ("Wolf"), whom they executed; their **heads** were brought to **Gideon** as grisly trophies of their triumph. The text is silent about whether this impromptu expansion of Gideon's army was sanctioned by the Lord.

> **MAIN IDEA REVIEW:** *God took Gideon—and his men—through a systematic reduction in military power in order that a powerful truth might be proclaimed: "'Not by might nor by power, but by my Spirit,' says the LORD Almighty" (Zech. 4:6b). God alone provides victory, and God alone is due glory.*

III. CONCLUSION

It Couldn't Be Done

Edgar Guest wrote a much beloved poem, "It Couldn't Be Done," which includes this stanza:

Somebody said that it couldn't be done,
But he with a chuckle replied
That "maybe it couldn't," but he would be one
Who wouldn't say so till he tried.
So he buckled right in with a trace of a grin
On his face. If he worried he hid it.
He started to sing as he tackled the thing
That couldn't be done, and he did it.

Much later some wag penned a forgettable parody:

He tackled the thing that couldn't be done;
With a will, he went right to it!
He tackled the thing that couldn't be done;
And found he *couldn't* do it!

We all face many challenges in life. The point is not self-assurance, self-confidence, self-determination (as in Guest's poem) nor is it self-defeat (as in its parody). When God is on your side, as Gideon and Israel learned, life's challenges take on an entirely different meaning. By yourself, you are . . . by yourself! A minority of one. But when it's "one-plus-God," you succeed every time—but on God's terms, and according to his definition of "success." Consider Paul the apostle and Nero the powerful emperor. From the world's perspective, Paul lost and Nero won. But as J. Vernon McGee poignantly remarked, "Nero was on the throne while Paul was being beheaded. . . . But history has already handed down its decision. Men name their sons Paul and call their dogs Nero."

PRINCIPLES

- God is extraordinarily patient with our fears and intimately aware of our concerns.
- God sees us differently than we see ourselves; those who are "in Christ" are eternal victors in his eyes.
- It is unwise to ascribe praise and glory to ourselves—every good thing in our lives (including our "natural" giftedness) is ultimately from God (Jas. 1:17).

- God is sovereign over all, including all enemies. Nothing touches us that has not first been sifted through his fingers.

APPLICATIONS

- Stay away from the mirror—life is not about you, but about how you may glorify God.
- Cast all your cares on God; he cares for you (1 Pet. 5:7).
- Stop fretting as though you were in charge and all results depended on you.
- Trust God's promises—he will direct your paths (Prov. 3:5–6; Josh. 1:8).
- Remember: one-plus-God is a majority—anytime, anywhere.

IV. LIFE APPLICATION

Encouraging the Discouraged

In 1888, one hundred and fifty young men tried to enter the ministry of a particular denomination. One young man passed the written exam and then had to preach his trial sermon in front of a panel of ministers. When the results were posted, one hundred and five were turned down, including that young man. He sent a telegram to his father with one word, "Rejected." His father shot back a six-word telegram, "Rejected on earth, accepted in heaven." That young man was G. Campbell Morgan, now acknowledged as one of the greatest expositors of Scripture and arguably the most effective pulpiteer of the last generation.

One Christian writer said, "Discouragement is dissatisfaction with the past, distaste for the present, and distrust of the future. It is ingratitude for the blessings of yesterday, indifference to the opportunities of today, and insecurity about strength for tomorrow. It is unawareness of the presence of beauty, unconcern for the needs of our fellowman, and unbelief in the promises of old. It is impatience with time, immaturity of thought, and impoliteness to God."

However true this may be theologically, I for one am thankful that God understands our emotional lives and does not pronounce such heavy condemnation on our heads during times of discouragement. Many of God's "prime ministers" suffered from discouragement—Abraham, Moses, Elijah, David, Peter, Paul, and Gideon!

In Acts 4:36 Joseph of Cyprus was nicknamed "Barnabas" (meaning "son of encouragement") by the apostles. The reason they did so is easily understood. This sophisticated Levite from Cyprus exemplified stewardship, servanthood, and submission to the apostles' teaching—qualities that deeply encouraged these former Galilean peasants. In my home I have a file in my cabinet simply labeled "Barnabas." It contains notes of encouragement from students, faculty colleagues, and other friends that were sent to me in a span of twenty-five years of college teaching and eighteen (concurrent) years of pastoral ministry. Remarkably, these notes often were sent to me at moments of personal discouragement—an evidence of God's timing. As William Arthur Ward put it,

> Flatter me, and I may not believe you.
> Criticize me, and I may not like you.
> Ignore me, and I may not forgive you.
> Encourage me, and I will not forget you.

There are times when the Lord comes alongside us with a unique sense of his presence and encourages us. This is what God did for Gideon. There are other times when we feel we are alone, but then God sends an agent alongside to encourage us. At the end of his life, Hudson Taylor was so enfeebled that he said to a friend, "I'm so weak that I can't work or read my Bible, and I can hardly pray. I can only lie still in God's arms like a little child and trust." But that is exactly where God wants us to rest (John 10:27–30).

V. PRAYER

Father, there are times when we must beseech you with the words, "I do believe; help me overcome my unbelief" (Mark 9:24). Forgive us when our faith is in what we can see rather than in your strength. Forgive us when we are so committed to our plans that we are insensitive to your Spirit. Forgive us when we absorb praise and glory to ourselves, as though you were not the source of every good and perfect gift that comes our way. May we listen to your word, and accomplish your will in your way. Through Christ our Lord. Amen.

VI. DEEPER DISCOVERIES

A. Honorable Discharge

God made gracious provision for men who were called to battle and permitted a man exemption from battle without penalty if he qualified in one of four areas: (1) he was building a home for his family, (2) he had invested in a vineyard for his family's livelihood, (3) he was betrothed to a woman, or (4) he was simply afraid to go into battle (Deut. 20:1–8). The reason for the last condition was presumably that fear is contagious, and a panicking soldier may cause greater harm to his fellow soldiers. In this situation, it is probable that no one who qualified for the first three exemptions showed up in the first place. However, the fourth criterion was the only one that was changeable prior to the battle and was the criterion that God invoked. (Notice, however, that Gideon was not given this option!)

B. A Curious Battle Cry

Nowhere else do we read of such a battle cry suggested by a military leader. For example, there was no cry "for the Lord and for *Moses*" or "for the Lord and for *Joshua*" or "for the Lord and for *David*." While Gideon's battle cry may be easily overlooked as innocent and without improper motivation, a careful reading of Judges demonstrates that the cry is a harbinger of things to come (see Judg. 8).

C. Gideon's Detours

There are interesting "detours" in the initial story of Gideon. By itself, the story line moves from his call (6:11–16) to the cleansing of his own household and the gathering of his army (6:25–35), then on to God's reduction in the size of the army (7:1–8), and finally through the conquest of the Midianites (7:16–25). One can read these verses and notice nothing amiss in a perfectly continuous and contiguous story. The "detours," however, tell us more about Gideon than they do about the Midianite conflict: his first request for a confirming sign (6:17–24), his second request for a confirming sign (6:36–40), and finally God's granting Gideon a third confirming sign (7:9–15).

D. Dreams Vs. Dreams

Students of the Bible are familiar with the non-canonical use God makes of dreams to reveal himself (or his plans, or warnings, etc.) to his beloved children. At times, however, God granted those outside the covenant varying degrees of revelation through dreams, such as Abimelech (Gen. 20), Pharaoh (Gen. 40), and Nebuchadnezzar (Dan. 2; 4). As it turned out, Nebuchadnezzar's last dream was apparently redemptive (Dan. 4:34–37). The dream recorded in this chapter seems to be entirely for Gideon's benefit.

VII. TEACHING OUTLINE

A. INTRODUCTION

1. Lead Story: One Huge Identity Crisis
2. Context: The Midianite oppression had resulted in Israelite depression (Judg. 6:6). God called Gideon as his deliverer, yet in the last segment of chapter 6 and through most of chapter 7 it was necessary for God to confirm Gideon's call and to affirm God's power to grant Israel a miraculous victory against overwhelming odds. Unfortunately, Gideon's reliance on the Lord diminished as the years passed (ch. 8).
3. Transition: God had been preparing Gideon to deliver the Israelites from Midianite oppression. Israel needed to know that their Lord, who had rebuked them (Judg. 6:8–10), would now rescue them—as Gideon's miraculous victory clearly demonstrates.

B. COMMENTARY

1. Condensing the Army (7:1–8)
    a. Test #1: Public (7:1–3)
    b. Test #2: Private (7:4–8)
2. Calming the General (7:9–15)
    a. Entering the enemy encampment (7:9–12)
    b. Eavesdropping on the enemy nightmare (7:13–14)
    c. Encouraging Israel's band (7:15)
3. Crushing the Enemy (7:16–25)

    a. The strategy (7:16–20)

    b. The success (7:21–25)

C. CONCLUSION: IT COULDN'T BE DONE

VIII. ISSUES FOR DISCUSSION

1. Here is a test with two true-false questions and one essay. First, God is unchanging. (True or False?) For the answer key, read James 1:17 and Hebrews 13:8. Second, God's methods are unchanging. (True or False?) For the answer to this one, simply scan the Bible, where the unchanging God considers the changing circumstances and the natures of the people involved and then acts with amazing creativity. Here is a final question, an essay discussion: How does the fact that God is unchanging, yet acts in unpredictable ways, affect one's own ability to know with certainty what God "ought" to do in one's life?

2. The Midianites had oppressed Israel for only seven years, but it felt like seventy. Through Gideon God provided security for this people at this time. Since September 11, 2001, Americans are deeply aware that we have been living in the illusion—not the reality—of national "security." The truth is, of course, that over the generations nations come and go, and "sovereign" borders on maps might as well be drawn with invisible ink, for all their permanence. What impact do you think God expects the fact that our citizenship is ultimately in heaven (Phil. 3:20) to have on the way we live our lives on earth?

3. Read through Judges 6 and 7. Identify the episodes where you think God might have become exasperated and impatient with Gideon. How are we like Gideon and unlike Gideon? What comfort may we derive from God's patience with Gideon?

Judges 8

Life: A Sprint, or a Marathon?

I. INTRODUCTION
Staying Strong in the Battle

II. COMMENTARY
A verse-by-verse explanation of the chapter.

III. CONCLUSION
Finishing Well

An overview of the principles and applications from the chapter.

IV. LIFE APPLICATION
Faithful to the End

Melding the chapter to life.

V. PRAYER
Tying the chapter to life with God.

VI. DEEPER DISCOVERIES
Historical, geographical, and grammatical enrichment of the commentary.

VII. TEACHING OUTLINE
Suggested step-by-step group study of the chapter.

VIII. ISSUES FOR DISCUSSION
Zeroing the chapter in on daily life.

"*All* power tends to corrupt;

absolute power corrupts absolutely."

Lord John Emerich Edward

Dalberg Acton

 IN A NUTSHELL

Gideon began well but ended poorly, and his life offers a sad warning: when we take our eyes off the eternal, our priorities go astray. We focus on temporal things that don't really matter, and then we appear little different from the rest of the world.

Life: A Sprint,
or a Marathon?

I. INTRODUCTION

Staying Strong in the Battle

*T*oday (as I write this) it is my birthday. Not five minutes ago I got a telephone call from a mortuary asking if I would like to prearrange my funeral plans. Their timing, in my view, was not good! But as Christians it is true that we must "live life backwards," that is, live the present in light of the future. God wants us to finish the race well, to persevere until the end when faith becomes sight. As we stand before the Lord, we want to hear "well done, good and faithful servant" (see Matt. 25:21,23). Not long ago I was visiting a friend in California, laughing together about the trauma of our doctoral studies and reminiscing. We played the game many old friends play, "Whatever happened to?" Unfortunately, an alarming number of our mutual friends were no longer living for the Lord.

The Bible is brutally honest about its "heroes"—they are cut from the fabric of reality, not fantasy action figures or a collection of "vignettes of victors." The truth is, Gideon did not finish well. In Galatians 3:3 Paul exhorted, "Are you so foolish? After beginning with the Spirit, are you now trying to attain your goal by human effort?" In a sense, Gideon began his race by the Spirit (after three false starts), but he ended in the flesh. He thought the race was a sprint, when in reality it was a marathon. After the "hall of faith" in which Gideon is lauded (Heb. 11), the next chapter of Hebrews begins with the exhortation to "run with perseverance the race marked out for us" (Heb. 12:1).

If Judges 8 were all you had of the story of Gideon, you would be confused whether he was a hero or a villain; most people do not know about this final chapter of Gideon's life. But there are helpful warnings here. First Corinthians 10:12 cautions, "If you think you are standing firm, be careful that you don't fall." In life you don't leave the battle until you leave the battlefield. And God wants us to finish well.

II. COMMENTARY

Life: A Sprint, or a Marathon?

> **MAIN IDEA:** *This chapter records Gideon's reactions to five confrontations. In four out of the five, he behaves abominably; in the first episode, he seems to behave appropriately. However, it comes as no surprise to see that victory over God's enemies may be followed by squabbling among God's people (see Acts 5:12–42 with Acts 6:1–7). Misplaced self-reliance over foiling an external attack made the Israelites vulnerable to internal disputes.*

A Dealing with Ephraim's Ego (8:1–3)

> **SUPPORTING IDEA:** *First, Gideon assuaged Ephraim with tact, but with questionable motives.*

8:1–3. **The Ephraimites** accused Gideon of ignoring them because he did not **call** them when he **went to fight Midian**, and so **they criticized him sharply**. The accusation was unwarranted; Gideon did not give offense, but the Ephraimites took offense anyway! (Some people simply cannot stand not being involved in other people's victories; rather than rejoice with those who rejoice, they become embittered.) While we are unsure of their motives—whether injured pride, jealousy, or loss of spoils of war—Gideon put a proverb into practice: "A gentle answer turns away [*defuses* and *diffuses*] wrath" (Prov. 15:1). Rather than respond with revenge or indignation, he responded with tact and diplomacy. He minimized the battle in which his forces were involved (calling it **the full grape harvest of Abiezer**) and maximized the mop-up operation in which Ephraim was involved (**the gleanings of Ephraim's grapes**). His ploy worked, for **their resentment against him subsided**.

Given Gideon's responses in the next four cases, one may wonder if his reaction to the Ephraimites was more a matter of political expediency than a passion for truth. Minimizing the role of his army of three hundred soldiers seems tantamount to minimizing God's powerful miracle. Was killing two kings *truly* a greater feat than routing an army at odds of four hundred fifty to one? Surely not! The Lord had given Gideon the victory, yet Gideon said nothing about God's role in the battle. He dealt with the Ephraimites entirely at a horizontal level. (We will see in chapter 12 that the Ephraimites learned nothing from the confrontation but rather became entrenched in terminal smugness.)

▣ Dealing with Succoth's Spitefulness (8:4–7,13–16)

SUPPORTING IDEA: *Second, Gideon behaved like a dictator and took revenge on the leaders of Succoth.*

8:4–7. The battle against the Midianites was not over, however. Gideon and his army were **keeping up the pursuit,** crossing from the east side of the **Jordan** (Cisjordan) to the west side (Transjordan), specifically within the portion occupied by the tribe of Gad (Josh. 13:24–28). Gideon with his very **exhausted** and **worn out** troops came to **the men of Succoth** requesting hospitality; he explained that he was **pursuing Zebah and Zalmunna, the kings of Midian.** These Israelite officials apparently did not respect Gideon's tiny "army" of **three hundred men,** and they ignored his authority as God's deliverer (in contrast to the Cisjordan Israelites in 7:23). Their challenge to Gideon was irascible and impossible (e.g., if a policeman were to ask a witness which way a suspect fled and he responded, "Show me the guy you're after and then I'll tell you which way he went!"). They asked illogically, **Do you already have the hands of Zebah and Zalmunna in your possession?**

Whether this challenge was meant literally (hands as trophies, cp. Judg. 7:25; 1 Sam. 18:25) or figuratively (leading captives by their hands, or with hands shackled) is uncertain. What is certain is that rather than respond (as with Ephraim) as a diplomat, Gideon responded as a dictator. He left them with a threat: **when the LORD has given Zebah and Zalmunna into my hand, I will tear your flesh with desert thorns and briers.**

8:13–16. Moving ahead in the story to verses 13–16 (see "Deeper Discoveries"), Gideon made good on his gruesome promise. As they **returned from the battle, . . . he caught a young man of Succoth and questioned him** about the leaders of the town, resulting in a list of the **seventy-seven officials of Succoth.** Gathering the leaders, he threw their challenge back in their faces and then fulfilled his promise to the letter **by punishing** (torturing) **them with desert thorns and briers,** sort of the land-based equivalent of being keel-hauled.

▣ Dealing with Penuel's Pettiness (8:8–9,17)

SUPPORTING IDEA: *Third, Gideon behaved like a despot and took revenge on all the men of Penuel.*

8:8–9,17. Still enraged, Gideon went **to Penuel and made the same request of them, but they answered as the men of Succoth had.** Apparently this town was fortified, and Gideon promised to remove their source of military defense against attacks from oppressors—strange behavior from a deliverer from Midianite oppression! For the second time, Gideon left a town of his fellow Israelites with a threat, **when I return in triumph, I will tear down this tower**. When he returned later, however, his ire extended beyond destruction of the **tower** but also included the people: He **killed the men of the town** (v. 17).

Gideon had changed. He who was fearful (Judg. 6) and then faithful (Judg. 7) became frightful (Judg. 8). The diplomat (Judg. 8:1–3) became the despot. These petty towns posed no threat to Gideon or to Israel; indeed, they were his brothers. Gideon did not torture and massacre Canaanites, but Israelites! In his fury he became a "loose cannon"—unmanageable, unrestrained, unruly, uncontrolled, and uninhibited.

Ⅾ Dealing with Zebah and Zalmunna (8:10–12,18–21)

SUPPORTING IDEA: *Fourth, Gideon behaved like a tyrant and murdered Zebah and Zalmunna out of revenge.*

8:10–12. A determined Gideon came upon the Midianite army of **about fifteen thousand men** and then **fell upon the unsuspecting army**. Although Zebah and Zalmunna escaped, Gideon **pursued them and captured them** (note that the odds were still against the Israelites, by fifty to one). After the episodes of revenge upon Succoth (vv. 13–16) and Penuel (v. 17), Gideon must have returned to his home (which we infer from the presence of his young son). Gideon held a military tribunal not to assess the guilt of these kings, nor to declare the verdict, but to decree their sentence—a process that contained a surprise both for the Midianites and for the readers of the story!

8:18–21. Gideon began by asking what would seem an irrelevant question: **What kind of men did you kill at Tabor?** Apparently this referred to an episode in which these kings held a public execution of specific Israelites, not some forgettable skirmish. Further, these two men were directly and personally involved in the executions. Their response may reflect either bravado or a terrifying realization: they were **men like you . . . each one with the bearing of a prince**. At this point Gideon unveiled a secret: **Those were my brothers, the sons of my own mother.** This fact helps explain both Joash's reluctance to turn his remaining son over to the Israelites (6:31) and Gideon's dogged pursuit of these two kings into Transjordan.

Gideon offered Zeba and Zalmunna a strange and irrelevant consolation: **If you had spared their lives, I would not kill you**. At this point it is clear that Gideon is not God's executioner but is carrying out his personal vendetta. He turned to his oldest son **Jether** and commanded the unsuspecting and unprepared boy to kill them. While the boy carried a sword, he apparently stood still, mute, **because he was only a boy and was afraid** (reminiscent of his father when we first met him). Zebah and Zalmunna filled the horrific silence with their own challenge: **Come, do it yourself.** "As is the man, so is his strength." Again, we are uncertain of their demeanor—whether defiant or diffident—but in either case they thought it would be more honorable (and presumably less painful!) to be killed by a proven warrior than by a child.

Gideon responded with two actions. First, he **stepped forward and killed them** in front of his son and all other witnesses. Second, he availed himself of the moon (crescent) **ornaments** with which these kings had adorned their **camels' necks**, a detail that anticipates the negative aspects of the legacy Gideon will leave.

E Dealing with Israel (8:22–31)

SUPPORTING IDEA: *Gideon's dealings with his supporters in Israel reflected an intention to live like a king—but without the title.*

8:22–23,28. *The Good News.* Prior to God's establishment of a Davidic monarchy, some of **the Israelites** brought a proposal to Gideon: **Rule over us**. This had to be flattering to Gideon. Imagine being offered prestige, power, and praise on a platter! Two elements of this offer are troubling. First, their motive had nothing to do with God's deliverance but reflected a horizontal view: **Because you have saved us out of the hand of Midian**. Second, not only was the proposal for Gideon to become king, but also for his family (**your son and your grandson**) to continue a hereditary dynasty. Israel had absorbed the paradigm of dynastic rule from the surrounding Canaanite culture rather than the non-hereditary pattern of judgeship.

Gideon's laudable response was to refuse the offers both of kingship and dynastic rule (**I will not rule over you, nor will my son rule over you**). Instead he proclaimed, **The LORD will rule over you**. Thankfully, **during**

Gideon's lifetime, the land enjoyed peace forty years (v. 28). The Midianite oppression was forcibly annihilated.

8:24–27,29–31. The Bad News. On the heels of the good news (civil stability and Gideon's rejection of kingship) came the bad news. Gideon didn't really mean it! He did not disabuse the Israelites of their idea of his prominence in their deliverance by explaining that it was the Lord who had delivered them from the Midianites (contrast his humility in 6:15–16 and even in 8:2–3). Indeed, he had already begun to compromise his lifestyle by gathering for himself the crescent symbols of kingship (v. 21). As Gideon positioned himself for the next four decades (v. 28), he continued down the path of self-aggrandizement that left a tragic legacy. He compromised in four areas: finances, faith, family, and fantasy.

8:24–26. His Finances. Gideon gathered to himself a royal treasury. He asked that each soldier (his faithful three hundred men plus all those involved in the mop-up operations) give him **an earring from your share of the plunder**. (The Midianites, apparently connected to the **Ishmaelites**, wore **gold earrings**). The Israelites were glad to comply, enriching Gideon (**seventeen hundred shekels**) and also symbolically securing the loyalty of the military as vassals to Gideon. Not only did Gideon amass gold; he also gathered **the pendants and the purple garments worn by the kings of Midian** and **the chains that were on their camels' necks**. Later in verse 30 we note that Gideon had funds to support a large harem—a far cry from his beginning as "the least" in the tribe of Manasseh (6:15).

8:27. His Faith. From the gold Gideon formed an object whose nature is uncertain. It may have been **an ephod**, the high priestly breastpiece which contained the Urim and Thummim (devices for discerning God's will—always a challenge for Gideon!). It may also have been a breastpiece used to clothe an image (an ironic twist; the Lord's Spirit had "clothed" Gideon, Judg. 6:34). In any case, the object was meant to fill a spiritual gap because the priesthood was either very corrupt or very inept at this time. But God had not dethroned Aaron and his family, so Gideon was not to enthrone himself or his family in the priestly role.

Sadly, this object eventually displaced the Lord from Israel's affections, so that the indictment from Judges 2:17 is here repeated for the first time in the book: **Israel prostituted themselves by worshiping it** (see also v. 33). This took place **in Ophrah**, Gideon's hometown, where the object also

became a snare to Gideon and his family. Gideon, whose faith had required visible signs from God and who did indeed have one great moment of faith, now turned entirely to the visible and chose sight over faith. For the first time in this book, idolatry is specifically linked to one of God's deliverers.

8:29–30. *His Family.* Gideon's family followed him into disobedience, not only in worship (v. 27, and his family), but also in lifestyle, as the next chapter will show. It also appears that his life became increasingly carnal. Gideon (who already had a family, 8:20, "oldest son") established a large harem, comparable to any Ancient Near Eastern king. Ordinarily harems were enlarged as one extended territorial influence and accumulated power. From these alliances **he had seventy sons.**

8:31. *His Fantasy.* Gideon's last compromised area (his fantasy) is more subtle but real nonetheless. He set up a mistress in the Canaanite city of **Shechem**, ignoring God's explicit command forbidding such alliances (Deut. 7:2–4). Presumably he frequented this Canaanite city, where his concubine **bore him a son, whom he named Abimelech** (there were three other people with this name in the Old Testament, all of them Philistines!), probably meaning, "my father is king."

Why would Gideon, who refused the title "king," choose this name? It may be significant that Gideon did not choose this name for any of his seventy sons in Israel, but he did give this name to the one son who was outside Israel. Others have observed that what Gideon *renounced* in Israel became constantly *pronounced* among the Canaanites.

If one does not interpret Gideon's legacy through a "best case" lens, then in truth all five confrontations in this chapter (with Ephraim, Succoth, Penuel, Zebah and Zalmunna, and Israel) reveal deep character flaws in Gideon. This lens also invites us to look backward to the battle cry that Gideon gave, "for the LORD and for Gideon" (7:18,20) and wonder why it's not simply, "for the LORD" or "for the LORD and for Israel." Kings demanded bequests from their vassals, kings amassed a royal treasury, kings displayed symbols of royalty (such as the crescent decorations, the pendants, the purple robes of the Midianite kings, and the royal neck bands worn by the camels), kings established and maintained harems. While he rejected the title of king, Gideon accepted the lifestyle of kingship.

F Epilogue (8:32–35)

SUPPORTING IDEA: *Gideon's legacy left no lasting heritage for the Lord; any positive impact of his life was soon forgotten as Israel continued her downward spiral.*

8:32–35. After forty years of peace, Gideon **died at a good old age and was buried in the tomb of his father Joash in Ophrah of the Abiezrites.** While Gideon was alive, open worship of the Baals was not practiced. However, Gideon had not availed himself of a forty-year window of opportunity to establish the worship of the true God. No judge left Israel in worse shape than did Gideon. After his death, the people showed what they had become: **The Israelites again prostituted themselves to the Baals.** Under forty years of Gideon's judgeship, Israel became totally Canaanized, while Gideon became totally comfortable. The people were idolaters long before they practiced idolatry. They returned from Gideon's funeral and broke out their old bottles of Baal Ale!

The author of Judges anticipates the next chapter by adding that the Israelites **also failed to show kindness to the family of Jerub-Baal (that is, Gideon) for all the good things he had done for them.** The generation who suffered under the oppression of the Midianites (and who remembered Gideon and his conquest) eventually died, and the new generation "knew neither the LORD nor what he had done for Israel" (Judg. 2:10). The cycle is complete. Almost.

MAIN IDEA REVIEW: *This chapter records Gideon's reactions to five confrontations. In four out of the five, he behaves abominably; in the first episode, he seems to behave appropriately. However, it comes as no surprise to see that victory over God's enemies may be followed by squabbling among God's people (see Acts 5:12–42 with Acts 6:1–7). Misplaced self-reliance over foiling an external attack made the Israelites vulnerable to internal disputes.*

III. CONCLUSION

Finishing Well

Beth DeCiantis tried to qualify in the marathon for the 1992 Olympics, which requires a female runner to complete the race in less than two hours, forty-five minutes. Beth was doing well but began having trouble around mile twenty-three. She reached the final stretch at two hours, forty-three minutes—with just two minutes left to qualify. Two hundred yards from the finish, she stumbled and fell. Stunned and dazed, she stayed down for twenty seconds. The clock kept ticking—two hours forty-four minutes, or less than a minute to go. She staggered to her feet and began walking. With ten seconds to go, she fell again. She began to crawl, and the crowd cheered her as she crossed the finish line on her hands and knees. Her time? Two hours, forty-four minutes, fifty-seven seconds (*Runner's World*, August 1991).

At the spiritual level many people are willing to expend their lives for the Lord, in the short run. As others have observed, God does not often ask us to give our lives in a rush of martyrdom. One man put it this way: "We think giving our all to the Lord is like taking a thousand dollar bill and laying it on the table—'Here's my life, Lord. I'm giving it all.' But the reality for most of us is that he sends us to the bank and has us cash in the thousand dollar bill for quarters. We go through life putting out twenty-five cents here and fifty cents there. Listen to the neighbor kid's troubles instead of saying, 'Get lost.' Go to a committee meeting. Give a cup of water to a shaky old man in a nursing home. Usually giving our life to Christ isn't glorious. It's done in all those little acts of love, twenty-five cents at a time. It would be easy to go out in a flash of glory; it's harder to live the Christian life little by little over the long haul" (Fred Craddock).

PRINCIPLES

- Diplomacy often succeeds when contention fails—a "gentle answer" does indeed defuse and diffuse difficult dilemmas (Prov. 15:1).

- Collectively, Satan's attacks may well be from without, but often he attacks the unity of the body of Christ—an attack from within.

- Satan often attacks believers after a moment of spiritual victory, when we are tempted to feel self-confident and thus are vulnerable. He knows that it is when we are weak (and dependent upon the Lord) that we are truly strong (2 Cor. 2:11).

- It is possible to be spiritual in the sprint but mired down in the marathon. God desires faithfulness "in the long run."

APPLICATIONS

- Don't take offense when none is given (like the Ephraimites), or even when it *is* given! Whenever possible, be at peace with all men (Rom. 12:18) and offer a "best case" interpretation of others' motives.

- Be a peacemaker. Take every opportunity to reinforce the "unity of the Spirit through the bond of peace" (Eph. 4:3).

- Plan actively for *your* legacy, to "live life backwards!"

- Memorize Hebrews 12:1–2, and think through the implications of these verses this week.

IV. LIFE APPLICATION

Faithful to the End

Often we think of our lives as set in the "right" patterns. I am not out robbing banks, I am faithful in my marriage, I am active in my church. Things look good, *from the outside!* But Satan tells you, "You know, you can have more. You can have that affair and no one will know. You can cheat just a little in business and no one will know." If it is true that believers are "not unaware of his schemes" (2 Cor. 2:11), neither is Satan ignorant of our weaknesses. Satan is a roaring lion seeking whom he may devour, and Christians look tender!

Gideon had some victories, but he fell short of greatness. Did you know that Gideon is found in the "hall of faith" of Hebrews 11? It is not a large entry—just his name, which flashes by, as though he were running a sprint. Hebrews 11 leads to Hebrews 12:1, in which all believers are exhorted to "run with perseverance the race marked out for us." Long ago C. H. Spurgeon reminded us, "By perseverance the snail reached the ark." Paul wrote to the Thessalonians and admonished them, "Never tire of doing what is right" (2 Thess. 3:13). Jesus praised the church at Ephesus because, he said, "You have persevered and have endured hardships for my name, and have not grown weary" (Rev. 2:3). He is, after all, our exemplar in faithfulness: Hebrews 12:3 encourages us to "consider him who endured opposition from sinful men, so that you will not grow weary and lose heart."

V. PRAYER

Lord, we recognize the truth that one day we will stand before you to render an account of our lives. Until that day, we ask that we will look unto Jesus, the exemplar of faithfulness. May our words and our deeds demonstrate your power, and may our lives not be explainable in terms of us, but point beyond us to the source of all strength. Through Christ our Lord. Amen.

VI. DEEPER DISCOVERIES

A. Structure of the Chapter

The chapter contains two "bookend" sections in which Gideon deals with Israelites on the east side of the Jordan River, the Israelites of Ephraim (vv. 1–3) and then presumably the larger population of Israel (vv. 22–35). The middle section deals with those outside Israel proper: the people of Succoth, Penuel, and the fleeing Midianite kings. The structure of these middle confrontations takes the form A, B, C, A', B', C' (Block, 288). For purposes of reading, the literary structure contains rapid-fire force. For purposes of oral communication, one might choose to group the verses dealing with each antagonist as a unit, as this commentary has done.

B. Gideon's Leniency

Gideon said he would have let the Midianite chieftains live (v. 19) in contradiction of God's explicit command (Deut. 7). At the same time, he had no qualms about killing Israelites (v. 17). His lack of consistency is exposed in the imprecation offered by the psalmist Asaph over the enemies of God, which reveals the motives of these kings: "Make their nobles like Oreb and Zeeb, all their princes like Zebah and Zalmunna, who said, 'Let us take possession of the pasturelands of God'" (Ps. 83:11–12; see Judg. 7:25).

C. Gideon's Polygamy (8:30–31)

Polygamy was never God's intention for marriage. This may be inferred by *principle* and by *pattern*. The *principle* that God established for marriage is a part of the creation ordinances of Genesis 2—God made one woman for one man (which excluded polygamy, polyandry, and homosexuality). Both Jesus and Paul refer to this pattern as normative. Second, by *pattern,* to the extent that we have information about polygamous households in Scripture, every single case is a dysfunctional family filled with extraordinary contention, jealousy, and strife. The New Testament makes it clear: a Christian man is to "aspire" to being a one-woman man in every possible way (1 Tim. 3:1–2,12).

D. Abimelech

The name Abimelech probably means "my father is king." Sympathizers may suggest that the name would be an encouragement to a boy raised in a family environment that was socially difficult. Block notes that the name may refer to a dynastic title for Philistine kings (Block, 304n), which serves as converging support for the view that functionally Gideon regarded himself as Israel's king.

VII. TEACHING OUTLINE

A. INTRODUCTION

1. Lead Story: Staying Strong in the Battle
2. Context: God had been faithful to Gideon; in Judges 7, the Lord *condensed* the army, *calmed* the general, and *crushed* the enemy. In Judges 8, however, Gideon showed almost no awareness of his dependence upon the source of his strength, and his life made little difference in Israel. In Judges 9, Gideon's legacy will bring at least as much trouble on Israel as the Midianite oppression from which Gideon delivered them.
3. Transition: Sometimes God uses bad examples to bring his children to an awareness of their need for spiritual vigilance. While the unfolding story of Gideon's later life may be less familiar than his early victories, it serves as a reminder that we must never grow weary in walking the walk.

B. COMMENTARY

1. Dealing with Ephraim's Ego (8:1–3)

2. Dealing with Succoth's Spitefulness (8:4–7,13–16)
3. Dealing with Penuel's Pettiness (8:8–9,17)
4. Dealing with Zebah and Zalmunna (8:10–12,18–21)
5. Dealing with Israel (8:22–31)
   a. The good news (8:22–23,28)
   b. The bad news (8:24–27,29–31)
6. Epilogue (8:32–35)

C. CONCLUSION: FINISHING WELL

VIII. ISSUES FOR DISCUSSION

1. Why do you think the Bible never puts human beings on a spiritual pedestal? After all, there were many admirable heroes of faith in Scripture. Similarly, why did the apostle Paul qualify his statement "follow my example" with the addition, "as I follow the example of Christ" (1 Cor. 11:1)?

2. What are the difficulties of serving the Lord through long years with faithfulness? What are the joys and benefits of serving the Lord through long years with faithfulness?

3. What do you think Gideon *should* have done with the people of Ephraim? With Succoth? With Penuel? With the two kings? With his fellow Israelites?

4. Speculate for a while: To what extent do you think the spiritual disease of pride played a role in Gideon's long-term ineffectiveness?

Judges 9

❧❧

Abimelech Ben-Gideon: The C.E.O. of Crime

" '*How* shall a man judge what to do in such times?'

asked Eomer. 'As he has ever judged,' said Aragorn. 'Good

and ill have not changed since yesteryear; nor are they one

thing among Elves and Dwarves and another among Men.'"

J .   R .   R . T o l k i e n

Judges 9

I N   A   N U T S H E L L

Judges 9 describes life without God. It tells a horror story of people who place their personal ambition over anything else in their lives, of people who do not believe because they will not believe.

Abimelech Ben-Gideon: The C.E.O. of Crime

I. INTRODUCTION

The Psychology of Practical Atheism

A businessman well-known for his ruthlessness once announced to writer Mark Twain, "Before I die I mean to make a pilgrimage to the Holy Land. I will climb Mount Sinai and read the Ten Commandments aloud at the top." "I have a better idea," replied Twain. "You could stay in Boston and keep them."

The truth is, many people feel they are morally upright people and that God is somehow pleased with them. They think, first, "Usually I'm a good person," second, "My good deeds outweigh my bad," and third, "I'm not as bad as some people." In other words, when these people measure themselves by *their own* standards, they come out pretty well. In the days of the judges everyone believed in what was true for them and behaved accordingly (Judg. 17:6; 21:25).

Unbelievers have an eternal stake in being right in their unbelief. If a personal God is there, then certain uncomfortable things are also true. First, I am no longer in control because God could break in, and his plan may conflict with my plan. Second, if a personal God is there, then he is able to communicate, and he has the right to tell me how to live. I can't do what is right in my own eyes. Because, third, if a personal God is there, then I am accountable to him for how I live, and my life is not going to be measured by my own personal moral code but by God's standards. People usually don't search among all the possible creeds and religions and try to objectively apply criteria for truth. People usually decide how they want to live and choose among religions or beliefs that permit that lifestyle.

In the last chapter we looked at Gideon's sad legacy. In this chapter we look at his tragic legacy: the story of his son Abimelech. Like a ruthless dictator, Abimelech did what he thought he had to do first to get ahead and then to stay ahead. Where is God in this chapter? He is there, "behind the seen."

This chapter is the story of practical atheism—of people who live their lives as though God did not exist, or at least is irrelevant to their lives.

II. COMMENTARY

Abimelech Ben-Gideon: The C.E.O. of Crime

> **MAIN IDEA:** *The life story of Abimelech exposes the evil hearts of men who reject God; he even allows them to use their own venom to poison one another. In the end, they reap what they sow (Gal. 6:7).*

A Fratricide: The Treachery of Abimelech (9:1–6)

> **SUPPORTING IDEA:** *Abimelech's evil heart was first exposed as he manipulated the people of Shechem to support the murder of his own brothers.*

9:1–3. *Securing His Mother's Relatives by Treason.* It has been observed that Gideon's story should have ended at 8:28 with "and they lived happily ever after—or at least for forty years." Unfortunately, his most significant—and tragic—legacy came through his son **Abimelech**, to whom we were introduced in the last chapter (8:29–35). On a superficial reading it appears that God has taken a leave of absence from human events; on closer reading (9:23,56–57) it is clear that God is present, "behind the seen." The key to unlocking this chapter is hung at the back door—"God repaid . . . God also made the men of Shechem pay" (9:56–57).

Abimelech was the son of Gideon's Canaanite concubine who continued to live in the Canaanite city of **Shechem**. The chapter begins as he challenged his mother's brothers with a false "either/or" dilemma: **Which is better for you: to have all seventy of Jerub-Baal's sons rule over you, or just one man?** There were several unfounded assumptions undergirding this question. First, there must be a human king or despot; second, these were the only two alternatives; third, the seventy sons of Gideon were planning to establish rule over the surrounding area; fourth, rule by a committee of seventy would not be good for the citizens of Shechem; and fifth, the human ruler(s) should of course be from the line of Gideon.

The question was framed as a political ploy to exclude thoughtful options, rather than as a quest for truth (like saying, "If you agree with me, then breathe!"). Further, Abimelech challenged them to **remember, I am your flesh and blood**. (Of course, he was also the flesh and blood of Gideon's sons, in the same degree). His uncles, and then **the citizens of Shechem**, were persuaded that following Abimelech would be in their best interest (**better for you**). After all, they reasoned, **he is our brother**, and therefore they could expect more favorable treatment from him than presumably they had received from Gideon, who had lived in Ophrah, not Shechem.

9:4–6. *Slaughtering His Father's Relatives by Treachery.* The citizens of Shechem dipped into the **temple** treasury—not of the Lord but of **Baal-Berith**—and secured **seventy shekels of silver**. It may be that the hit men Abimelech hired were to be paid for each of Gideon's seventy sons, one piece of silver per head. The funds were sufficient for the **reckless adventurers** whom Abimelech hired—who probably were not mercenary soldiers but criminals. Abimelech went to his father's home in Ophrah and captured the town, very likely by surprise. He **murdered his seventy brothers** (minus Jotham, the youngest, who had escaped by hiding). Abimelech did not want any of them alive and available should the Shechemites change their minds.

This slaughter was systematic and serial—one at a time **on one stone** (see 1 Sam. 14:33–34), an astonishing horror for these lads. One after another, like the victims of Nazi atrocities, they were herded toward their inevitable doom. After this gruesome ceremony was complete, another ceremony began: **the citizens of Shechem and Beth Millo gathered . . . to crown Abimelech king**.

Israel had become morally anesthetized. The nation should have been outraged, but there was not one blip of protest on their moral radar screen. As long as no one bothered them, they did not care what happened to other people. Abimelech should have received *condemnation;* instead, he received *coronation*. Only one voice was raised in trembling protest (vv. 7–21).

B Fable: The Indictment by Jotham (9:7–21)

SUPPORTING IDEA: *With prophetic voice, Jotham publicly denounced the wickedness of Shechem and Abimelech, using a parable that invoked justice on both for their crimes.*

9:7–15. *The Story.* Gideon now had only two sons remaining alive. After learning about his half-brother's coronation and the complicity of the men of Shechem (very likely he **was told about this** by those who hid him), **Jotham**, the youngest of Gideon's sons, took the bold step of public confrontation, even though there was a price on his head. **He climbed up on the top of Mount Gerizim** which overlooked the city of Shechem and shouted from this acoustically beneficial location (Josh. 8:30–35; Mark 4:1; 6:34–44), uttering a carefully crafted story designed to make a significant point. He began by asking the **citizens of Shechem** to listen to him, **so that God may listen to you**—offering the possibility of forgiveness despite their complicity.

In Jotham's parable **the trees** (who were **cedars of Lebanon**, v. 15) **went out to anoint a king for themselves.** Their nominating committee had a short list of candidates and approached them one by one. First, they **said to the olive tree, "Be our king."** But the olive tree declined because it was too involved with fulfilling what olive trees do best, producing oil **by which both gods and men are honored.** Olive oil was used in anointing (honoring) people but also in the more mundane matters of medicine, giving light (fuel for lamps), and cooking. It would seem pointless for olive trees to be "anointed" with olive oil (the very thing they produced).

Second, the trees made the same offer **to the fig tree,** which gave the same response. The fig was too busy being useful as a food and as sweetener to be demoted by trading its role for kingship. Third, the trees offered the same **to the vine,** which responded in similar terms. The fruit of the vine brings joy. Why abandon such a noble role for a role of dubious "nobility"?

Finally, having run out of options, the trees approached the bramble, or **thornbush**—whose existence was part of the curse of Genesis 3. Whereas the other three candidates contributed positive joys or values to life, the thornbush contributed nothing but prickles. The point of Jotham's analogy was not that Abimelech was less desirable than three other candidates, but that he was less suitable than any other candidate possible! The bramble promised, **If you really want to anoint me king over you, come and take refuge in my shade; but if not, then let fire come out of the thornbush and consume the cedars of Lebanon.** The liason was not based on love or loyalty but on convenience and expediency. Of course, the thornbush did not offer cover or "shade" (an absurd idea!) or provide "refuge." By its very nature it hurt those who came near; it could not do otherwise. The point of the story was that the trees were self-destructive; they sought a false security that would turn and consume them.

9:16–21. *The Application.* The application of Jotham's obvious fable was in two parts: a *challenge* (vv. 16–19) and a *curse* (v. 20). He began by addressing the issue of corporate integrity with an ironic and emotional prelude to a question: **If you have acted honorably and in good faith when you made Abimelech king, and if you have been fair to Jerub-Baal and his family, and if you have treated him as he deserves**—the implication being negative. Serial slaughter was not "good faith" or "honorable," and Gideon's family did not deserve such treatment.

The application also pulses with emotion, as Jotham interrupted the first half of his conditional sentence with an accusation: **And to think that my father fought for you, risked his life to rescue you from the hand of Midian** and that **you have revolted against my father's family, murdered his seventy sons on a single stone, and made Abimelech, the son of his slave girl, king**.

Jotham continued, **But if you have not, let fire come out from Abimelech and consume you, citizens of Shechem and Beth Millo, and let fire come out from you, citizens of Shechem and Beth Millo, and consume Abimelech**. Jotham's imprecation was theologically hideous but understandable. In essence, it was this: "May you both get what you deserve." For a second time **Jotham fled, escaping to Beer**, and was never heard from again.

🅲 Fulfillment: The Justice of God (9:22–55)

> **SUPPORTING IDEA:** *In a downward spiral of conflict, compromise, and contention, Abimelech and his "allies" consumed each other; Jotham's curse came true.*

9:22–25. *The "Spirit" of Unrest.* Abimelech did not exactly live happily ever after. The next time we see him he had **governed Israel three years**. His alliance with the men of Shechem was not based on mutual trust but on mutual benefit. It was assumed that Abimelech would be a more benevolent ruler over Shechem than his brothers would have been and that he would help the Shechemite economy.

Apparently Abimelech set up one of his lieutenants (Zebul, v. 28) as governor in Shechem, while he ruled from Ophrah. Resentment was percolating, and when **God sent an evil spirit between Abimelech and the citizens of Shechem** hostilities erupted. Whether this "spirit" was a personal demonic being or a coalescing of circumstances that served as a catalyst is unimportant (see 1 Sam. 16:14–23). For the first time we see God actively involved in this chapter, guiding the mutually destructive relationship between the king and his Shechemite vassals. The specific *reason* for this is stated: **In order that the** crime against Jerub-Baal's seventy sons . . . might be avenged on their brother Abimelech and on the citizens of Shechem, who had helped him murder his brothers. Scripture is clear: "Do not be deceived: God cannot be mocked. A man reaps what he sows" (Gal. 6:7).

The *result* was that friends became foes, allies became adversaries. The men of Shechem began to ambush and rob all travelers and caravans, and because this could seriously affect the economy of several towns, it was reported to Abimelech.

9:26–29. *The Conspiracy of Gaal.* Intensifying the hostilities the men of Shechem already felt against Abimelech, a new Canaanite family moved into town, Gaal son of Ebed, and his brothers. This man, about whom we know almost nothing, quickly gained the allegiance of the citizens. After harvesting the grapes and making wine, they held a festival in the Baal-B'rith temple, the same temple whose treasury had provided the money to exterminate Abimelech's seventy brothers. The party turned into a complaint session against Abimelech, whom they cursed. For the second time in this chapter, the men of Shechem were swayed by slick talk.

Gaal made three essential points. First, Abimelech was not worthy to rule over Shechem. He was the son of a Jew and not a pure-blooded Shechemite (playing the "race card"; he did not mention that Abimelech's mother was a Shechemite). Second, Shechemites should serve only other Shechemites (Gaal considered himself a citizen in this brief time). Third, if the Shechemites were under his own command, he would defeat the army of Abimelech. Gaal expelled a lot of hot air (fueled with wine) to float a trial balloon with the men of Shechem.

9:30–34. *The Strategy of Abimelech.* Abimelech's surrogate governor became furious and secretly sent messengers to Abimelech to report the insurrection and also suggested a strategy: During the night you and your men should come and lie in wait, thus catching Gaal and his cohort by surprise. This Abimelech did, separating his men into four companies.

9:35–41. *Defeating Shechem's Champion, Gaal.* When Gaal and his men were outside the city gate, he realized he was trapped when Abimelech and his soldiers came out from their hiding place. If Zebul were atop the gate manning the retreat route, the ensuing conversation makes sense. Gaal tried to distract Zebul (presumably so that Zebul would in turn warn Abimelech and his army to back off from some unseen threat). Zebul would have none of it and instead taunted, **Where is your big talk now, you who said, "Who is Abimelech that we should be subject to him?" Aren't these the men you ridiculed? Go out and fight them!** Since he had no other option, **Gaal led out the citizens of Shechem and fought Abimelech.** Abimelech's army thrashed the followers of Gaal and **chased him** into retreat. Possibly with other pressing matters in nearby **Arumah**, he left **Zebul** to drive **Gaal and his brothers out of Shechem.**

9:42–43. *Disrupting Shechem's Countryside.* Abimelech did not need to retaliate further; Gaal and his family were expelled, Zebul was again established in Shechem, and there were thousands of people in Shechem who would give no further trouble. But Abimelech wanted revenge. The common **people of Shechem went out to the fields**, assuming that the conflicts among the rulers and warriors did not extend to the citizens of the city. They found that they were wrong (it was not wise to impute peaceful intentions to a man who massacred his own family). As soon as the vulnerability of the people was reported to Abimelech, he **divided** his army **into three companies**, set an **ambush**, and attacked the unsuspecting citizens. He no longer desired their allegiance; he desired their blood.

9:44–45. *Destroying Shechem's City.* **Abimelech and** his three **companies** not only struck down **those in the fields**; he **pressed his attack against the city,** . . . **captured** it, and butchered its citizens. Still not satisfied, the vengeful ruler tore down **the city and scattered salt over it**, insuring its future infertility and undesirability (it was not rebuilt until about 150 years later under Jeroboam, 1 Kgs. 12:25).

9:46–49. *Demolishing Shechem's Citadel.* Thus far, Abimelech had dispensed with Gaal and his family, with the warriors of Shechem, with the farmers in the field, with the merchants in the city, with the city walls and buildings, and with the land on which the city was built. There was one last **stronghold** left to which many of the citizens had fled. The pagan temple had a fortress attached to it, apparently set apart from the city. **When Abimelech heard that they had assembled there,** . . . **he took an ax and cut off some branches** that he (and his men following his example) piled **against the stronghold.** He set the wood on fire and thus killed **about a thousand men and women.** Shechem's destruction could not be more complete. The "thornbush" in whose brambles the trees had taken "shelter" had ignited and consumed them, like a wolf eating the foolish sheep that had elected him shepherd. The first part of Jotham's fable found fruition (vv. 15,20a).

9:50–52. *Excess and Egotism.* One would think Abimelech's rampage would surely be sated. But he was not finished. Apparently the city of **Thebez** either had joined Shechem in its duplicity or else had offended Abimelech in some other way during his three-year reign. So Thebez was Abimelech's next target. **Abimelech . . . besieged it and captured it,** following the same strategy that was successful at Shechem. He was again planning to conquer through conflagration, so **he approached the entrance to the tower to set it on fire.**

9:53–55. *Epitaph.* Things did not turn out as Abimelech anticipated, however; **a woman** took **an upper millstone** (the smaller of the two stones used in grinding grain—although still large and formidable) and **dropped** it **on his head and cracked his skull.** As he lay dying, he begged **his armorbearer** to finish the job, lest people adopt the saying **a woman killed him** as his epitaph. The soldier complied with the request, but everyone knew the truth. Abimelech was not killed by another noble, or by another soldier, or even by another man; he was killed by a woman—to his ego-inflated pride yet another death blow. Since the military campaign itself had no intrinsic value other than Abimelech's personal vengeance, **when the Israelites saw that Abimelech was dead, they went home.**

Block perceptively observes, "The man who had shamelessly played the female card to seize the throne (vv. 1–2) now shamefully falls victim to a representative of this gender. Indeed the story of Abimelech the macho man is framed by two women: the first, who gave him life (8:31), and the second, who took it (9:53)" (Block, 333–334).

🄳 Epilogue (9:56–57)

9:56–57. These last verses show that God was involved all along. He was active "behind the seen," not only working things for good to those who love him (Rom. 8:28), not only using the evil intentions of men to accomplish good results (Gen. 50:20), but using the venom of evil men to poison one another. **Thus God repaid the wickedness that Abimelech had done to his father by murdering his seventy brothers. God also made the men of Shechem pay for all their wickedness.**

The chapter that began with assassination on one stone (possibly a lower millstone) ended with execution by means of another stone (the upper millstone). The second part of Jotham's fable found fruition (v. 20b). Abimelech and his victims ended like venomous snakes, entwined in a death dance, fatally biting one another.

MAIN IDEA REVIEW: *The life story of Abimelech exposes the evil hearts of men who reject God; he even allows them to use their own venom to poison one another. In the end, they reap what they sow (Gal. 6:7).*

III. CONCLUSION

Playing the Odds

In 1982, *ABC Evening News* reported on an unusual work of modern art—a chair with a shotgun fastened to it. Yes, the gun was loaded but would not fire—probably! The artist used a timer to trigger the mechanism so that the gun would fire at random sometime during the next hundred years. Art viewers were to "enjoy" the exhibit in this way: they were to sit down in the chair and look directly down the gun barrel. Did people actually do this? Yes! There were long lines of those who waited to look down into the chamber and contemplate death and eternity for one minute. Everyone who took that risk knew that the gun could splatter them at any second, but they were playing the odds, gambling that it would not happen during their minute in the chair.

We all will face death sooner than later; we are in a life-and-death gamble that we will not win. The odds are impressive; one out of one die!

> The clock of life is wound but once,
> And no man has the power
> To tell just when the hands will stop.
> At late or early hour.
> To lose one's wealth is sad indeed.
> To lose one's health is more.
> To lose one's soul is such a loss,
> That no man can restore.

In the time it took you to read this little poem aloud, over forty people died. It is unwise to risk living our lives as though God did not exist, or were irrelevant. As far as eternity is concerned, unbelievers are gambling that God's standards will conform to their standards.

Those who live their lives choosing to ignore God need to realize three things. First, they may be ignoring God, but he is not ignoring them. His hand is present in their lives, whether they acknowledge him or not. Second, they must face life's eternal questions (questions of origin, purpose, destiny). These questions do not politely fade away simply because they cause discomfort. Third, unbelievers are gambling with their souls at stake; eternity is on the table. Sadly, many people have thought: "I'm fine without God. My good deeds outweigh my bad. I'm not as bad as some people. Usually I'm a good person. So I think I'll play the odds, thank you."

But ultimately moral relativism does not work; in fact, it doesn't even survive logical scrutiny. Someone who is on trial for murder, or for molesting a child, should not rely on the defense, "You know, my good deeds outweigh my bad. I'm not as bad as some people. Usually I'm a good person." Besides, Jesus has told us what his standards are. If one has ever felt hate, Jesus said that's in the same category as murder as far as separating one from the absolute holiness of God (Matt. 5:21–22). If someone claims, "I've never committed adultery," then has he or she ever lusted (Matt. 5:27–28)?

Is it wise to play those odds? To gamble one's eternal destiny on the hope that, despite what the Bible says, God will change his mind and conform to our standards? Salvation is not something we achieve or win, but something we receive as a gift. Even so, this is a gift that must be received with *empty* hands.

PRINCIPLES

- People often choose to ignore God not because of evidence but because of their wills; to acknowledge the Sovereign of the universe is to acknowledge their individual accountability.
- Many people would do anything at anyone's expense to advance themselves and their goals. This chapter makes it clear that the old saying is true: "There is no honor among thieves."
- Sometimes in a fallen world innocent people are hurt when cruel people pursue their greed. God is not mocked; the sowing-and-reaping principle (Gal. 6:7) applies both to this life and to the next.

APPLICATIONS

- Never try to evict God from your life! (If you are a believer he won't go anyway.)
- Don't treat others poorly; you will likely be treated poorly in return.
- Don't be surprised when unbelievers persistently resist your best efforts to evangelize them (this is the pattern about which Scripture warns us, Rom. 1:18–25).

IV. LIFE APPLICATION

Pascal's Wager

Blaise Pascal was a young man of astonishing accomplishments. He pioneered developments in such diverse areas as the vacuum, calculus, hydrostatics, conic sections, mass transit, and literature. He became a Christian and lived faithfully until his untimely death. At one point he laid out a challenge to his unbelieving friends, who spent much time in the gambling houses of Paris, as well as in the opera and theatre, because otherwise (said Pascal) they would have to think about their lives and eternal issues. Of course, people who reject God are not neutral seekers after truth; they have a huge, eternal stake in being right in their unbelief. His challenge is often called "Pascal's Wager," and here is my paraphrase (with explanation):

- If Christianity is false and I have not believed, then I gain finitely. (I've been right about something in this life, but the significance of being right ends when this life ends because Christianity is wrong after all.)
- If Christianity is false and I have believed, then I lose finitely. (I've been wrong in this life, but again there are no eternal consequences. The most that I've lost is that I've tried to live a happy and moral life for untrue reasons.)
- If Christianity is true and I have not believed, then I lose infinitely. (I've been wrong in this life, and my error has eternal consequences—I am forever under the wrath of God!)

- If Christianity is true and I have believed, then I gain infinitely. (I've been right in this life, and the truth that I have embraced follows me into eternity where I shall experience eternal bliss!)

"So," Pascal challenged his gambling friends, "what are the odds? Is it more prudent to believe, or not to believe?"

V. PRAYER

O Lord, we know that you desire that no one perish, but that all will come to repentance (2 Pet. 3:9). We do ask that unbelievers would become aware of your presence in their lives before it is too late. We also ask that those of us who are believers would never live as though you were irrelevant to our lives, but that our thoughts would inhabit the grace in which you enfold us. We have accepted Jesus by faith as our Savior for eternal life; may we live for him in our daily life. Through Jesus Christ our Lord. Amen.

VI. DEEPER DISCOVERIES

A. "Flesh and Blood" (9:2)

The NIV has translated the meaning for modern English, but the Hebrew reads "bone and flesh." The idea is similar to Genesis 2:23, where Adam exclaimed that Eve was "bone of my bones and flesh of my flesh."

B. "Seventy Shekels of Silver" (9:4)

Although the unit of measurement was not specified in the Hebrew, all currency was measured in shekels. Life is presented as cheap in this chapter. The price for a live slave varied from fifty to thirty shekels (Lev. 27:3–7). Note the extravagant amount Delilah received for Samson (Judg. 16:5).

C. Jotham (9:5,7)

Jotham's name is a compound of "Yahweh" and the word grouping that meant "honesty" or "truthfulness" (Block, 315n); the resultant meaning of his name may be close to "Yahweh is truthful." Note these themes in the only speech we have from Jotham, particularly in verses 16 and 19.

D. Jotham's Fable (9:7–15)

The form of the story was a "fable," the first of its kind in Scripture. A fable is a specialized form of parable, in which animals or inanimate objects (like trees) can speak and behave like humans to convey the point of the story.

E. God's Evil Spirit (9:23)

Any systematic observer will note that there are different levels of causality within Scripture. In Genesis 50:20, Joseph calmed his brothers by telling them that while they meant evil against him (at the human level), God meant it for good (at the divine level). In Acts 2:23, it was God's eternal plan (borne out of the motive of his love for humanity) to send his Son to the cross, but even so it was done by the hands of evil and godless men (motivated by hatred and jealousy). Similarly, Paul's "thorn in my flesh" (2 Cor. 12:7) was both "a messenger of Satan," and yet was "given" by God. Certainly different intentions were at work when Jesus was led by the Holy Spirit to be tempted by Satan (Matt. 4:1). Similarly, Judges 9:23 is a part of the same pattern which indicates that God works with all things ("an evil spirit") to accomplish his eternal plan.

F. A Veritable Bevy of Verbs

The flame of the rhetorical questions in verses 28–29 was fueled by the action of progressive verbs in verse 27: gone out, gathered, trodden, held a festival, eating, drinking, cursed. These verbs move from activity to wildness in a very brief time. It is quite clear that Gaal did not plant Shechemite resentment against Abimelech; he simply harvested it.

VII. TEACHING OUTLINE

A. INTRODUCTION

1. Lead Story: The Psychology of Practical Atheism
2. Context: In chapter 6, we were introduced to Gideon, God's *fearful* servant. In chapter 7, he became a *faithful* warrior. In chapter 8, unfortunately, he became a *frightful* warlord. In Judges 9, the Gideon cycle is completed as Gideon's tragic legacy is played out through his son Abimelech.

3. Transition: In the last chapter we were introduced to Abimelech. In this chapter we learn his tragic story. Abimelech thought he had out-smarted everyone. He killed his seventy half-brothers (except Jotham). He destroyed Gaal and his followers. He killed all the people of Shechem. He was intent on establishing himself as supreme dicta-tor, no matter the cost. He was the Adolph Hitler of the Old Testa-ment. But he forgot someone: not Jotham, but Jehovah.

B. COMMENTARY

1. Fratricide: The Treachery of Abimelech (9:1–6)
   a. Securing his mother's relatives by treason (9:1–3)
   b. Slaughtering his father's relatives by treachery (9:4–6)
2. Fable: The Indictment by Jotham (9:7–21)
   a. The story (9:7–15)
   b. The application (9:16–21)
3. Fulfillment: The Justice of God (9:22–55)
   a. The "spirit" of unrest (9:22–25)
   b. The conspiracy of Gaal (9:26–29)
   c. The strategy of Abimelech (9:30–34)
   d. Defeating Shechem's champion, Gaal (9:35–41)
   e. Disrupting Shechem's countryside (9:42–43)
   f. Destroying Shechem's city (9:44–45)
   g. Demolishing Shechem's citadel (9:46–49)
   h. Excess and Egotism (9:50–52)
   i. Epitaph (9:53–55)
4. Epilogue (9:56–57)

C. CONCLUSION: PLAYING THE ODDS

VIII. ISSUES FOR DISCUSSION

1. Discuss the implications of these definitions: justice is getting what we deserve; mercy is not getting what we deserve; grace is getting what we do not deserve.
2. If you were to try to evict God from your life, do you think he would go? Why or why not? Can you support your answer from Scripture?

3. Scripture was given for both positive and negative purposes. Read 1 Corinthians 10:11–15, and reflect further on the Old Testament events presented in this chapter.

4. How do you explain the moral apathy of Israel (vv. 4–6)? Were they any different from us?

5. In light of passages like 2 Corinthians 4:4 ("The god of this age [Satan] has blinded the minds of unbelievers, so that they cannot see the light of the gospel of the glory of Christ, who is the image of God"), how are we to evangelize in a world that is hostile to the gospel of grace?

Judges 10

A Duet, a Solo, and Oppression in Stereo

"*L*earn from the mistakes of others. You can't live long enough to make them all yourself."

Eleanor   Roosevelt

BIOGRAPHICAL PROFILE: TOLA

- Name means "worm"
- Family was from the tribe of Issachar
- Lineage includes Puah and Dodo
- Lived in and judged from the central portion of the land (hill country of Ephraim), not in Issachar
- Judged Israel for twenty-three years, the longest span of any "minor" judge

BIOGRAPHICAL PROFILE: JAIR

- Name means "may (God) enlighten"
- No family pedigree or background given
- Lived in and judged from the land of Gilead, east of the Jordan River
- Became a man of wealth and status
- Was known for his sons, to whom he apparently delegated responsibility for securing peace for the region
- Was a "minor" judge who served for twenty-two years

IN A NUTSHELL

*T*he chapter begins with a record of two full judgeships (a "duet" of Tola in vv. 1–2 and Jair in vv. 3–5), while the rest of the chapter (vv. 6–18) prepares us for the judgeship of Jephthah (11:1–12:7). The two "minor" judges in verses 1–5 logged major time serving Israel (forty-five years together), while the judgeship of Jephthah spanned only six years (12:7). Judges 10:6–18 is a solo of sin, where the nation speaks with a single voice as a prelude that exposes the shallowness of any human-centered religion.

A Duet, a Solo, and Oppression in Stereo

I. INTRODUCTION

Good News and Bad News

*I*n the film *Dead Poets Society*, the main character, played by Robin Williams, brings a group of young boys into the school hall, where they observe the photographed faces of past generations of students, now long dead—faces that the boys had always ignored as if they had never existed. His point is that all these faces at one time were boys just like them. They all thought they were invincible and planned great things for their lives. Now those fires of anticipation, in every case, have been extinguished. So his message to these boys is, "Seize the day!" God's message to us goes far deeper: "Make a difference now . . . for eternity!"

The first portion of this chapter records the lives of two "minor" judges. In fact, these five verses contain the names of six people, but our knowledge of these individuals (other than the notorious Abimelech) is sketchy at best. One doesn't have to go very far to find names of individuals whose lives made a difference, people about whom we know little but God knows much! Let's try a couple: Do you know Mel Seguine, or Betty Brynoff—both now with the Lord?

Mel pastored churches all his life, led a denomination, and influenced hundreds of young men who are now pastors (including this writer). His greatest joy, after preaching, was reading stories to groups of children (a prototypical "granddaddy" who never had any grandchildren). Betty was a career missionary teacher who courageously finished her Ph.D. in English amidst painful chemotherapy treatments, all the while inspiring two generations of students toward excellence.

Both of these people had eternal impact; both chose to serve God humbly, "behind the seen."

Look around at the plaques posted at your church, your school, your civic center—they record the names of people whose lives were invested for good. As one couplet puts it, "One short life will soon be past; only what's done for Christ will last." God wants us, like Tola and Jair, to invest our lives to make a difference.

But this chapter contains both "good news" (vv. 1–5) and "bad news" (vv. 6–18). Even a nation salted with individuals whose lives are exemplary can be subject to failure collectively. The bad news is that Israel hedged her religious bets with other gods, and Judges 10:6–18 offers the most forceful confrontation between God and his prodigal people in this book. They chose to regard all the gods as "true," in willful defiance of God's Word. Edward Gibbon, in *The Decline and Fall of the Roman Empire,* said that during the last part of the empire, all religions were regarded by the people as equally true, by the philosophers as equally false, and by the politicians as equally useful! Israel served all the rival gods (after all, why risk offending one?).

In the same spirit, poet Alexander Pope wrote his well-known "Universal Prayer":

> Father of all, in every age,
> In every clime adored
> By saint, by savage, or by sage,
> Jehovah, Jove, or Lord.

In modern American culture, embracing religious pluralism is becoming more and more the norm. Ironically, we are just catching up to the world of the Bible here. Throughout the pages of Scripture, we see the clash of cultures and religious systems, whether in Egypt or Canaan, Greece or Rome. Today, however, many people seem to think that it's not important *what* you believe, just as long as you believe something (the validity of faith is subjective—tied to the believer—rather than objective—tied to whether what one believes is true or false). And the more pluralistic and inclusive one is, the more sophisticated one is perceived to be! From God's standpoint, Israel's position is utter nonsense and treachery (and from the human standpoint, it would not be the wisest husband who enthusiastically proclaims, "Sweetheart, I love you so much, I think I'll add three other wives!").

Of course there is more to it. In a culture where religious truth is relative (whatever religion you like becomes "true for you"), moral relativism is not far behind ("everyone did as he saw fit"; see Judg. 17:6; 21:25). Israel's choice to include the practices of other gods was an attempt to put a veneer of virtue over their moral bankruptcy. We begin to enjoy immorality and adjust our beliefs accordingly. The Israelites engaged in "Canaanicity"—they became like the people they were supposed to overcome through both religious and moral compromise. But God does not want us to forget who we are and whose we are.

II. COMMENTARY

A Duet, a Solo, and Oppression in Stereo

MAIN IDEA: *Two judges (Tola and Jair) live faithful lives of quiet service; however, Israel is lulled into a false security and begins to think it doesn't need God. Other "gods" and religious systems made less moral demands and were quite attractive. But God is not mocked, and when Israel is oppressed, he is not impressed or fooled by false sincerity. Even when we are unaware, God is always deeply involved in our lives, "behind the seen."*

A The Judgeship of Tola (10:1–2)

SUPPORTING IDEA: *The faithful service of Tola spanned twenty-three years, during which there is no report of apostasy or rebellion.*

10:1–2. After Abimelech's death Tola and Jair are the second and third "minor" judges—so designated by the amount of space devoted to their stories. **Tola** was a man of the tribe of **Issachar** (*Tola* was a recurring family name in the tribe; see Gen. 46:13; Num. 26:23) who evidently did not put himself forward, in stark contrast to Abimelech. We know his pedigree but little else. Even his name ("worm") bespeaks lowliness and humility. Rather than be destructive of Israel, again in contrast to Abimelech, Tola was a national hero who **rose to save Israel**—terminology reserved for the major judges and not used for any other minor judge (though the terminology for Shamgar is similar).

Little space is devoted to Tola's life and service. No enemy is specified. He ruled from **Shamir**, a location **in the hill country of Ephraim**, which is at present unidentified but central within the land. There he lived, **died, and was buried**. His life and faithful service to God and God's people endured **twenty-three years**, the longest of any of the minor judges.

B The Judgeship of Jair (10:3–5)

SUPPORTING IDEA: *The faithful service of Jair spanned twenty-two years and serves as a picture of political and social stability.*

10:3–5. Similar in duration, **Jair** judged Israel for **twenty-two years**. He served in the Transjordan area of **Gilead** and, as with Tola, no enemy is specified. Unlike Tola, however, he is not identified by his genealogy—his past—

but more by his progeny—his future. Jair **had thirty sons, who rode thirty donkeys**, a description which seems strange to us today (see 5:10).

What is a criterion of value in one culture may be different in another. (History buffs will remember that when Herbert Hoover campaigned to become the thirty-first president of the United States, his 1928 motto was "a chicken in every pot and a car in every garage.") In this culture and at this time, people who rode horses were regarded as less civilized, whereas the riding of donkeys and mules bespoke wealth, security, and at times royalty (see also 12:14; Gen. 49:11; Zech. 9:9). The picture here is one of family stability and regional political stability.

The next judge will also be a man of Gilead: Jephthah (11:1). Jair joins Ibzan (12:8–10) in briefly "framing" the family context within which the saga of Jephthah will fit. Both had thirty sons, while by contrast Jephthah had only one child, a daughter, whose fate is an integral part of his story.

Ⓒ Prelude to Jephthah's Judgeship: Oppression by the Ammonites (10:6–18)

SUPPORTING IDEA: *God allows spiritual recession to lead to political oppression so that his people will repent and return to him. However, remorse and repentance are not the same thing, and God is not fooled.*

10:6. *Sin.* The Israelites were guilty of becoming like those whom they were supposed to drive out of the land. This verse catalogs the most extensive description of apostasy found in the book. There is a sevenfold litany of gods; in other words, their apostasy was complete. Not only did they serve these gods; they now ignored the one true God. Their actions were dangerously close to Paul's portrait of a culture of decadence (Rom. 1:21–25).

There is two-part irony here: first, a sevenfold apostasy yields a sevenfold oppression (Judg. 10:11–12). Second, the intentional placing of **the gods of the Ammonites** and **the Philistines** last in the list underscores how, rather than being served by their gods, the Israelites were enslaved by the people of the gods they chose. They betrayed God, and then the gods whom they chose betrayed them. The seriousness of the sin of Israel is the catalyst that would spill over not only into this cycle (Jephthah with the Ammonites) but also into the next. While the Philistines played no immediate role in the story of

Jephthah, their mention at this point in the book anticipates what will follow with Samson (chs. 13–16).

10:7–9. *Servitude.* Even though God was faithful to his covenant promises, Israel again refused to learn from the past. Thus, God **sold them** into servitude (notice how the terms used are an identical fulfillment of the template in 3:7–8, only with different names filled in). For the first time since the first cycle, God's anger is explicitly stated to be the emotion behind their servitude and also presumably behind God's response when they pretended to "turn" to him. It is clear that God is sovereign over their servitude, in contrast to the powerlessness of the gods whom they chose to serve.

The oppressions under the **Philistines** and **Ammonites** were probably contemporaneous, with the Ammonite oppression beginning first with Jephthah, to be followed by the story of the Philistines with Samson (Judg. 13–16). This pincer strategy (intentional or not by Israel's enemies) has been described as "oppression in stereo." The **Amorites** who had lived in the hill country of Gilead (on the east side of the Jordan River) were not the oppressors, however. The Ammonites who lived west of the Jordan River would cross over and cause Judah, Benjamin, and Ephraim **great distress.**

There may have been an initial simultaneous oppression of Israel by both the Ammonites and the Philistines for a year, likely the year of Jair's death; after that the Ammonite harassment overwhelmed Israel for a total of **eighteen years.** We are not to understand that this was like a random attack by a British highwayman or like the occasional stagecoach robbers of the American old west. These bands were not like gnats occasionally annoying the more powerful Israelites; rather, they were predators on the prowl who took whatever they wanted whenever they wanted to take it.

10:10. *Israel's Remorse: "We're Sorry."* This is the first confession of sin we see from Israel in the Book of Judges, and certainly the most extensive response to sin in the entire book, but it was hollow. There was no genuine sorrow or weeping over sin (see 2:4). It is the wise parent who discerns the difference between a child's genuine sorrow over sin as opposed to regret over getting caught. From the context it is clear that Israel viewed God as the cosmic parent they tried to manipulate, using the end (getting God to "fix it") to justify the means (repeating formulas of remorse with no genuine repentance).

10:11–14. *God's Rebuke: "You're Playing Games."* We do not know what form God's communication took (most likely through a prophet), but his point is clear: God would have nothing to do with their crocodile tears. He did not accept their confession because it was not genuine. God's response to them was fourfold.

First, God *reminded* them of his faithfulness to them in several occasions of past deliverance (vv. 11–12). Second, he *rebuked* them because, despite his grace toward them, they repeatedly turned their backs on him and went after other gods (v. 13a). Third, God *rejected* their plea and *refused* to come to their aid in the present (v. 13b). Finally, there was *ridicule,* forcing an acknowledgement of stark *reality:* since they trusted in other gods, let them turn to those gods for deliverance in the future (v. 14)! God holds in derision all attempts to find deliverance apart from him.

Just as there is a listing of seven pagan deities the Israelites served in verse 6, so there is a listing of seven episodes of deliverance by God (vv. 11–12). Every time they cried out to him, he delivered them. The point is clear: God's *past* faithfulness to them is unalloyed, is complete, and should have served as a *present* motivation for their faithfulness to him. We are reminded of Romans 2:4, "Do you show contempt for the riches of his kindness, tolerance and patience, not realizing that God's kindness leads you toward repentance?"

The rebuke consists of a simple terse statement: **You have forsaken me and served other gods** (v. 13a). This is a twofold slap in God's face, trampling on God's loyal love. It's one thing for a husband or wife to be rejected; the humiliation is deepened when the beloved pursues another person. The pain is deepened further still when the rival is unworthy and even despicable. The agony is complete when the rival is complicit in the cause for the present repentance—in this case, the beloved Israel returned only because she was spurned! The honest truth is, if Israel were not presently in servitude, she would still be worshiping at the altars of the false gods. They rejected God for himself, and now they did not want him for himself but for what he could do for them. They didn't want the creator, lover, husband, king—they wanted a cosmic handyman to fix their problem. Religion had become for them a purely pragmatic matter.

Probably to their amazement, God rejected their confession (v. 13b). They didn't manipulate God; if anything, it was the opposite. They had been presuming that God "owed" them his grace and, too late, they learned that God was not domesticated.

Indeed, God tells them to direct their pleas to the gods for whom they rejected him (v. 14). The wording is very pointed: not merely are they taunted to cry out to *your* gods (a simple possessive); rather, they are to **cry out to the gods you have chosen**, highlighting their deliberate preference (while things were going well, of course) to have the kind of god that made no moral demands on their lives. The element of ridicule is enhanced by the questions of truth and reality. In truth, they were false gods. Further, they had no reality to them and could rescue no one (Isa. 41:7,21–23). They were impotent.

10:15–16. *Israel's Repentance: "We're Wrong."* Israel realized the first lesson of "Repentance 101"—God is not stupid and will not be manipulated by false sincerity.

Verse 15a records *Israel's confession.* While they still wanted God to "fix" their problems, the people realized that God, and God alone, is the only true God. If one appeals to the one true God, one must accept his authority over one's life. We cannot pick and choose from among God's guidelines—it's all of a piece. Thus Israel now stood in submission to God's will, whatever form that might take, casting themselves on his mercy.

The second half of the verse (15b) contains *Israel's petition.* They beseeched God to deliver them because they recognized that he, and only he, is the great deliverer. Other gods are impotent (Jer. 10:2–5); only God is omnipotent.

Verse 16 records *Israel's action* and God's reaction. Again Israel uttered words of repentance, but this time their petition was accompanied by appropriate action. **They finally got rid of the foreign gods among them and served the LORD.** God was not willing to deliver on their terms, but on his terms, which they had now met. While some scholars debate the exact meaning of these words (due to some interpretive options in the Hebrew), God seemed to relent when they repented. There was again forgiveness and grace from the loving Father who **could bear Israel's misery no longer.**

10:17–18. *Israel's Research: "Who Will Lead Us?"* The Ammonites **camped in Gilead**, prepared for what could become a "winner-take-all" battle. It is both embarrassing and disheartening when the enemy has the freedom to amass its army behind enemy lines, but as yet there was no strong leadership among the Israelites. Now at the end of eighteen years of oppression the Israelites had a new commitment to their Lord. They **assembled** with a renewed heart. Perhaps he would not deliver them, but then again perhaps he would (v. 15).

Although they gathered their forces in **Mizpah** ("lookout point," a common descriptive name but also possibly a Gileadite town), there was no **head**. Even among the captains of their forces, there was no leader who commanded the respect necessary for guiding a military coalition against the Ammonite aggressors. The stage was now set for Jephthah to emerge as one of God's most colorful leaders.

> **MAIN IDEA REVIEW:** *Two judges (Tola and Jair) live faithful lives of quiet service; however, Israel is lulled into a false security and begins to think it doesn't need God. Other "gods" and religious systems made less moral demands and were quite attractive. But God is not mocked, and when Israel is oppressed, he is not impressed or fooled by false sincerity. Even when we are unaware, God is always deeply involved in our lives, "behind the seen."*

III. CONCLUSION

God, the Pigpen, and Roadside Service

Throughout the cycles of Judges, God is very much like the father of the prodigal son, patiently waiting for his beloved to come home. God could have written the nation off as a loss many times, but he is also a God of longsuffering and mercy. In Luke 15, the prodigal son left the pigpen in order to return. Even though the son was still covered with filth as a reminder of his tragic choices, he was welcomed. In our chapter Israel's first cry to God was uttered while the nation chose to remain in the pigpen and had every intention of staying there.

There is a kind of spiritual insanity about sin—it makes no logical sense. It doesn't matter how smart you are or how spiritually mature you perceive yourself to be. Anyone who is separated from God by sin is also separated from reality. Then, if you are a believer, you eventually come back to reality. In the story of the prodigal son, the boy sitting in the pigpen "came to his senses" (Luke 15:17). Here Israel, wallowing in the mire and plopped in the pigpen of paganism, "came to her senses." But it took a two-stage process to get there.

They began at the level of superficial religion, which (to use computer terminology) may be our human "default setting." By nature we resist going deep with God. We are more comfortable reciting expected traditional religious platitudes. They thought of God as an emergency 911 number, to be called only when they were in trouble. Surely, they thought, God would be on call "24/7" and waiting in the wings to render emergency roadside service.

But God was not impressed. And with Israel, God was unmoved. He took the call but explained in no uncertain terms why he would not respond to their self-made predicament. To be sure, before we become Christians, God will make "housecalls," even to a pigpen! But if we have been born again and then choose to wallow in some sin (Rom. 6:1,15), God wants our remorse (half-hearted repentance) to become true repentance (whole-hearted submission to God). It was only when Israel stopped wallowing in the mire of other gods and left their evil practices behind them that the Father's heart was touched for his prodigal nation. Israel left the pigpen and put away the other gods, and God was deeply moved.

PRINCIPLES

- God uses people who want to make a difference, not necessarily those who want to make a splash.
- Truth is not measured by the size of the group that agrees with us but by the standard of God's revelation.
- No one is beyond the point where God's grace cannot reach them.
- God is patient with us, but we may not presume upon his grace as though it were something God *owed* us.
- Truth is to be valued above expediency.

APPLICATIONS

- Check your motive: do you want to serve God because of who he is, for his glory, or because of what you can get out of him?
- God forgave the Israelites—again! Is it any surprise that he calls on you, who would follow him, also to forgive repeatedly (Matt. 18:22)?
- You have no right to call on God if you plan to stay in the pigpen.

- Don't just mouth the right words; put your commitments into practice.
- Stay in fellowship with God; it keeps you out of trouble.

IV. LIFE APPLICATION

The Power of Service

We began this chapter by stating that there was good news (two faithful men) and bad news (Israel's hypocrisy). The good news is that God uses faithful service. In 1994 missionary Doug Nichols wrote a description of his experience with Operation Mobilization in India in 1967. His quiet account of one difficult opportunity to be a servant speaks louder than many a sermon (warning: it's rated "PG").

I spent several months in a TB sanitarium with tuberculosis. After finally being admitted into the sanitarium, I tried to give tracts to the patients, doctors, and nurses, but no one would take them. You could tell that they weren't really happy with me, a rich American (to them all Americans were rich), being in a government sanitarium. They didn't know that serving with O.M., I was just as broke as they were! I was quite discouraged with being sick, having everyone angry at me, not being able to witness because of the language barrier, and no one even bothering to take a tract or Gospel of John.

The first few nights, I would wake around 2:00 a.m. coughing. One morning as I was going through my coughing spell, I noticed one of the older (and certainly sicker) patients across the aisle trying to get out of bed. He would sit up on the edge of the bed and try to stand, but because of weakness would fall back into bed. I really didn't understand what was happening or what he was trying to do. He finally fell back into bed exhausted. I then heard him begin to cry softly. The next morning I realized what the man was trying to do. He was simply trying to get up and walk to the bathroom! Because of his sickness and extreme weakness he was not able to do this, and being so ill he simply went to the toilet in the bed. The next morning the stench in our ward was awful. Most of the other patients yelled insults at the man because of the smell. The nurses were extremely agitated and angry because they had to clean up the mess, and moved him roughly from side to side to take care of the problem. One of the nurses in her anger even slapped him. The man, terribly embarrassed, just curled up into a ball and wept.

The next night, also around 2:00 a.m., I again awoke coughing. I noticed the man across the aisle sit up to again try to make his way to the washroom. However, still being so weak, he fell back whimpering as the night before. I'm just like most of you. I don't like bad smells. I didn't want to become involved. I was sick myself but before I realized what had happened, not knowing why I did it, I got out of my bed and went over to the old man. He was still crying and did not hear me approach. As I reached down and touched his shoulder, his eyes opened with a fearful questioning look. I simply smiled, put my arm under his head and neck, and my other arm under his legs, and picked him up. Even though I was sick and weak, I was certainly stronger than he was. He was extremely light because of his old age and advanced TB. I walked down the hall to the washroom, which was really just a smelly, filthy small room with a hole in the floor. I stood behind him with my arms under his arms, holding him so he could take care of himself. After he finished, I picked him up and carried him back to his bed. As I began to lay him down, with my head next to his, he kissed me on the cheek, smiled, and said something which I suppose was "Thank you."

It was amazing what happened the next morning. One of the other patients whom I didn't know woke me around 4:00 with a steaming cup of delicious Indian tea. He then made motions with his hands (he knew no English) indicating he wanted a tract. As the sun came up, some of the other patients began to approach, motioning that they would also like one of the booklets I had tried to distribute before. Throughout the day people came to me, asking for the Gospel booklets. This included the nurses, the hospital interns, the doctors, until everybody in the hospital had a tract, booklet, or Gospel of John. Over the next few days, several indicated they trusted Christ as Savior as a result of reading the Good News! What did it take to reach these people with the Good News of salvation in Christ? It certainly wasn't health. It definitely wasn't the ability to speak or to give an intellectually moving discourse. Health and the ability to communicate sensitively to other cultures and peoples are all very important, but what did God use to open their hearts to the Gospel? I simply took an old man to the bathroom. Anyone could have done that! (Doug Nichols, *World,* March 12, 1994, p. 26).

This deeply moving story illustrates how God uses faithful service. But let's not ignore the negative portion of Judges 10, because there are lessons to be learned there as well. In ancient Greece the actors (who could not be seen easily in huge amphitheatres) wore masks, which conveyed the appropriate emotions at the appropriate time. The term for these actors is the root for our English word *hypocrite.* In Scripture hypocrisy was the sin of pretending to be someone you were not, the wearing of a spiritual mask. God wants us to avoid wearing masks before one another and before him. The first time Israel came to God in this chapter, she wore a mask of repentance that was only skin deep—it had no depth beyond mere words. That was a mistake, because God is not stupid, and he saw through their performance.

The difference between King Saul (whom God rejected) and King David (a man after God's heart) was not to be found in their sins. In fact, David's sins were arguably greater (coveting, adultery, conspiracy, disloyalty, and murder). What was the difference in the way God viewed these two men? This difference was they way each responded when confronted with his sins. Saul blamed everyone around him. David, however, accepted his culpability and the consequences of his failures, and in Psalm 51 put his wounded and penitent heart on display for all to see. This is the hard lesson Israel learned in Judges 10. As a father, I would much rather hear from my children, "Dad, I blew it—I was wrong," than superficial pretension. The Lord, our heavenly Father, knows the depths of our hearts.

V. PRAYER

God, you know that right now we are simply uttering words. We have just learned that sometimes words are cheap, that even in prayer true believers can try to use you to accomplish their purposes, rather than be used by you to accomplish your purposes. You are not fooled, but you wait for us to enter your presence with submissive and repentant hearts. We ask that our hearts would align with your heart, and that we would put your truth into action. We ask that the words of our mouths, and the meditations of our hearts, would be acceptable in your sight, O Lord, our rock and our redeemer (see Ps. 19:14). Amen.

VI. DEEPER DISCOVERIES

A. Minor League Judges? (10:1–5)

The six minor judges are distinguished from their contemporaries by the absence of the cycle of sin, servitude, supplication, salvation, and silence—almost exclusively the criterion for how much space is (or is not) devoted to telling their stories. Other than their being included in this book for the sake of completeness, we know almost nothing about them. However, we do see that five of them ruled Israel (or parts of Israel) for seventy years in total (to this we would add the length of Shamgar's judgeship in 3:31, which is not given). Very likely all six together judged for a shorter span than did Ehud (eighty years, 3:30). Apparently most of them did not have to fight an enemy but devoted their lives to judicial issues, became arbiters of claims and disputes, and in general helped maintain order.

B. "Canaanicity" (10:6)

Many of the Canaanites worshiped the Baals and the Ashtoreths (Judg. 2:11–13). The Moabites worshiped Chemosh (Num. 21:29), the Ammonites worshiped Molech (1 Kgs. 11:5), and the Philistines served Dagon (Judg. 16:23). While some may infer that the only kingdom contiguous to Israel which did not make any impact on God's people was Edom, it is more likely that the seven-fold litany of apostasy is intended to mean that their apostasy was absolute and complete. This seems clear from God's response to their first "repentance."

C. "Shattered and Crushed" (10:8)

The Ammonites, the immediate oppressors of Israel in this cycle, were well-known in ancient times for their cruelty (1 Sam. 11:1–2). The collective damage they and the Philistines inflicted is described by two terms that are almost poetically linked in the Hebrew: to say they were "shattered" and "crushed" would be like saying they were "bombed and blasted," or "devastated and destroyed"—the words are related both in sound and in meaning and indicate a total demoralization of Israel.

D. The Deliverer (10:11–12)

God's record of deliverance is thorough and extensive. He delivered the Israelites from the Egyptians (Exodus), then the Amorites (Num. 21:21–35), the Moaabites (Judg. 3:15–30), and the Philistines (Judg. 3:31). God also delivered them from the Sidonians (probably Judg. 4:1–3), the Amalekites (Judg. 3:13; 6:3,33; 7:12), and the Maonites (10:12; apparently connected with the Midianites, see Judg. 6–8).

E. Does Jephthah Wear a White Hat? (10:16)

Some scholars debate the exact meaning of God's reaction to Israel—whether he was moved to pity, or he was even more disgusted with them. The Hebrew may read that God "could bear *them* no longer" or "could bear *their misery* no longer." The implications of this decision involve whether the deliverance under Jephthah was of God or of man. If the latter is true, then Jephthah was not *God's* deliverer at all. This writer believes that the subsequent story of deliverance and God's role in Jephthah's life supports the view that God was definitely and actively involved in the Jephthah cycle. Jephthah looked to God as the source of deliverance (Judg. 11:9,21,23–24). God was invoked as a covenant witness between Jephthah and Israel (11:10–11), was the one who empowered Jephthah by his Spirit (11:29), and granted the victory over the Ammonites (11:32). In addition, Jephthah is seen in the New Testament as one of the heroes of faith (Heb. 11:32). While Jephthah's "white hat" may not fit extraordinarily well (he was a rough man in rough times, as we shall see in the next chapter), the NIV has it right: God "could bear Israel's misery no longer" (Judg. 10:16).

VII. TEACHING OUTLINE

A. INTRODUCTION

1. Lead Story: Good News and Bad News

2. Context: Judges 9 records the story of Gideon's son Abimelech, the man who would be king. His rise and fall demonstrate the futility of man's attempt to be sovereign over God. In Judges 10, again God is sovereign over both the movements of nations and the movements of hearts. The next two chapters continue the story of a rough and violent man who wants to be used by the sovereign God, although at times he blunders (as George Will once said of an uninformed but feisty political activist, "Even a bad shot is dignified by accepting the challenge of a duel").

3. Transition: The author of Judges has taken us through the highs and lows of the story of Gideon and his family. After the discouraging saga of Abimelech, we begin to wonder if there will again be stories of people who lived faithfully for the Lord. Even though the judge-ships of Tola and Jair are told in terse terms, we find deep refreshment in their prolonged faithfulness.

B. COMMENTARY

1. The Judgeship of Tola (10:1–2)
2. The Judgeship of Jair (10:3–5)
3. Prelude to Jephthah's Judgeship: Oppression by the Ammonites (10:6–18)
   a. Sin (10:6)
   b. Servitude (10:7–9)
   c. Israel's remorse: "We're sorry" (10:10)
   d. God's rebuke: "You're playing games" (10:11–14)
   e. Israel's repentance: "We're wrong" (10:15–16)
   f. Israel's research: "Who will lead us?" (10:17–18)

C. CONCLUSION: GOD, THE PIGPEN, AND ROADSIDE SERVICE

VIII. ISSUES FOR DISCUSSION

1. Romans 16 contains a greeting-card list from Paul to twenty-six peo-ple (twenty-four named, two nameless), about whom we know almost nothing (Ampliatus, Rufus, Patrobas, Nereus, etc.). Yet there

they are, recorded for us to read their "plaques" on the pages of Holy Scripture. They are referred to as "friend," "fellow worker," "my relatives," and so on. They were well-known to the early church but are unknown to us. Like Tola and Jair, their lives will count for eternity. Does your church have plaques or pictures of people whose names you do not know? Have you ever thought of discovering their stories?

2. From the standpoint of the Israelites, they were brought back to truth and reality after dabbling with false gods. Whenever we place anything (a person, a possession, a goal) above our allegiance to God, that becomes a false "god." List a dozen or so false gods people may have in their lives. As you look down the list, is there any fulfillment in them? Any help or any comfort? Do any of these things deliver eternally?

3. Probe the illogic of sin. If God is the only Creator, does it make sense to place anything in the creation above him? If God wants our best and, accordingly, has told us how to live fulfilling lives of peace and joy, does it make any sense at all to ignore his guidebook and its principles? Consider this statement: "I have always regretted acts of disobedience to God, but have never once regretted an act of obedience." If this is a biblical perspective (and it is), what are the implications for how we live our lives?

4. Read Romans 1:21–25. These words describe a declining culture. Can you think of ways in which these words describe our society today?

Judges 11

The Mystery of the Missing Miss

| Q u o t e |

---

*"**In** great matters men show themselves as they wish to be seen, in small matters, as they are."*

G a m a l i e l   B r a d f o r d

HISTORICAL PROFILE: THE UNIQUENESS OF JEPHTHAH'S JUDGESHIP

- Only cycle in which God rebukes false repentance (10:11–15)
- Most extensive description of the "rebellion" component
- Only cycle containing dialogue between God and the people
- Most detailed account of Israel's response to their persecution
- First confession of sin we see from Israel in the Book of Judges
- Only judge recruited by men
- Worst recorded family background
- Only judge who tried to use diplomacy to avert armed conflict
- Used the personal name for God (YHWH) more than any other judge
- Following his military victory, his judgeship was the shortest (six years)
- No mention of "rest" after Jephthah's judgeship
- Most unique offering (or controversy for interpreters)

 I N   A   N U T S H E L L

Jephthah was a rough man who experienced God's grace late in life, yet God's grace did not cancel the consequences of his unwise choices.

The Mystery of the Missing Miss

I. INTRODUCTION

The Character of a "Real Character"

My friend (I'll call him Charlie) was a new Christian during the Korean War. He had enlisted in the army but at the same time was a "conscientious objector." His faith was unsophisticated, rough, and blatant. He said that he didn't want to be responsible for killing any non-Christians. Instead he became a medic and placed himself in harm's way numerous times. As a new Christian he was told he should read the Bible, but he didn't have one. So he got a Bible the same way he got other things—he stole it. After he had been a Christian about a year, Charlie was reading his Bible and had a flash of perception about how he had procured the very Bible he was reading! Charlie matured greatly over the years, eventually earned an ivy league Ph.D. and became a beloved Christian professor. One thing did not change about Charlie: either you were wholly committed to Jesus or you were not. There was nothing in-between. Like Jephthah.

It has been observed that nothing about Jephthah was drawn in pastel colors; everything is painted in deep, brilliant, bold tones. He was a man with a past, with scars placed on his soul by his family. The kind of religious sophistry that characterized Israel's first response to God would have been inconceivable to Jephthah. Total commitment was something he understood—there was nothing in-between.

II. COMMENTARY

The Mystery of the Missing Miss

MAIN IDEA: *Jephthah had much to overcome in his life. He came from a dysfunctional family from which he was evicted; yet through his natural leadership skills he became a sought-after warrior. His choices sometimes reflected wisdom, sometimes foolishness. However, even when it meant great personal agony, he remained a man who valued truth and integrity over compromise.*

A Jephthah the Disowned (11:1–3)

SUPPORTING IDEA: *Through no fault of his own, Jephthah was cruelly evicted from his family.*

11:1–3. The Israelites were desperate; they had been victims of Ammonite oppression for eighteen years (10:8). Despite the family rivalries among siblings (or half-siblings), the elders of Gilead called on the only man they knew who could rise to the threat: **Jephthah the Gileadite**. His name means "[God] has opened," a reference to the womb. Jephthah may be compared to and contrasted with our last major character, Abimelech, in four ways.

First, the birth status of both was viewed with contempt; unlike Abimelech, however, Jephthah's **father** (**Gilead**) had not married **his mother**; rather, she **was a prostitute**. Whether she was of the religious cult status or an independent agent is not known. Second, unlike Abimelech, who was raised away from both his father and his brothers, apparently Gilead acknowledged his illegitimate son and took him into his household to be raised. Third, unlike Abimelech whose father Gideon had many wives, Gilead apparently had only one **wife**, whose sons **drove Jephthah away**. It is likely that this event took place near or after the death of their father, due to their stated reason for excluding him: **You are not going to get any inheritance in our family**. Since receiving an inheritance in Israel did not depend on the mother but on the father, they were stealing his future fortune. Fourth, unlike Abimelech who slaughtered his brothers in revenge, Jephthah later saved **his brothers** through the rescue of God's people (whether or not they appreciated it).

Consequently **Jephthah fled** to **the land of Tob** where in time he became a natural leader. His men were military mercenaries, **a group of adventurers** (the same term from 9:4); they were "The Dirty Dozen" of the Old Testament writ large.

B Jephthah the Desperado (11:4-11)

SUPPORTING IDEA: *In time Jephthah became a skilled warrior and leader. He was willing to forgive his family and take leadership over his clan.*

11:4-11. It may well be that many years passed, so that **some time later** (during which time Jephthah himself married and had his only child, a daughter), **the elders of Gilead went to get Jephthah from the land of Tob.** (We are now brought back into the mainstream of the story from chapter 10:17-18.) By this time he had become a notorious military leader. Even so, Jephthah was not considered a criminal—he was not a Robin Hood who supported the people's needs, but neither was he an Al Capone who lived off their greeds. Also of great significance was that he was not under the thumb of Ammonite dominance.

In desperation the Gileadites approached the desperado; the elders made Jephthah an offer: **Be our commander, so we can fight the Ammonites.** The word "commander" in this context refers only to a military leader, nothing more—in contrast to the offer on the table when the Gileadites were discussing a "head" from among their own kind (10:18).

Jephthah's initial response was resistance and rebuke: **Didn't you hate me and drive me from my father's house? Why do you come to me now, when you're in trouble?** Here the "you" is generic to the people of Gilead, who sanctioned by their silence Jephthah's earlier treatment. Rather than try to hide or deny their earlier conduct, the Israelites admitted their wrongdoing (a perspective that reflects the genuineness of their repentance in 10:15-16) and repeated their offer, making it stronger. They were now **turning** to Jephthah not only as commander, but also to be their **head,** or ruler.

This enlarged offer apparently stunned Jephthah, who (possibly with incredulity) repeated it: If indeed the Lord does give victory over the Ammonites, **will I really be your head?** Since Jephthah placed these events as contingent on the sovereign action of the Lord in granting freedom from oppression, **the elders of Gilead** answered in like manner with an oath: **The LORD is our witness; we will certainly do as you say.** The result was that

Jephthah went with the elders of Gilead, and the people made him head and commander over them.

This was no secular ceremony but was accompanied by commitments made **before the LORD.** Jephthah had made a choice. He would now serve as ruler over a people who had rejected him years before, yet he would establish that rulership under the sovereign rule of the Lord of the covenant.

Ⓒ Jephthah the Diplomat (11:12–28)

> **SUPPORTING IDEA:** *Jephthah learned not to resort to violence whenever diplomacy was an option (provided it did not compromise his integrity).*

11:12–28. If we now expect the man of action to spring to battle, we are surprised. Jephthah functioned as a ruler, not just a general. He was the only judge who tried to use diplomacy to avert armed conflict with an enemy of Israel. He **sent messengers to the Ammonite king** asking the reason for the oppression, a preliminary question to open negotiations toward a hopeful truce. The Ammonite king made the outrageous claim that all of the land **from the Arnon to the Jabbok, all the way to the Jordan** was his, and he demanded it back (this is the first time we are given understanding of the motive behind the eighteen-year oppression.)

Jephthah's response was clear: First, he told him to "check your history" (vv. 15–22)—it never was your land. Second, he told him to "check your theology" (vv. 23–25)—this land was given to Israel by the Lord. Third, he told him to "check your chronology" (v. 26)—if your claim were legitimate, why wait over three hundred years to act on it?

Check your history (vv. 15–22). Jephthah's first point was that **Israel did not take the land of Moab or the land of the Ammonites.** The Ammonite claim was guilty of revisionist history, so Jephthah gave the leaders of Ammon a history lesson in the troop movements of Israel from the time they left **Egypt** through the time of the conquest. Jephthah maintained that Israel studiously avoided violating the territorial rights of **Edom, Moab,** and Ammon and intentionally avoided fighting against Moab and Ammon (Deut. 2:5,9,19), even when they were hostile to Israel. However, Israel had been given no such prohibition against the Amorites. When they requested safe passage through the Amorite lands and were themselves attacked without provocation by the suspicious **Sihon king of the Amorites**, they defended themselves. The result was that **the LORD, the God of Israel**, brought about victory.

Jephthah's point was this: it never was *your* land to begin with. Israel took no land controlled by the Edomites, the Ammonites, or the Moabites. The land in question was a part of the spoils of the Amorite war.

Check your theology (vv. 23–25). Second, the victory over the Amorites came about only because **the LORD, the God of Israel**, drove them out. Jephthah appealed, for the sake of argument, to their own theology: if they believed they should possess what they thought their **god Chemosh** gave them, did it not make sense that Israel should possess what they knew the Lord gave them? The Ammonite aggression was entirely illogical; even **Balak son of Zippor, king of Moab**, whom they would understand to be the royal representative of Chemosh, did not attack Israel over land disputes.

Check your chronology (v. 26). Third, Jephthah invited the Ammonites to consider the timing of their oppression. Israel had possessed this land and these towns **for three hundred years**. Why wait so long? **Why didn't you retake them during that time?** To suddenly press a claim when Israel could not easily withstand oppression smacked of opportunism, not nobility.

In sum, as Israel's representative Jephthah claimed innocence: **I have not wronged you, but you are doing me wrong by waging war against me**. He then invoked not "the gods" or Chemosh, but the name of the only true **LORD, the Judge**, to **decide the dispute this day between the Israelites and the Ammonites**. The sad but predictable result was that **the king of Ammon . . . paid no attention to the message Jephthah sent him**. The wheels were already in motion for military resolution.

D Jephthah the Defender (11:29,32–33)

> **SUPPORTING IDEA:** *Jephthah was empowered by the spirit of God to achieve victory.*

11:29,32–33. Armed conflict could not be avoided, and **the Spirit of the LORD came upon Jephthah** as he advanced against the Ammonites. The result was that **Israel subdued Ammon**, including **twenty towns from Aroer to the vicinity of Minnith, as far as Abel Keramim**. The brevity of the battle's report is surprising. The writer (and Jephthah) made it clear that the glory for the victory rested not in a single man or even in an army; rather, **the LORD gave them into his hands**. The legendary words of Julius Caesar were "I came, I saw, I conquered (*veni, vidi, vici*)." In contrast, John III Sobieski, king of Poland in the late seventeenth century, was the man who saved central Europe from invading armies of Turks in 1683. His rescue of Vienna was one of the decisive battles in European history. In announcing his victory the king paraphrased the famous words of Caesar by saying, "I came; I saw; God conquered." This was Jephthah's attitude.

E Jephthah the Doubter (11:30–31)

SUPPORTING IDEA: *However, Jephthah's view of God was still immature. In an attempt to bargain with his Lord, he made a foolish vow.*

11:30–31. Prior to the battle already described, and even though Jephthah had the empowerment of God's Spirit, he had hesitated. His problem was not knowledge of God's will but weak faith. Whether due to innate doubts arising from a superficial knowledge of the covenant God, or simple misunderstanding of God's nature, he made a bargain with God. The **vow** consisted of this pledge: **If you give the Ammonites into my hands, whatever comes out of the door of my house to meet me when I return in triumph from the Ammonites will be the LORD's, and I will sacrifice it as a burnt offering**. This phrase almost always refers to an animal sacrifice. By means of this vow Jephthah tried to manipulate God, even though God had already said he was with him. Few verses in the Old Testament have given rise to more speculation and debate than the interpretation of this vow.

In his role as defender, God granted Jephthah victory. At this point one would expect to read, "and the land had rest for twenty years." Instead, we read not of rest but of tragedy.

F Jephthah the Daddy (11:34–40)

SUPPORTING IDEA: *The execution of Jephthah's vow robbed him and his family of joy and of any future; even so, to them truth was more important than private happiness.*

11:34–40. Jephthah was now accepted by his countrymen, successful by any criterion, flush from victory, and ready to return to a life of respect and responsibility as the "head" over God's people. It should have been the most joyous day of his life. However, as he **returned to his home in Mizpah, who should come out to meet him but his daughter**. The text makes it clear that **she was an only child** and then repeats, for effect, **Except for her he had nei-**

ther son nor daughter. Jephthah's irrational anguish is understandable: **Oh! My daughter! You have made me miserable and wretched, because I have made a vow to the LORD that I cannot break.** Jephthah believed that he now had to "sacrifice" his daughter.

Four things are clear about Jephthah's only child. First, she had a deep sense of respect for her father and his integrity. Second, she had a sense of responsibility. Third, she shared with her father a deep reverence for the Lord (**you have given your word to the LORD, and the LORD has avenged you**), which was her motivation. Fourth, she loved her father. In essence, she was willing to sacrifice herself based on two ideas: (1) you promised the Lord, and (2) the Lord granted victory.

She made only one request: **Give me two months to roam the hills and weep with my friends, because I will never marry.** This concession was a small thing and was granted: **He let her go for two months. She and the girls went into the hills and wept because she would never marry.** Thus it became an annual **Israelite custom** that the young girls would commemorate the "sacrifice" of Jephthah's daughter.

This unbreakable vow of Jephthah has been the cause of much speculation and is the top candidate for the most controversial interpretive problem in the Book of Judges. Jephthah definitely "sacrificed" his daughter. But did he sacrifice her life (a dead sacrifice), or did he sacrifice her future (a living sacrifice)? Was she killed, or was she separated for tabernacle (or similar) service? Strong arguments (and weak ones!) go both ways, and the bottom line is that we do not know. I believe that the preponderance of biblical information allows us to understand that she was not killed, although any exposition and explanation of these verses should make sure no explicit biblical statement is diminished in its clear force when examining the data.

Most interpreters who adopt the view that she was killed do so on the basis of the grammar of his original *intention* to make a burnt offering in 11:31. However, I would suggest that the meaning of Jephthah's vow was to give "him" (whatever emerged, in Hebrew masculine singular) to the Lord, and that the manner of consecration was not the primary part of the vow, or perhaps even part of the vow at all. Further, even if there was an original intention to make a burnt offering, that would not mean Jephthah actually followed through in that way; some vows were commuted. Consider the following reasons that argue for the view that Jephthah *changed* that intention (see "The Sacrifice of Jephthah's Daughter" below).

First, human sacrifice clearly violates God's law (Exod. 20:13; Deut. 12:31–32; Lev. 18:21; 20:2–5). If Jephthah were motivated to serve the Lord, he would not render service that would be an abomination to God.

Second, one would expect that the God whose spirit came upon Jephthah to provide his victory (after the vow was made) would not grant victory at this time or else would intervene either directly (e.g., Gen. 22:11–12, when God stopped Abraham from killing his "only son") or providentially (e.g., 1 Sam. 14:45) to prohibit a misguided murder. Indeed, there is only one human blood sacrifice acceptable to God, that of the Lord Jesus Christ (Heb. 10:12).

Third, it would seem from the *masculine* verb and suffix in Judges 11:31 that Jephthah had an animal in mind for a burnt offering, not his child, a female. But it was his daughter who greeted him. Such a disturbing development would not change the meaning of the vow ("it will be the Lord's") but could change the manner of its fulfillment ("sacrifice it as a burnt offering").

Fourth, sacrifices were offered at the central sanctuary, and it is certain that no human sacrifice would be permitted in the tabernacle or any other sacred location. This would have been considered by the Israelites a worse abomination than the notorious sacrifice of a pig on the temple altar by Antiochus Epiphanes (168 B.C.).

Fifth, there was a band of "consecrated virgins" devoted to tabernacle service at this time (Exod. 38:8; 1 Sam. 2:22), and it may well be that this or some other sanctuary served as the location for the daughter's permanent servitude.

Sixth, there is no explicit statement that Jephthah's daughter was killed or any indication later that she was dead; the only statement made ("and she knew no man") bewails her virginity and thus the cessation of the family line, which sets Jephthah in contrast with the two judges on either side, Jair and Ibzan, each of whom had thirty sons.

Seventh, one would expect the primary stated reason for her grief to be her death; instead, it was **because I will never marry** (literally, "I and my friends will weep over my virginity").

Eighth, there was provision in the law for removal and presumably commutation of foolish vows (Lev. 27:1–8). If Jephthah were not familiar with these guidelines, any priest at any sanctuary would inform him.

Ninth, there is no negative evaluation of Jephthah in Scripture. Later reference to Jephthah in a morally positive context (particularly Heb. 11:32) would seem extraordinarily incongruous if he actually had killed his daughter.

One should not leave these verses without attention to the character of Jephthah's daughter. Like earlier heroines in Judges (Deborah, Jael) she is calm in the chaos. She did not flee, for to do so would bring dishonor on her, her father, and the Lord. She was as much concerned that her father would not have grandchildren as she was that she would have no children. She allowed her father to have her be his sacrifice.

MAIN IDEA REVIEW: *Jephthah had much to overcome in his life. He came from a dysfunctional family from which he was evicted; yet through his natural leadership skills he became a sought-after warrior. His choices sometimes reflected wisdom, sometimes foolishness. However, even when it meant great personal agony, he remained a man who valued truth and integrity over compromise.*

The Sacrifice of Jephthah's Daughter

Jephthah Sacrificed His Daughter's Life (A Dead Sacrifice)

Simplest reading: "burnt offering" usually a literal fiery sacrifice

Tradition: most earlier commentators until Middle Ages thought her life was forfeited

Pattern: this is another example of the "Canaanicity" of Israel at this time

Jephthah Sacrificed His Daughter's Future (A Living Sacrifice)

Violates teaching of law (Exod. 20:13; Deut. 12:31–32; Lev. 18:21; 20:2–5)

If her life, God would intervene (as with Isaac, and in Jephthah's victory)

Grammatical uncertainty: "*or* I will offer" (11:31)

Role of the tabernacle, as the place for making sacrifices and fulfilling vows

Public outcry absent (1 Sam. 14:45)

No explicit statement of death; instead repetition of "she knew no man"

Possibility of "consecrated virgins" (Exod. 38:8; 1 Sam. 2:22)

Provision for removal of foolish vows (Lev. 27)

Jephthah's inclusion in "Hall of Faith" (Heb. 11:32)

III. CONCLUSION

Power Through Suffering

Alexander Whyte (1836–1921) was one of the greatest preachers of the nineteenth century. When he preached on Jephthah, these were his words: "Jephthah the Gileadite was the most ill-used man in all the Old Testament, and he continues to be the most completely misunderstood, misrepresented, and ill-used man down to this day. Jephthah's ill-usage began when he was born, and it has continued down to the last Old Testament commentary and last Bible dictionary that treats of Jephthah's name. The iron had entered Jephthah's soul while yet he lay in his mother's womb; and his father and his brothers and the elders of Israel helped forward Jephthah's affliction, until the Lord rose up for Jephthah and said, 'it is enough!'" (cited in Barber, *Judges: A Narrative of God's Power,* p. 140).

The reason Whyte sounded so passionate about Jephthah reaches back into Whyte's own background. He was born as an illegitimate child in Scotland, which meant in that day (the 1840s) that all his young life he was the object of whispers, scorn, and rejection. His mother committed her life to Jesus Christ and raised Alexander in poverty and piety. Through his own hard work, he was able to study first at Aberdeen and then later at Edinburgh. When Whyte preached, he was known as a man who identified with those who suffer—but especially Jephthah! Jephthah also went through life's schools of hard knocks—he had a bachelor's degree in rejection, minoring in suffering, a master's in violence, and a Ph.D. in leadership. But God used it all for his glory.

PRINCIPLES

- Sometimes integrity is a deeply painful value to embrace in a fallen world.
- God is not bound by human stereotypes to the kind of person he uses.
- It may be that the things God has permitted you to endure in your life are those very things that make you usable for his glory.

APPLICATIONS

- Check your impulses; don't say the first thing that comes into your mind (Eph. 4:29).

- Keep your word—your commitments, your promises, your appointments. All reflect on you and your Lord.

- Remember: no matter how desperate your past may be, you are not a prisoner of your past. His grace is greater than all your sin.

- Forgive those who caused you emotional scars. You will be in good company (Luke 23:34).

IV. LIFE APPLICATION

Victims of the Victor's Vow

In a sense both Jephthah and his daughter were victims of his foolish vow. One cannot help but respect the sense of honor that would keep one's word once it is given. Even in painful circumstances, this may be a testimony.

Years ago when I was in seminary I was across town from where I lived, but tried to write a check in a grocery story that was a part of the chain where we usually shopped. In this store the assistant manager said he couldn't cash the check for me. At that time the manager came in and heard the conversation. He caught my address, looked at me, and asked, "Do you go to the seminary?" I said, "Yes," and he told his assistant to cash the check. He explained to him that he had worked for years at the branch a few blocks from the seminary and then added, "Those people don't write bad checks." I'll never forget how I felt in that moment. Wouldn't it be wonderful if the church, collectively and individually, had the reputation in this world of being people of honor and integrity?

V. PRAYER

O Lord, sometimes we find ourselves in messes of our own making. We don't ask that you undo our past choices, but we do ask that you minimize the pain we have caused those whom you love, and that you use these circumstances for your glory. As we obey your Word, may we be people of our word, but may our words be wise. Through Christ our Lord. Amen.

VI. DEEPER DISCOVERIES

A. An Ancient Land Grab (11:13)

"The present claims arise not only from a desire for more land but also out of a need for fixed and definable borders, such as these rivers would provide. But the Ammonite's claim is based more on wishful thinking than on historical reality. According to the biblical record the Arnon served as the border between Moab and the Amorites (not the Ammonites), and the Israelites had gained title to the land between this river and the Jabbok by defeating the Amorite king Sihon, who ruled in Heshbon" (Block, 359).

B. Jephthah the Diplomat (11:12–28)

By word count this segment comprises about three hundred and forty-five of the almost one thousand words (Hebrew) devoted to the Jephthah cycle, or over one-third of his story (Block, 357n). Clearly in the writer's mind these attempts at negotiations were important for understanding the full story of Jephthah. He was a man given to impulses, but he was not driven by impulses.

C. Jephthah's Legacy

The heritage of Jephthah cannot be measured in his progeny but (maybe) in his ensuing peace. The next three judges ("after him") knew no oppressors or enemies. Whether there is a cause-and-effect relationship is a question we are unable to answer right now.

VII. TEACHING OUTLINE

A. INTRODUCTION

1. Lead Story: The Character of a "Real Character"

2. Context: In chapter 10 Israel had been served well by two judges (Tola and Jair). Jephthah is the next judge and was succeeded by three more "minor" judges (Ibzan, Elon, and Abdon). The next major judge will begin with the saga of Samson (chs. 13–16).

3. Transition: Again Israel turned her back on God and descended into sin, and again God permitted the nation to be oppressed—this time by the Ammonites for eighteen years. Israel became desperate for deliverance and asked for someone to be "head" over Gilead. Chapter 11 introduces us to that man and his story.

B. COMMENTARY

1. Jephthah the Disowned (11:1–3)
2. Jephthah the Desperado (11:4–11)
3. Jephthah the Diplomat (11:12–28)
4. Jephthah the Defender (11:29,32–33)
5. Jephthah the Doubter (11:30–31)
6. Jephthah the Daddy (11:34–40)

C. CONCLUSION: POWER THROUGH SUFFERING

VIII. ISSUES FOR DISCUSSION

1. Many interpret Jephthah's vow as a "worst case" scenario. Read 1 Samuel 12:11 and Hebrews 11:32 to see if you agree.

2. Describe the values of respect and integrity undergirding the brief speech of Jephthah's daughter. Look carefully at verses 34–37 and try to answer this question: What do you think motivated her?

3. If you can, enter the emotions of this chapter. For example, Jephthah experienced the truth that seeing your children (or someone you love) suffer is the hardest thing to bear. C. S. Lewis asked God to relieve the suffering of his dying wife by transmuting some of the pain to his body. In moments of anguish, what parent of a sick child has not uttered a similar prayer? As we observe the emotional suffering of Jephthah, reflect on the emotional suffering of God, who chose to send his Son to die on the cross for our sins.

Judges 12

The First Deadly Sin

I. INTRODUCTION
Pride and Prejudice

II. COMMENTARY
A verse-by-verse explanation of the chapter.

III. CONCLUSION
Win, Lose, or Draw?

An overview of the principles and applications from the chapter.

IV. LIFE APPLICATION
The Envy of Egotistical Ephraim

Melding the chapter to life.

V. PRAYER
Tying the chapter to life with God.

VI. DEEPER DISCOVERIES
Historical, geographical, and grammatical enrichment of the commentary.

VII. TEACHING OUTLINE
Suggested step-by-step group study of the chapter.

VIII. ISSUES FOR DISCUSSION
Zeroing the chapter in on daily life.

"*If* you don't learn from your mistakes,

there's no point in making them."

Anonymous

Judges 12

IN A NUTSHELL

The story of Ephraim and Jephthah graphically portrays the head-on collision of pride and jealousy with raw anger—in both cases the unrestrained outcome of sin. Even so, this very brief chapter concludes with a legacy of twenty-five years of continuous peace for God's people as they were governed by three minor judges.

The First Deadly Sin

I. INTRODUCTION

Pride and Prejudice

*A*n old story is told of two merchants who were bitter rivals. Their stores were across from each other, and they spied on the other endlessly, each tracking the other's business. Each storekeeper was more concerned about the customers who entered the store of his rival than he was about servicing his own customers. One night an angel appeared and promised one of the shopkeepers that he could have one wish, but the wish had one condition attached: His rival would receive double what he requested. Rather than bear the thought of having his rival twice as happy, twice as healthy, or twice as rich, he said to the angel: "Strike me blind in one eye!"

When pride is coupled with jealousy, the mixture is self-destructive. The Ephraimites had a difficult time enduring the success of someone else. They were unable to bear having their Israelite brothers enjoy freedom from Ammonite oppression, even though Jephthah's victory marginally benefited them as well. Rather than "rejoice with those who rejoice," they chose to challenge the champion—with calamitous consequences.

II. COMMENTARY

The First Deadly Sin

> **MAIN IDEA:** *Through the downward spirals of the Book of Judges, we are moved from Jephthah to Samson in a transitional chapter: first, the closing chapter of Jephthah's tragic story is recorded; second, a trio of minor judges is remembered.*

A Jephthah as Judge, Jury, and Executioner (12:1–7)

> **SUPPORTING IDEA:** *The clash of Jephthah and Ephraim, which could have been avoided more than once, reveals the consequences of stubborn sin.*

12:1–3. *Confrontation.* Once before we saw **the men of Ephraim** reacting with an inflated sense of self-importance. They challenged Gideon in Judges

8 and whined because they were not called upon to participate in the victory. Here they went further. They charged Jephthah with similar neglect (**Why did you go to fight the Ammonites without calling us to go with you?**) but then threatened him with a horrible death. They said they would burn him alive in his own house. Their army of forty thousand lent undue bravado to their boasts. Their focus was not on the nation but on themselves, and they expressed no appreciation for the removal of a serious threat to the nation.

Jephthah's response was not that of a patient parent offering a soft answer to turn away the wrath of a people behaving collectively like an immature teenager (cp. 8:2). Instead, he responded with clipped words and clenched fists, offering the Ephraimites a between-the-teeth rebuke. Jephthah said that he and his people the Gileadites (11:11) **were engaged in a great struggle with the Ammonites** and that the Ephraimites were indeed **called** to help. While this was the first time readers are aware of his overture, it probably took place because earlier, with an astonishing sense of self-importance, the Ephraimites had demanded glory and praise in connection with their minor role in the Midianite victory (8:1–3).

However, this time the Ephraimites had not even shown up! Instead, their outrage fueled Jephthah's indictment: **Although I called, you didn't save me out of their hands. When I saw that you wouldn't help, I took my life in my hands and crossed over to fight the Ammonites.** Instead of help from the Ephraimites, Jephthah received help from **the LORD** who **gave me the victory over them.**

Jephthah's rebuke of the Ephraimites was well-deserved and ended with an incredulous question: **Now why have you come up today to fight me?** The Ephraimites had the wrong time, the wrong place, the wrong attitude, and the wrong enemy. They whined for justice; Jephthah resolved that they would get it and more.

12:4. *Conflict.* Unfortunately, the Ephraimites apparently chose to ratchet up the hostilities by responding with an untested claim of battle prowess: **You Gileadites are renegades from Ephraim and Manasseh.** The choice of the word *renegade* was particularly unfortunate because it would have acted like salt on a raw wound, reminding Jephthah of his life when he lived as an outcast from his people. A paraphrase may help us understand their puzzling taunt: "You are such pathetic warriors compared to us, that not only are our least powerful soldiers greater than your strongest warriors; even our deserters are superior to your champions!"

The Ephraimites threatened to destroy the house of a man who had lost his home and had little else to lose. They had taunted him about the prowess of his loyal men. (It would be like Don Knotts spitting in Clint Eastwood's face, telling him, "Go ahead, punk, make my day.") Unfortunately, they got what they asked for, as Jephthah called their bluff. He quickly gathered his men and they **fought against Ephraim**. Soon the issue was settled, and the Ephraimites chose to run. They retreated in disarray across the Jordan River.

12:5–7. Carnage. While Jephthah's *confrontation* with them was correct, (vv. 1–3) and his *conflict* with them was regrettable but understandable (v. 4), the *carnage* at the river ford (vv. 5–6) was a blot on the history of the nation; here Jephthah went too far. Rather than let the Ephraimites escape with their tails between their legs, Jephthah's men captured the Jordan fords and in effect forced the frightened Ephraimites, attempting to return home, to lie in order to save their lives.

Over the hundreds of years of occupation of the land, dialectical differences had emerged, so that the Ephraimites no longer used the aspirant "sh." (This should not be surprising, given the dialectical differences within the United States after only two hundred years despite widespread mass language unifiers, such as the oral media of radio and television.) All who would escape at the ford were given a speech test. The password was "head of grain," **shibboleth**. (There is a recent parallel: during World War II, the Nazis identified Russian Jews by the way they pronounced the word for corn, *kookoorooza*.) If the traveler was unable to pronounce the "sh" (saying instead **sibboleth**) he was summarily slaughtered.

The Ephraimites had expected to be stroked, soothed, mollified. It is at once both ironic and pathetic that those whose inflated pride in being Ephraimites had brought them to this place were able to escape only by denying their tribal identity as Ephraimites. Instead of *mollifying* them, Jephthah *murdered* them. Jephthah became the triad of judge, jury, and executioner, all in one.

Rather than end Jephthah's story with a statement of "rest," the text ends with a report of retribution: **Forty-two thousand Ephraimites were killed at that time**, almost wiping out the entire tribe. Possibly depressed by the loss of his daughter and perhaps even by the cruelty of his own vengeance, Jephthah ruled only **six years** before he died (the shortest of all the judges), **and was buried in a town in Gilead**. In every other case, the judge ruled until he died, which one must assume holds true here; this would very likely mean that Jephthah went to an early grave.

Why was Jephthah so harsh with the Ephraimites? (1) He was emotionally depressed, drained, and devastated over his daughter. (2) He *had* tried to call them, and they did not respond (their bravery began after the battle was over, which did not sit well). (3) They were motivated by a mixture of pride and jealousy. (4) They had done this once before (with Gideon, Judg. 8); this time they were even more hostile. (5) For eighteen years the Ammonites had overrun the land, and Ephraim ignored their brothers; they were aware of their *rights*, but never their *responsibilities*.

𝔹 Ibzan (12:8–10)

> **SUPPORTING IDEA:** *Ibzan, in contrast to Jephthah, had a large family and served Israel for seven years. He was the fourth "minor" judge.*

There are six minor and six major judges in the Book of Judges, measuring by the criterion of the amount of space devoted to them. We have already studied three of the minor judges: Shamgar (3:31), Tola (10:1–2), and Jair (10:3–5). Of course the major judges are Othniel, Ehud, Deborah/Barak, Gideon, Jephthah, and Samson, who is next in our exposition. Before we launch into the complex and puzzling cycle of Samson, the last three "minor" judges are recorded: Ibzan, Elon, and Abdon.

12:8–10. Ibzan (Heb., "swift") was from **Bethlehem**. These verses contain the first and only reference in the cycles of the judges to the city that would become prominent in the epilogue to the book (chs. 17–21). Just as Jair before him—and in intentional contrast to Jephthah—he also had **thirty sons**. But he "out-Jaired" Jair. In addition to his sons, Ibzan also had **thirty daughters**! Contextually this is important to mention after the story of Jephthah (a man whose life was wrapped up in the destiny of his only child).

Ibzan extended his tribal influence (and no doubt his power) by giving **his daughters away in marriage to those outside his clan**—within Israel, to be sure, but outside his immediate clan and possibly his tribe. Similarly, he brought in thirty young women as wives from outside his clan for his sons, further extending his influence and prestige. The total time he judged Israel was **seven years**. After his death he was **buried in Bethlehem**.

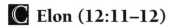 Elon (12:11–12)

SUPPORTING IDEA: *Elon of Zebulun served the Lord as judge for ten years. He was the fifth of the "minor" judges.*

12:11–12. After him, Elon (Heb., "oak tree") . . . **led Israel**. Nothing is said of Elon's family (sons or daughters) or wealth; we know only that he was of the tribe of **Zebulun**. How God gave him recognition among the people as a judge is again unknown, but God's ways are not limited. Perhaps he was simply a man of integrity or leadership ability and thus respected by the people. He judged for **ten years**, and **died**. Like Ibzan, who was buried in his native home, Elon also was buried in Zebulunite land, specifically **in Aijalon**.

Abdon (12:13–15)

SUPPORTING IDEA: *Abdon faithfully judged Israel for eight years. He was the sixth and last of the "minor" judges.*

12:13–15. Abdon (Heb., "service") was the **son of Hillel**, from the town of **Pirathon**, a town near Shechem, and **led Israel eight years**. Not only did Abdon "out-Jair" Jair (10:4); he "out-Ibzaned" Ibzan! In contrast to Elon, Abdon was known by his family. Like Gideon, he had seventy descendants, although they were **forty sons and thirty grandsons** (not "nephews" as in the KJV; no daughters or granddaughters are indicated). Like Jair, his seventy descendants **rode on seventy donkeys**, a sign of prosperous and peaceful times. After he died he was buried in his town **Pirathon in Ephraim, in** (what used to be) **the hill country of the Amalekites**.

MAIN IDEA REVIEW: *Through the downward spirals of the Book of Judges, we are moved from Jephthah to Samson in a transitional chapter: first, the closing chapter of Jephthah's tragic story is recorded; second, a trio of minor judges is remembered.*

III. CONCLUSION

Win, Lose, or Draw?

L. M. Boyd writes about a boxer from the 1930s named C. D. "Bigboy" Blalock. He was boxing for Louisiana State University against an opponent from Mississippi State. In the second round the six-foot, six-inch giant threw a sweeping roundhouse punch at the same time that the boxer from Mississippi State had unexpectedly stepped in. The man's head caught Blalock's arm at the elbow, acted as a lever, and "Bigboy's arm whipped around in almost full circle, connecting with haymaker force on Bigboy's own chin. He staggered, grabbed the rope, walked almost all the way around the ring, and then fell flat for the count—the only prizefighter who ever knocked himself out with a right to his own jaw." Sometimes the Israelites became their own worst enemies.

Who wins in the story of Jephthah? Nobody. First, Jephthah kept his vow, and his daughter became a (living) sacrifice; second, this admirable young girl supported her father, even though she became the victim of the circumstances which he brought about! Third, the Ephraimites entered the story with pride, envy, and stubbornness at a time when Jephthah was emotionally raw. He lived the rest of his life (which probably was only six years) knowing the pain he had brought on his own daughter and his nation.

It is hard to observe the suffering of someone you love when you are powerless to fix it! It is harder to observe the suffering of someone you love when you are the cause of it! It is hardest to observe the suffering of someone you love, when you caused it, and you can do something about it, but you will not because of what you consider greater reasons! For right or wrong, this seemed to be the motivation both of Jephthah and his daughter. But it rendered him vulnerable to anger and violent eruption when confronted with the arrogant Ephraimites!

PRINCIPLES

- Sometimes people behave irrationally for rational reasons; we must be sensitive to the person and to the Holy Spirit in knowing how to respond to people in deep pain.

- Satan is aware when people who desire to serve the Lord are vulnerable to attack.
- It is possible for hurtful opposition to conceive, to gestate, and to be born among the very people for whose spiritual well-being we are deeply concerned.

APPLICATIONS

- Get involved! Don't sit on the sidelines and take shots at those who are on the field.
- Rejoice with those who rejoice, and weep with those who weep (Rom. 12:15).
- Keep the batteries in your "ego-meter" fresh; be aware of when you are more concerned about your rights than about being right.
- Turn jealousy into love by the only means possible—pray for the person whose success you envy!

IV. LIFE APPLICATION

The Envy of Egotistical Ephraim

Benjamin Franklin said, "There is perhaps no one of our natural passions so hard to subdue as pride. Beat it down, stifle it, mortify it as much as one pleases, it is still alive. Even if I could conceive that I had completely overcome it, I should probably be proud of my humility." The godly Scottish preacher Andrew Bonar penned a diary entry. He wrote, "This day twenty years ago I preached for the first time as an ordained minister. It is amazing that the Lord has spared me and used me at all. I have no reason to wonder that He used others far more than He does me. Yet envy is my hurt, and today I have been seeking grace to rejoice exceedingly over the usefulness of others, even where it cast me into the shade. Lord, take away this envy from me!"

How do we handle our envy? The Ephraimites were quite proud of their history. The tabernacle was located in their territory (Shiloh), Bethel was within their borders, and Joshua (the leader of the conquest) was an Ephraimite. They had developed, as we say, an "attitude." But the Ephraimites were spectators, not participants. They weren't on the field with Jephthah; they weren't even in the stands; they were watching the action from a safe distance. Too many Christians are like the Ephraimites, willing to let others do the work and then complain about how it was done.

D. L. Moody was once criticized by a man who didn't like the way he preached the gospel. Moody asked, "Well, sir, what method do you use to present the gospel?" When the man admitted he didn't have one, Moody replied, "I like the way I do it better than the way you don't do it."

V. PRAYER

O Lord, we are people who are vulnerable to pride. We recognize that nothing of lasting value in our lives is the result of our own labor, but that every good and perfect—and eternal—gift is from your hand. You have dealt with us in grace, not according to our merit. We ask that we would likewise treat others in grace. May we be slow to speak, slow to wrath, slow to anger, and slow to criticize. Through Christ our Lord. Amen.

VI. DEEPER DISCOVERIES

A. "Bad Timing"

From the larger context readers may add another element to the Ephraimites' confrontation with Jephthah: they had terrible timing. Although the sequence of events is unknown, this confrontation must have taken place shortly after the Ammonite victory, since it was in a cause-and-effect relationship with the battle. If it happened immediately after the battle, then Jephthah's daughter was gone for her two months of mourning, or possibly right after his daughter had left his life forever (see ch. 11). The Ephraimites could not have selected a worse time to antagonize the new Gileadite leader.

B. Majoring on Minor Judges

The inclusion of minor judges within this period of Bible history is an indication of the completeness and accuracy of the storyteller. Otherwise, they would simply be omitted. As far as Ibzan, Elon, and Abdon are concerned, we know very little about these men (cp. the litany of names in Rom. 16:1–23). We do know four things. Collectively, we know that the total number of years they ministered totaled twenty-five years, that those years were consecutive—they didn't overlap (each episode begins with the time marker, "after"), that they all apparently judged during times of peace (no enemies are identified nor battles recorded) and that each one "judged" for a longer time than Jephthah did!

VII. TEACHING OUTLINE

A. INTRODUCTION

1. Lead Story: Pride and Prejudice
2. Context: There are six "minor" judges (by criterion of space devoted to them), and three of them are found in this chapter. The story line, however, takes us from one major self-destructive judge (Jephthah) to another self-destructive judge (Samson, ch. 13). With Jephthah, we sympathize; for Samson, we will have little sympathy (chs. 13–16).
3. Transition: The sad epilogue to the story of Jephthah reminds us of the sad epilogue to the story of Gideon. Both of these judges made choices that had consequences that destroyed their families. All seventy of Gideon's sons were murdered (Jotham escaped, but he disappears from history) by their step-brother Abimelech, who became a dictator and then died as a result of his greed. Jephthah made the tragic vow that destroyed his daughter's future and curtailed his family line. In both cases, however, their legacies were cancelled. But they had something else in common: the egomania of Ephraim. However, they had different strategies of dealing with these men: Gideon *soothed* them; Jephthah *slaughtered* them.

B. COMMENTARY

1. Jephthah as Judge, Jury, and Executioner (12:1–7)
   a. Confrontation (12:1–3)
   b. Conflict (12:4)
   c. Carnage (12:5–7)
2. Ibzan (12:8–10)

3. Elon (12:11–12)
4. Abdon (12:13–15)

C. CONCLUSION: WIN, LOSE, OR DRAW?

VIII. ISSUES FOR DISCUSSION

1. Do we ever act like the Ephraimites? To what extent do we sit on the sidelines and criticize rather than invest ourselves in the challenge of the game?
2. Do we ever act like Jephthah, allowing circumstances to trump our reason and lashing out at others? At our loved ones?
3. Consider the reaction of the early church when Jews steeped in the law learned that the Gentiles had received grace and did not have to obey the law in order to maintain continued favor with God (Acts 10–11). How do you think you would have reacted?

Judges 13

Samson: The Early Years

I. INTRODUCTION
An Angel of Few Words

II. COMMENTARY
A verse-by-verse explanation of the chapter.

III. CONCLUSION
Insulated or Isolated?

An overview of the principles and applications from the chapter.

IV. LIFE APPLICATION
Separation—in Reverse!

Melding the chapter to life.

V. PRAYER
Tying the chapter to life with God.

VI. DEEPER DISCOVERIES
Historical, geographical, and grammatical enrichment of the commentary.

VII. TEACHING OUTLINE
Suggested step-by-step group study of the chapter.

VIII. ISSUES FOR DISCUSSION
Zeroing the chapter in on daily life.

Quote

"*How* little people know who think that holiness is dull. When one meets the real thing, it is irresistible."

C .   S .   L e w i s

Judges 13

IN A NUTSHELL

When God raises up leaders, he desires that they be holy, in the world but not of the world, and separated unto him.

Samson: The Early Years

I. INTRODUCTION

An Angel of Few Words

*T*he thirtieth president of the United States was Calvin Coolidge, known as "silent Cal." He once said, "Four-fifths of all our troubles in this life would disappear if we would only sit down and keep still." His last will and testament was only twenty-three words long: "Not unmindful of my son John, I give all my estate, both real and personal, to my wife, Grace Coolidge, in fee simple." That was it. Nothing more. His motto was, "If you don't say anything, you won't be called on to repeat it." Coolidge even refused to use the telephone while he was in office. He was so notorious for saying so little that a White House dinner guest once made a bet that she could get the president to say more than two words. When she told the president about her wager, he replied, "You lose."

The main character in the chapter before us has a strange role. He was a messenger from God who revealed—yet his revelations were repetitive and uninformative, at least in terms of what the human characters wanted to know! In some ways we identify with Manoah; he wanted to know everything! It borders on the comical as he attempted to wheedle information from the angel four times! (vv. 11,12,15,17). As angelic announcers go, the angel who came to Manoa was an "angel of few words." He operated on a "need to know" basis, and what he shared with Manoah and his wife was what they— and we—need to know. It contained a core message about holiness that will become central in the saga of Samson.

II. COMMENTARY

Samson: The Early Years

MAIN IDEA: *The story of Samson is unique in several ways, the most obvious being the judge himself. This time God did not send a national liberator but an individualist who fought all his battles alone. Chapter 13 records the announcement to Samson's parents by "the angel of the LORD." It carries Samson from intention to conception through gestation to birth and mentions the growing years—until the Spirit of the Lord began to stir within him. So far, so good.*

A The Background (13:1–2)

SUPPORTING IDEA: *While there was anguish in the nation of Israel over the Philistines, there was also private anguish in the lives of two people that was entirely unrelated to Philistine oppression. But God was at work and would cause these two stories to intersect.*

13:1–2. Once **again the Israelites did evil in the eyes of the LORD**. The definite article (Heb.), as before, indicates the specific evil of serving other gods and rejecting the Lord (2:10–13). Accompanying this cause is the promised effect that **the LORD delivered them into the hands of the Philistines**, a people who have already been introduced as the "five rulers of the Philistines" (see 3:1–4) and later appeared in the story of Shamgar (3:31). They were reintroduced still later as part of a military pincer movement (from the west) along with the Ammonites (from the east, 10:7). The present oppression continued **for forty years** prior to Samson's birth and would continue until it was finally vanquished under King David.

We would expect at exactly this point to read that Israel cried out in repentance to the Lord, who sent them a deliverer to relieve them from Philistine oppression. Instead, the next verses introduce the family of God's deliverer in a story that is entirely independent from the presence (or absence) of any repentance on the part of Israel. We are introduced to the main male character of this chapter gradually through increasing specificity: by gender (**a certain man**), by geography (**of Zorah**), by tribe (**of the Danites**), and by name (**Manoah**). This reflects the Hebrew order (cp. the NIV order). The meaning of his name is uncertain, but may be related to "Noah," and carry the idea of "resting place." The important half of this couple, however, was the unnamed **wife who was sterile**, thus rendering the couple **childless**.

Ⓑ Announcement to Samson's Mother (13:3–7)

SUPPORTING IDEA: *The angel of the Lord appeared to proclaim God's intervention in enabling the birth of Samson, God's deliverer. He was to be a Nazirite, separated unto the Lord.*

13:3. *The Wife's Elation: Promise of a Son.* Perhaps to the surprise of the reader, rather than appear to Manoah, **the angel of the LORD appeared to** Manoah's wife, who (despite her prominence as the only level-headed human being in this chapter) remains unnamed. We are not told how she responded to the welcome announcement that she would **conceive and have a son**, although presumably it was received with great joy.

13:4. *The Wife's Restriction: Special Nutritional Regimen.* However, in contrast to all other women in Scripture who were given the promise of a child, this woman was given a specific dietary regimen that we later learn accords with a provision in the law. At the beginning, however, she was simply told that she was to **drink no wine or other fermented drink**, nor was she permitted to **eat anything unclean**. The reason for this restriction would shortly be made clear.

13:5a. *The Angel's Explanation: Nazirite Vow.* The **son** that she was to **conceive** and **give birth to** would be a life-long **Nazirite** and would be **set apart to God from birth**. Even prior to birth, his post-natal regimen was known to be the same as his pre-natal regimen "shared" by his mother. The Nazirite vow (Num. 6; see "The Nazirite Vow" below) included proscriptions against the fruit of the vine, against the cutting of hair, and against contact with the dead. Two of these three were specifically mentioned.

13:5b. *The Boy's Mission: Deliverance.* Finally, we arrive at the nexus between this interlude and its context of the Philistine oppression: this child would be involved in **the deliverance of Israel from the hands of the Philistines**. However, unlike all previous judges, his work would only **begin** the process of deliverance (which would not be completed until the time of King David, 2 Sam. 5:17–25).

13:6–7. *The Wife's Description: Announcement to Her Husband.* No words of dialogue between the woman and the angel of the Lord were recorded. She asked no questions, nor did she seek confirming signs about this special birth as Gideon had done (6:17) and Zachariah would do (Luke 1:18). Instead, she **went to her husband** and reported first on the looks of the visitor: **he looked like an angel of God, very awesome**. Her meaning was that whoever this being was, he was more than a mere man (Manoah apparently did not share this opinion and thought of him as no more than a prophet—13:16b). She added two negations: what she did not ask (**where he came from**) and what he did not volunteer (**he didn't tell me his name**). But, positively, she reported that the man told her that she would **give birth to a son** and that there was a dietary regimen that she was to follow. Not only was she to **drink no wine or other fermented drink**; she was also warned against eating **anything unclean** (a prohibition in effect for all Israel, but which needed to be repeated in this age of spiritual laxness).

She recited everything the man said accurately with three divergences. First, she omitted that he had pointed to her as the barren member of the marriage. Second, she added (and perhaps rightly assumed) that the son would be **a Nazirite of God from birth until the day of his death**. Third, she omitted the stated prohibition of cutting the boy's hair, which when coupled with the mention of his death, was almost prophetic. This cycle would end when the cutting of his hair brought about his death.

In addition, there were departures here from the normal pattern of the Nazirite vow mentioned in Numbers 6. Normally the vow was to be voluntary; here it was mandated. Normally the vow was to be temporary; this was permanent. The uniqueness of the birth and the uniqueness of the vow lead us to anticipate the uniqueness of the child.

C Announcement to Samson's Father (13:8–14)

SUPPORTING IDEA: *The angel of the Lord appeared again (by God's grace) to the woman and also to Manoah in order to confirm the birth of the child.*

13:8–14. Again we are surprised at another interlude. Rather than recount the birth of the child, Manoah pursued divine guidance (using the less specific divine name *Adonai*). He asked God to send the man again in order **to teach us how to bring up the boy**. Although God heard Manoah, and the angel of God appeared again, he came not to Manoah but **to the woman while she was out in the field**. She was eager to have her husband involved in the loop of information and therefore **hurried to tell her husband** that the man had appeared again.

After confirming that this was indeed **the one who talked to** his wife, Manoah asked, **When your words are fulfilled, what is to be the rule for the boy's life and work?** The response was terse and added nothing new about the boy's nature or career. The angel simply repeated the litany for prenatal care of the child. Manoah attempted to wheedle all the information he could from the divine visitor, but at the end he knew nothing more. While the return visit was evidence of God's grace in confirming the birth to Manoah (first, that she was faithful to him, and second, that she was not delusional!), it was frustrating for Manoah. As angelic announcers go, the visitor was an "angel of few words."

The Nazirite Vow

It was to be voluntary
Dedicated *himself* (Num. 6:2)
Separated *himself* (Num. 6:5)
Aspects of the vow as *his* (eighteen times in Num. 6)
It was to have a hallowed purpose
Before the Lord (mentioned two times)
To the Lord (mentioned seven times)
It was to be symbolic
Avoid fruit of vine (Num. 6:3–4)
Avoid cutting hair (Num. 6:5)
Avoid contact with dead people (Num. 6:6–12)
It was to be temporary
Until the period of separation is over (Num. 6:5)
When the period of separation is over (Num. 6:13)

Note: Other Nazirites include Samuel (1 Sam. 1:11), arguably John the Baptist (Luke 1:15), Paul (Acts 18:18), and four unnamed Christians (Acts 21:23–24). Scripture records only three life-long Nazirites (Samson, Samuel, and John the Baptist). Jesus was *not* a Nazirite (Matt. 11:18–19)!

Ⓓ Recognition of the Angel of the Lord (13:15–23)

> **SUPPORTING IDEA:** *As Manoah persisted in gaining more specific information, he found out less about "what" and more about "who" it was that stood before him.*

13:15–23. Still seeking information, Manoah told the visitor that he **would like** him **to stay until we prepare a young goat for you.** This was not an expression of piety or submission in any way but merely an expression of hospitality—not sacred but secular. To Manoah's surprise the angel of the Lord replied, **Even though you detain me, I will not eat any of your food.** Manoah's inadequate view of his visitor (**Manoah did not realize that it was the angel of the LORD**) was about to be corrected. The appropriate response was not a (secular) meal but a (sacred) offering: **If you prepare a burnt offering, offer it to the LORD.**

Manoah's response to this exhortation is interesting. Rather than ask if the visitor spoke for the Lord, he asked about the prophecy for his son. If that word should come true, he would want to **honor** the prophet, so he insisted, **What is your name?** (Literally, the Hebrew reads, "Who is your name?"— probably a grammatically awkward conflation of "what is your name?" and "who are you?" The grammar probably reflects Manoah's stammering frustration.)

Instead of responding, the visitor answered a question with another question: **Why do you ask my name?** And before Manoah could respond he added that his name was **beyond understanding** ("wonderful," NASB). This messianic appellation (also found in Isa. 9:6) enlarges our awareness that this person was more than a man or a prophet or even an angel. He was "the angel of the LORD!" Again, the visitor did not answer all of Manoah's questions—and the questions he did answer evoked more questions!

Rather than pursue this fruitless line of questioning further, Manoah did as he was bidden and offered a sacrifice to the Lord. While they looked on, **the LORD did an amazing thing.** He caused a flame to blaze up **from the altar toward heaven,** and **the angel of the LORD ascended in the flame.** Their response was to fall **with their faces to the ground** in fear, awe, and obeisance. Things were now clear. The visitor had ascended to the Lord. **Manoah** reacted in near hysteria, **"We are doomed to die! . . . We have seen God!"** (see "Deeper Discoveries").

His wife calmed him and applied logical analysis to their situation: first, **the LORD** (note her use of God's covenant name for the first time) received the offering from them, rather than reject it. Second, God had **shown us all these things**—the implication being, why would God communicate anything to them if his intention was to kill them? Third, a promise has been given: God was to give them a special child, which required that they live.

⒠ Birth and Growth of Samson (13:24–25)

> **SUPPORTING IDEA:** *God's promise through the angel was fulfilled as the promised child was conceived, was born, and grew to manhood.*

13:24–25. Later Manoah's wife **gave birth to a boy and named him Samson**. It was not unusual for women to name children, but what was unusual was the meaning of the name itself: "shemesh" ("sun") plus the diminutive ("on"), or "Shimshon." Its meaning was "little sun" or "Sunny-boy!" (Block, 416; rather like James to Jimmy). The name may mean that the Lord had brought light into their dark existence. **He grew and the LORD blessed him**, among other things, with extraordinary health. At the appropriate time, **the Spirit of the LORD began to stir him while he was in Mahaneh Dan, between Zorah and Eshtaol**. The promised child was intended to live a life of special holiness—*in* the world, but not *of* the world.

> **MAIN IDEA REVIEW:** *The story of Samson is unique in several ways, the most obvious being the judge himself. This time God did not send a national liberator but an individualist who fought all his battles alone. Chapter 13 records the announcement to Samson's parents by "the angel of the LORD." It carries Samson from intention to conception through gestation to birth and mentions the growing years—until the Spirit of the Lord began to stir within him. So far, so good.*

III. CONCLUSION

Insulated or Isolated?

Years ago a boy lived out his brief existence inside a bubble. His plastic dome isolated him from germs that could prove fatal to him. His air was filtered, his food and water were sterilized, and his life was lived without direct human touch. Such a tragedy is often replicated at the spiritual level by Christians who misunderstand God's mandate for holiness. Of course we are to remain unpolluted by the world (Jas. 1:27). However, as Vance Havner said, "We are not to be isolated but insulated, moving in the midst of evil but untouched by it." We are to be *in* the world but not *of* the world. Our pattern is Jesus, who was "holy, blameless, pure, set apart from sinners" (Heb. 7:26), yet he was "a friend of tax collectors and 'sinners'" (Luke 7:34).

PRINCIPLES

- Holiness may not be quantified; it is not a matter of *lists* but of *love* for the Lord.
- God does not always explain to us the future details of his plan for our lives; he simply wants us to "trust and obey" him.
- God is not passive; even in his providence he is active. "In him all things hold together" (Col. 1:17); "in him we live and move and have our being" (Acts 17:28).
- Though concerned with individuals, this chapter demonstrates that God will not abandon his chosen people. Even though in this cycle there is no repentance, no prayer, no change, God will not let go of this nation (2 Tim. 2:15).

APPLICATIONS

- Be holy, because God, in whose image you were created, is himself holy (1 Pet. 1:15–16).
- List the number of friendships you have with unbelievers. Are you functioning as "salt" and "light" (Matt. 5:13–14)?
- When you don't understand why things happen in your life, trust the Lord. The crucial truth is not *why* but *who*.
- God wants you to be *in* the world but not *of* it—how are you doing?

IV. LIFE APPLICATION

Separation—in Reverse!

Donald Grey Barnhouse, the beloved pastor of Tenth Presbyterian Church in Philadelphia, led a young soldier to the Lord during World War I. When the young man returned from war, where he had been an outspoken witness for Christ, he was apprehensive about reentering the levels of high society from which he had come prior to being saved. He was afraid that the temptations of his former life would tug so strongly at him that he would succumb and revert to his old habits. The "front line" of spiritual conflict among family and friends was more intimidating than the front line of military conflict! Barnhouse advised him to tell the first ten people of his old crowd about his newfound faith. He followed through and was met with frozen smiles and cold shoulders. He was not obnoxious, but he was bold. Word got around quickly, and soon he didn't have to worry—his old friends gave him up (cited in J. M. Boice, *Christ's Call to Discipleship,* Moody, 1986, 122–123).

God calls believers to walk a thin line; we are to be holy and at the same time we are to make a difference in a world that offers enticements that would nullify holiness. While the Nazirite vow was a vow of separation, many misunderstand its meaning and its application. Separation *from,* by itself, is mere legalism. Separation was not only to be *from* but also to be *unto.* The issue is not *how much can I get away with,* but rather, *how holy can I be?* God will set no limits on how holy you can become! Think about it: aren't you the only person who sets those limits?

V. PRAYER

O Lord, we know that you want us to be a holy people. Too often we try to quantify holiness into lists of do's and don'ts, but you know our motives and observe our hearts. When we are tempted, may we see sin for what it truly is: that which removes us from the deep joy that you have planned for your children. Through Christ our Lord. Amen.

VI. DEEPER DISCOVERIES

A. The Philistines

The origin of the Philistines is uncertain, but they apparently arrived in Israel from two directions: overland through Anatolia, and by means of the sea (through Crete and Cyprus), initially leaving paths of destruction in their wake like Vikings (Block, 394). Five Israelite leaders dealt with them: Shamgar, Samson, Samuel, Saul, and finally David (who ended the Philistine threat, 2 Sam. 5:17–25).

B. Zorah

Zorah was "a small Israelite town on the north side of the fertile Sorek Valley, a few miles north of Beth Shemesh" The Hebrew indicates Manoah was "*from* Zorah" (speaking of origin) rather than "*of* Zorah" (speaking of present location) which suggests that he had "settled in a more felicitous location up the valley toward Eshtaol" (Block, 400).

C. Pre-Natal Equals Post-Natal

One should note that the pre-natal conditions were related to the spiritual separation of the Nazirite, and thus one may infer that there were implications for personhood and the scriptural view of pre-natal life here: "he" was the same person from conception through birth and beyond, not merely tissue. What was of spiritual benefit after his birth (as infant) was of spiritual benefit before his birth (as embryo and fetus).

D. "Seeing God"

The expression "face to face" is a figure of speech, and refers to knowing God intimately. Exodus 33:11 says that "the LORD would speak to Moses face to face, as a man speaks with his friend." The point of these words was not that Moses actually saw the face of God but rather that he spoke *intimately* with God (this becomes particularly clear in Exod. 33:18–23, especially vv. 20,23). God spoke to Moses "face to face," but he would not allow Moses to "see His face." They are not the same thing.

E. The Boredom of Sin

If you were to step away from this book of the Old Testament and get a bird's eye view, what would you see? First, you would see that again, sin gets more and more boring, always the same old thing. It's hard to think up new categories of sin. So in the Book of Judges the reports of the kind of sin that collectively send a nation into a moral tailspin are simply reduced, in effect, to "they did it again (yawn)." There's not much more to say. Second, by contrast, you will notice that God's deliverance is interesting (to say the least)! As we consider the fascinating stories of Gideon, Jephthah, and now Samson, there is nothing boring here!

VII. TEACHING OUTLINE

A. INTRODUCTION

1. Lead Story: An Angel of Few Words
2. Context: After the painful episode of Jephthah, we have completed the study of six minor judges and five major judges. Our last judge is Samson, whose story takes us from chapter 13–16, leading up to three "Bethlehem" stories (Judg. 17–18; 19–21; Ruth 1–4).
3. Transition: After the disappointing story of Gideon and his tragic legacy (Abimelech), followed by Israel's chronic apostasy and subsequent servitude, God again proves himself faithful to his covenant. This time, however, deliverance will be through an individual and not by an army.

B. COMMENTARY

1. The Background (13:1–2)
2. Announcement to Samson's Mother (13:3–7)
   a. The wife's elation: promise of a son (13:3)
   b. The wife's restriction: special nutritional regimen (13:4)
   c. The angel's explanation: Nazarite vow (13:5a)
   d. The boy's mission: deliverance (13:5b)
   e. The wife's description: announcement to her husband (13:6–7)
3. Announcement to Samson's Father (13:8–14)

4. Recognition of the Angel of the Lord (13:15–23)
5. Birth and Growth of Samson (13:24–25)

C. CONCLUSION: INSULATED OR ISOLATED?

VIII. ISSUES FOR DISCUSSION

1. Reflect on this observation by theologian John Murray: "They who are of the world may be able to keep up a good front . . . but they do not hunger and thirst after righteousness. Their aspirations are not heavenly. They are not strangers and pilgrims on earth. [By contrast, Christians] have been translated from the realm of sin and death to that of righteousness and life. Sin [now] becomes their burden and plague. They are no longer at home with it. This is now foreign soil."

2. Note the growing awareness through the chapter of who "the angel of the LORD" actually is. First, he is a "man of God" (vv. 6,8), then he is "beyond understanding" (v. 18), then a messenger of God (v. 21), and finally "God" (v. 22). Discuss this proposition: This part of the story is not about Samson or about his family; it's about God.

3. It is easy to read this chapter and glance away without understanding its essence: holiness. God wanted Samson, who would represent him before a watching world, to be holy. The Nazarite vow is not an interesting afterthought but is the very core of the story. At the moment of regeneration, each believer is set apart unto God, declared positionally righteous and holy in his sight (note 1 Cor. 6:11, "you were sanctified" and 2 Thess. 2:13, "chose you . . . through the sanctifying work of the Spirit"). But after regeneration, each believer is charged with living a life of holiness. Read carefully the following exhortations for bringing our practice into conformity with our position: Ephesians 4:1; 1 Thessalonians 4:3; 5:23; 1 Peter 1:16.

Judges 14

The Lion, the Witch, and the Wardrobe

Quote

"*A* man without a purpose is like a ship

without a rudder."

T h o m a s   C a r l y l e

Judges 14

I N   A   N U T S H E L L

*O*ur introduction to the appetites and exploits of Samson also exposes us to his character. He is a spoiled child who gives his passions primacy over people. In this chapter his poor choices lead him into episodes with a lion, a nagging fiancée (the witch), and a gambling debt that requires him to murder people for their clothes (the wardrobe). Even so, while Samson appears to have abandoned God, God has not abandoned Samson.

The Lion, the Witch, and the Wardrobe

I. INTRODUCTION

God Is No Fool

*L*ois Cheney writes this parable in her book *God Is No Fool* (Abingdon Press, 1969):

> Once, a man said, "If I had some extra money, I'd give it to God, but I have just enough to support myself and my family." And the same man said, "If I had some extra time, I'd give it to God, but every minute is taken up with my job, my family, my clubs, and what have you—every single minute." He also said, "If I had a talent I'd give it to God, but I have no lovely voice; I have no special skill; I've never been able to lead a group; I can't think cleverly or quickly, the way I would like to."
>
> And God was touched, and although it was unlike him, God gave that man money, time, and a glorious talent. And then he waited, and waited, and waited. . . . And then after a while, God shrugged his shoulders, and he took back all three gifts from the man.
>
> After a while, the man sighed and said, "If I only had some of that money back, I'd give it to God. If I only had some of that time, I'd give it to God. If I could only rediscover that glorious talent, I'd give it to God."
>
> And God said, "Oh, shut up."
>
> And the man told some of his friends, "You know, I'm not so sure that I believe in God any more."

God gave Samson amazing gifts, yet he squandered them. In spite of his potential, his victories were all personal. He did less for God's people than did any judge. Block put it this way: "On the one hand he is born and buried as a hero, but on the other he is a bandit, a trickster, and one who frivolously fritters away his extraordinary calling and gifts" (Block, 421).

II. COMMENTARY

The Lion, the Witch, and the Wardrobe

> **MAIN IDEA:** *Samson's character was exposed in the unfolding conflicts of his life. He pursued the wrong woman in defiance of his God and his parents. He repeatedly violated his Nazirite vow in defiance of God's command. He tried to cheat his wedding guests in defiance of social protocols. He insulted and embarrassed his fiancée; he used his abilities to kill his enemies for all the wrong reasons, and he thoughtlessly abandoned his fiancée to public ridicule.*

A Animal Desire (14:1–4)

> **SUPPORTING IDEA:** *Samson's character was exposed when he pursued the wrong woman, in defiance of God and his parents.*

14:1–4. Samson intentionally went to visit the Philistine city of **Timnah**. He was on no spiritual pilgrimage nor was he an emissary with worthy goals; he simply planned to party. There he saw **a young Philistine woman**. After returning home, he demanded of his parents: **Get her for me as my wife.** He refused to listen to their reasonable protests—was there no **acceptable woman among your relatives or among all our people?** Scripture is clear: Believers are to marry only other believers. His parents objected to an alliance with a family whose allegiance was to the god Dagon, but Samson refused to listen. His criterion was not hidden; it was clear (and shallow)—"She looks good to me" (NASB). The Hebrew phrase is the same as that found in Judges 17:6 and 21:25—she was "right in his own eyes" (NASB).

Samson, however, had no respect for God and his laws, much less respect for his parents or concern for their objections. He was like a beast whose appetites must be fed. It has been observed that beasts want only food and sleep and their next sexual encounter (like some humans who only want to eat and sleep and await their next sexual encounter). When one stops living for something bigger than one's appetites, one stops being recognizable as human.

From the midst of Samson's pursuit of his fleshly appetites, there is this statement that is both disconcerting and astonishing: **His parents did not know that this was from the LORD, who was seeking an occasion to confront the Philistines.** God was working behind the scenes to accomplish his purposes, even to the extent of using the ungodly desires of fallen men (see Acts 2:23). The Israelites were content with Philistine domination, and for the first time did not cry out to the Lord. They had lost any sense of mission or national purpose and had become content to be less than God wanted them to be. Samson was unaware of God's sovereignty over his circumstances. He lived his life as though God were disconnected from his private life. For him, God was reduced to a benign grandfather. But God was about to stir the pot—the *status* would no longer be *quo*.

B Lion Attack (14:5–9)

SUPPORTING IDEA: *Samson's character was shown in his violation of the Nazirite vow and his lack of respect for his parents.*

14:5–9. While going **down to Timnah together with his father and mother**, Samson became separated from his parents. A "best case" interpretation would be that he went exploring without them; a "worst case" interpretation would be that he planned to go to **the vineyards of Timnah** where he was going to enjoy some wine (as he probably had done on his previous trip) and didn't want his parents to witness the ongoing violation of his Nazirite vow. He was not with his parents at this time, nor did he mention to them what happened. As far as he was concerned, his business was not their business.

Suddenly a young lion attacked him, but **the Spirit of the LORD** empowered him to slaughter the lion **with his bare hands**. Samson apparently took his astonishing abilities for granted; never did he pause to ask why he should be so gifted or to what divinely ordained use those gifts should be placed.

Samson **talked with the woman**, and the marriage plans were confirmed—**he liked her**. What she thought about him is unknown to us. On his way **back to marry her, he turned aside to look at the lion's carcass**. This was another violation of his Nazirite vow (Num. 6:6—contact with the dead, which presumably included "road kill"). To his surprise (Heb., "behold") the carcass was not a host to maggots but to bees! It is said that in the summer heat of the Arabian desert, carcasses can dry up and mummify within almost twenty-four hours. Apparently the lion had almost by-passed the stages of decay and being putrified and went straight to being petrified! Again, God was at work, bringing about an integral part of an unfolding story.

Samson intentionally visited the carcass; further, he desecrated his parents by sharing the honey—**he gave them some, and they too ate it. But he did not tell them that he had taken the honey from the lion's carcass.** His action is not unlike giving one's parents a gift one has stolen from a store. Block reminds us, "His parents had sanctified him, but now he desecrates them" (Block, 430).

Stag Party (14:10–14)

> **SUPPORTING IDEA:** *Samson's character is shown in his attempt to cheat his wedding guests.*

14:10–14. Samson's **father went down to see the woman,** and all marriage arrangements were made. **Samson made a feast there, as was customary for bridegrooms.** This "feast" was a week-long bachelor party at the end of which he was to claim his bride and consummate the marriage union. Much drinking took place—again a violation of the Nazirite vow, this time in front of pagan observers (apparently Samson cared little about testimony). At this point the two strands of the story (the lion and the liaison) coalesce into one. Samson was perceived to be somewhat dangerous, and **thirty companions** were to guard him (not, as NIV, **given**). We are unsure why—possibly his warlike appearance and extreme self-confidence were unsettling.

Samson, however, saw this as an opportunity for gain, and his greed triumphed over his good sense. He proposed a gamble on a riddle with thirty-to-one odds against him. Samson knew, however, that he possessed the "ace card" because only he could possibly know the answer.

The riddle was clever and elegant: **Out of the eater, something to eat; out of the strong, something sweet.** The first line was mischievous and misleading because it would invite the revelers to recall the traditional gluttonous feasts where the guests vomited what they had just eaten—in order to eat still more. This may have been going on around them at that very time. But this would have been a wrong guess because that was not Samson's meaning. Further, the second line (**strong . . . sweet**) had no easily decoded meaning. The result was seen in their escalating frustration: **For three days they could not give the answer.**

D Heifer Tears (14:15–20)

SUPPORTING IDEA: *Samson's character was shown in his abuse of his gifts (using them for the wrong reasons) and in the horrible treatment of his fiancée (insulting her and exposing her to public ridicule).*

14:15–20. In seething frustration these soldiers told Samson's betrothed wife to find out the answer for them, and made this threat: **We will burn you and your father's household to death.** All that she held dear was hostage to their demands. Rather than explain the dilemma to Samson (whose love was questionable enough that she was uncertain if he would be willing to trade the lives of her family for clothing), she tried to wheedle the answer out of him through incessant nagging and emotional blackmail. She **threw herself on him, sobbing, "You hate me! You don't really love me. You've given my people a riddle, but you haven't told me the answer."**

This was the first time we hear her voice, and unfortunately it is shrill and hysterical. A man who was attuned to understanding his future wife would be more concerned to probe the reason for her panic, but not Samson. His callous response was revealing: **I haven't even explained it to my father or mother.** The implication was, if he had not told his parents, then (*a fortiori*) what made her think he would tell her? She was engaged to a man who had no desire for intimate companionship with her beyond what he would receive in the bedroom. The symmetry is interesting. She was willing to deceive and betray her betrothed husband to save her parents, while he saw nothing wrong in being more attached to his parents than to his wife.

But her nagging was relentless and finally **on the seventh day**, motivated by his own desire for peace and quiet, **he finally told her.** In turn she **explained the riddle to her people.** In anything but a spirit of comradeship over the celebration of the wedding, the guests waited until the last possible moment (**before sunset on the seventh day**) and snatched victory from Samson's hands at the last moment. They answered by asking two rhetorical questions—as though the answer were a matter of obvious deduction—**What is sweeter than honey? What is stronger than a lion?**

They apparently did not know about the source of the honey or the attack of the lion, in which Samson was indeed proven stronger than a lion! But while they may not have known the meaning, they knew the right answers to

Judges 14

write into the blanks; like children who cheat on a math test by copying the final number, they had no idea how that answer was reached.

Samson realized that he had been betrayed by his fiancée, and he knew that they knew that he knew (**if you had not plowed with my heifer, you would not have solved my riddle**). Heifers were not used in plowing, so his insult, while intentionally cruel and unflattering to her, was true enough. Again, **the Spirit of the LORD** "came upon" him (see v. 6), empowering him to fight, overpower, and strip the clothing and armament from **thirty . . . men** in the city of **Ashkelon**, one of the five cities of the Philistine Pentapolis (3:3, Ekron, Gath, Ashkelon, Ashdod, and Gaza; see Judg. 1:18). Rather than consummate the marriage to a woman he believed had betrayed him out of tribal loyalty, he sulked and pouted and went home to his mother—a strange response for a serial bandit.

In order to avoid ridicule (and also to hopefully cement ties with his townsmen), the father of the betrothed girl gave her in marriage to the chief among the companions. (Samson will learn about this in chapter 15; he will not be pleased.) Consider the sovereignty of God: Samson planned to live with the enemy, but God intervened. Rather than securing an alliance with the Philistines, Samson would be at enmity with them. God was stirring the pot.

> **MAIN IDEA REVIEW:** *Samson's character was exposed in the unfolding conflicts of his life. He pursued the wrong woman in defiance of his God and his parents; he repeatedly violated his Nazirite vow in defiance of God's command; he tried to cheat his wedding guests in defiance of social protocols; he insulted and embarrassed his fiancée; he used his abilities to kill his enemies for all the wrong reasons, and he thoughtlessly abandoned his fiancée to public ridicule.*

III. CONCLUSION

Great Expectations

The story of Samson began in Judges 13:24, where we learned that the woman gave birth to a son and named him Samson; we also learned that the boy grew and that he was blessed by the covenant Lord. After a miraculous conception and God's promise of divine intention and attention, one would expect the next verses to bespeak great promise. This was true of the other

224

two life-long Nazirites in Scripture: "And the boy Samuel continued to grow in stature and in favor with the LORD and with men" (1 Sam. 2:26). "And you, my child, will be called a prophet of the Most High; for you will go on before the Lord to prepare the way for him, to give his people the knowledge of salvation through the forgiveness of their sins, because of the tender mercy of our God" (Luke 1:76–78).

However, the reader who has never before heard the story of Samson would be in for a surprise. Samson was exposed as a man far more concerned with his appetites than with God's glory. God gave Samson amazing gifts, and he squandered them. The tragedy of his life was not that he never got the woman he wanted, but that he never became the man God wanted.

PRINCIPLES

- God is not surprised, dismayed, or his plan derailed over the sinful choices of sinful men.
- Even though God's plan incorporates our evil choices (Gen. 50:20), we are still accountable for our sins (Gal. 6:7; Acts 2:23).

APPLICATIONS

- Don't loiter where you lust! If you remove yourself from temptation, there will be nothing to yield to.
- Trust your Lord! He knows what he's doing in the details of your life.
- In hard circumstances ask God what you can learn that will make you more godly.
- Honor your parents! Samson's life would have been much less tragic if he had heeded their counsel.
- Cherish your spouse! Samson treated his like dirt and ended with a mess.

IV. LIFE APPLICATION

Temptation

Chuck Swindoll tells the story of how we plan ahead for temptation. "Son," ordered a father, "don't swim in that canal."

"OK, Dad," he answered. But he came home carrying a wet bathing suit that evening.

"Where have you been?" demanded the father.

"Swimming in the canal," answered the boy.

"Didn't I tell you not to swim there?" asked the father.

"Yes, sir," answered the boy.

"Why did you?" he asked.

"Well, Dad," he explained, "I had my bathing suit with me and I couldn't resist the temptation."

"Why did you take your bathing suit with you?" he questioned.

"So I'd be prepared to swim, in case I was tempted," he replied.

Samson had no intention of resisting temptation; indeed, he planned ahead to indulge himself. Not much good can be said about Samson in this episode.

To what temptations did Samson yield? First, self-indulgence (going to Timnah in the first place, going to the vineyard). Second, lust (he saw the girl, desired her, pursued her—all based on her physical appearance). Third, greed (he proposed a riddle—desiring to add to his holdings on his wedding day! He was not content with his wife as the main issue of the wedding). Fourth, petulance (he left his betrothed, with no explanation offered or promise of return, and went off to sulk with no thought for her or her family). Fifth, anger (twice, really—he left to kill men, return with spoils, left again, and then when he discovered she had been given to another, had a fit of revenge—which resulted in the next chapter in getting his "beloved" and her family killed!). Samson never wrestled with temptation—he simply always yielded! There is a serious warning here: We are to remove ourselves from what tempts us!

V. PRAYER

O Lord, you have given us natural talents and spiritual gifts. At times we are tempted to use good gifts to fulfill selfish goals. May we be good stewards of what you have entrusted into our hands, so that when we stand before you one day we will hear, "Well done, good and faithful servant" (Matt. 25:21,23). Through Christ our Lord. Amen.

VI. DEEPER DISCOVERIES

A. Samson: Arnold or Donald?

If Hollywood were to produce a movie of Samson's life today, who would get the starring role? Originally Victor Mature played opposite Hedy Lamarr in the 1949 movie *Samson and Delilah*. But if the movie were to be made these days, the leading role would most certainly go to someone like Arnold Schwarznegger. However, did Samson look like someone who just stepped out of the gym or the professional wrestling ring? Possibly. But I'd like to suggest an alternative view:

- Scripture does not actually *say* Samson had a robust appearance (it *does* say this about Saul, David, and Absalom).

- Clearly his strength was not in his muscles, or else when the hair was cut and the muscles remained, his strength would not have been affected (unless there was a miracle of degeneration—an immediate atrophy, like letting the air out of a balloon—but then when his hair was growing back, were his muscles again filling out, and should the Philistines have noticed that before they permitted him to rest against the two pillars supporting the coliseum?).

- Delilah's relentless questioning was about the source of his strength, not the source of his muscles or the size of his frame. If his muscles were unusually huge, the answer would be obvious. (Similarly, the restoration of his strength would have been noticeable by the Philistines when he was brought to the temple of Dagon.) Instead, her questioning seems to be along the lines, "Why is your strength so disproportionate to your ordinary frame?"

- God's pattern of empowerment would seem to require that it was clear that Samson's strength was not natural but supernatural (consistent with Judges; so that accomplishments are unexplainable in human terms but point beyond us to God, from whom all blessings flow). The appearance of unusual musculature would leave that in doubt.

It is possible that his appearance would have been closer to Don Knotts than to Arnold Schwarznegger. Probably he was somewhere in-between, sort of average; maybe he looked like *you!*

B. God's Puzzling Sovereignty (14:4)

It is a mystery, but the text informs us that Samson's foolish choices were "from the LORD, who was seeking an occasion to confront the Philistines." This does not mean that God made Samsons' evil choices for him; rather, God was using the evil choices of men whom he knows exhaustively and infinitely to bring about his plan for the universe. In this story there is an inexorable chain of cause-and-effect relationships that moves toward the upsetting of the Philistine-Israeli truce. God was not in heaven wringing his divine hands, biting his celestial fingernails, uncertain about either the "end" or the "means to the end" in Samson's life.

Ephesians 1:11 refers to God as the one "who works out everything in conformity with the purpose of his will." There is comfort here. This means that nothing that happens to us is a surprise to God. It has first passed through his sovereign hand. It also means that there was, or is, or can be, a purpose for the circumstances of our lives.

C. Unequally Yoked

Scripture is clear that believers are to marry only other believers. This makes perfect sense, since otherwise the one thing that *should* be the most important thing in your life (your faith) is the one thing that you *cannot* share with the most important person in your life. Not only is it illogical; it is also unbiblical (1 Cor. 7:39, 2 Cor. 6:14–17; 1 Pet. 3:7, "heirs"). The reason why Abraham stopped asking God if the presence of ten righteous people would spare Sodom was because Lot and his wife had six children (which made eight), and two of them were married, which—since surely Lot would not allow his daughters to marry unbelievers—made ten!

D. A Constant Dripping

While Samson called his fiancée a "heifer," more accurately (in a worst case interpretation) she was a "nag." Proverbs paints verbal pictures of the "contentious woman" (Prov. 19:13; 21:9,19; 27:15) who wears down her husband with sharp words. By contrast, Proverbs paints a picture of the "adulterous woman" (Prov. 2:16; 5:3; 6:24; 7:5,21) as one who uses her words to flatter and entrap the unwary man. Even worse, how much more vulnerable is the man who is the target for the "adulterous woman" but who is married to the "contentious woman"? By way of contrast, God's pattern is laid out for the "noble," or "excellent," woman (Prov. 31:10–31).

VII. TEACHING OUTLINE

A. INTRODUCTION

1. Lead Story: God Is No Fool
2. Context: Samson's story divides into two geographical groupings: the Timnah Tales (chs. 14–15) and the Gaza Sagas (ch. 16). Both segments conclude with a statement of his time as a leader in Israel (15:20; 16:31) and are separated in time by twenty years.
3. Transition: At the end of chapter 13, readers have great hopes. God has intervened and sent a deliverer into the world, one who will surely serve him as a pious Nazirite all his days! Thus we enter the story of Samson's life entirely unsuspecting that the man he became was very different from the promise he foreshadowed. No matter where we turn in the life of Samson, there are negative lessons to be learned—patterns not to follow, warnings to be heeded. "We've only just begun."

B. COMMENTARY

1. Animal Desire (14:1–4)
2. Lion Attack (14:5–9)
3. Stag Party (14:10–14)
4. Heifer Tears (14:15–20)

C. CONCLUSION: GREAT EXPECTATIONS

VIII. ISSUES FOR DISCUSSION

1. Study these passages: Hebrews 12:1–2; 1 Corinthians 9:27; 10:12; 2 Peter 2:19. Make two columns and list the things in your life that

are "wings" (that encourage you spiritually) as opposed to "weights" (that drag you down).

2. People with little ability sometimes make a huge difference, and people with great ability sometimes make very little (positive) difference. Speculate: What is the difference that makes the difference? (Hint: think about the motto of John the Baptist, found in John 3:30.)

Judges 15

When God Becomes a Hobby

I. INTRODUCTION
I'll Fix Anthony

II. COMMENTARY
A verse-by-verse explanation of the chapter.

III. CONCLUSION
Walking the Walk That We Talk

An overview of the principles and applications from the chapter.

IV. LIFE APPLICATION
Vengeance Is . . . Whose?

Melding the chapter to life.

V. PRAYER
Tying the chapter to life with God.

VI. DEEPER DISCOVERIES
Historical, geographical, and grammatical enrichment of the commentary.

VII. TEACHING OUTLINE
Suggested step-by-step group study of the chapter.

VIII. ISSUES FOR DISCUSSION
Zeroing the chapter in on daily life.

Judges 15

I N   A   N U T S H E L L

*S*amson treated God as though he were a hobby, to attend to if there were time, but otherwise to be placed neatly on the shelf.

When God
Becomes a Hobby

I. INTRODUCTION

I'll Fix Anthony

*I*n Judith Viorst's children's book, *I'll Fix Anthony* (New York: Simon & Schuster, 1988), the younger brother complains about the way his older brother Anthony treats him:

> My brother Anthony can read books now, but he won't read any books to me. He plays checkers with Bruce from his school. But when I want to play he says, 'Go away or I'll clobber you.' I let him wear my Snoopy sweatshirt, but he never lets me borrow his sword. Mother says deep down in his heart Anthony loves me. Anthony says deep down in his heart he thinks I stink. Mother says deep, deep down in his heart, where he doesn't even know it, Anthony loves me. Anthony says deep, deep down in his heart he still thinks I stink. When I'm six I'll fix Anthony . . . When I'm six I'll float, but Anthony will sink to the bottom. I'll dive off the board, but Anthony will change his mind. I'll breathe in and out when I should, but Anthony will only go glug, glug.
>
> When I'm six my teeth will fall out, and I'll put them under the bed, and the tooth fairy will take them away and leave dimes. Anthony's teeth won't fall out. He'll wiggle and wiggle them, but they won't fall out. I might sell him one of my teeth, but I might not . . . Anthony is chasing me out of the playroom. He says I stink. He says he is going to clobber me. I have to run now, but I won't have to run when I'm six. When I'm six, I'll fix Anthony.

Those of us who have had older siblings understand that feeling, and smile at the childish set of the jaw toward miniature revenge. But an insatiable appetite for revenge can corrode the soul, as evidenced in the cynical remark by Heinrich Heine (1797–1856): "One should forgive one's enemies, but not before they are hanged." However, even though we may want to get even with someone who treats us badly, at the same time we don't have omniscience to know all the circumstances and motives behind their behavior. That's why God said in Romans 12:19: "Vengeance is mine; I will repay" (KJV; see Rom. 12:18–21).

Samson allowed vengeance to become the consuming motive of his life. He had one thought: "I'll fix the Philistines." He was neither concerned for God's glory nor for the well being of his people Israel. He wanted to satisfy his selfish desire for revenge.

II. COMMENTARY

When God Becomes a Hobby

MAIN IDEA: *Samson steers a course of vengeance as violence escalates from individual retribution to national revenge. In this chapter he is exposed as manipulative and self-centered.*

A Visitation (15:1–3)

SUPPORTING IDEA: *The catalyst for Samson's vendetta was his displacement as the groom of his own wedding.*

15:1–3. After a time of letting his seething anger simmer down, **Samson took a young goat and went to visit his wife.** We are informed that this visit took place **at the time of wheat harvest** (around the month of May), a detail that is significant for two reasons: first, because months have passed with no communication whatsoever with his "wife," and second, because the harvest will become a factor in the unfolding story (v. 5). Samson's insensitivity to his "wife"—returning to consummate the union as though he had not abandoned her—was astonishing. But it does inform us that when he left, Samson never planned to break off the marriage. He brought her a gift ("a young goat"), possibly a second millennium B.C. equivalent to a bouquet of roses, to assuage his guilt and her residual anger.

Her father, however, **would not let him go in** and explained, **I was so sure you thoroughly hated her . . . that I gave her to your friend** (or companion; see 14:20). The father suggested a solution that he hoped would be acceptable but which reveals his own callousness toward his daughters: **Isn't her younger sister**

more attractive? **Take her instead**. After all, by Samson's own stated criterion ("she looks good to me," 14:3 NASB), the younger daughter would also qualify.

However, Samson had been offended, and someone must pay! Rather than take revenge on the father or the daughter, he regarded all the Philistines as conspiring to disrespect him, and he was determined to make sure that they would regret it! He threatened that **this time** he would **get even with the Philistines**; he would **really harm them**. Samson felt morally justified (**I have a right**) in what he was about to do.

B Retribution (15:4–5)

> **SUPPORTING IDEA:** *Samson took revenge by destroying the Philistine harvest and insulting the Philistine religion.*

15:4–5. Samson embarked on an elaborate plan for revenge—one with both flair and cruelty. He **caught three hundred foxes and tied them tail to tail in pairs**, the reason for which will become apparent. Then he **fastened a torch to every pair of tails, lit the torches** and released the foxes **in the standing grain of the Philistines**. If he had released the animals singularly, in their terrified frenzy they would have run in one direction until the torch was extinguished; but tied tail to tail, they might zig-zag frantically to and fro. One may justly wonder if this were not a prank that Samson had done before; thus Samson knew what the foxes would do.

The added benefit of attaching one hundred and fifty mobile torches makes clear the point of Samson's revenge: he planned to destroy the local Philistine economy. His plan was successful. Four targets were effectively destroyed: First, "the standing grain"; second, **the shocks** (of harvested grain); third, **the vineyards**; and fourth, the **olive groves**. In so doing, Samson insulted their god Dagon, who was known (among other things) as the god of grain or harvest.

C Escalation (15:6–9)

> **SUPPORTING IDEA:** *After the Philistines retaliated by killing the only woman Samson ever intended to marry, he again avenged himself; as the conflict with Samson expanded through Israel, the Philistines tracked him down in Judah.*

15:6. *Philistine Revenge.* Dismayed at the destruction, **the Philistines asked, "Who did this?"** The collective reply, of course, was **Samson**, but the specific direction of their revenge was curious: he was identified as **the Timnite's son-in-law, because his wife was given to his friend.** They apparently would have agreed with Samson that the girl was indeed his wife, because instead of taking revenge on Samson for his action, they took revenge on the cause of Samson's action. They **burned her and her father to death** (nothing was said about the fate of the young Philistine to whom she had been given in marriage). Sadly, she fell victim to the very terror that had caused her to betray Samson in the first place (14:15).

15:7–8. *Samson's Revenge.* Presumably Samson was distraught over the consequences of his prank. Rather than be secretly pleased that father and daughter had gotten what they deserved, he determined to seek further revenge. After all, the only woman Samson ever intended to marry was now dead as a result of his actions. The chain reaction continued as Samson responded: **I won't stop until I get my revenge on you** (Heb., "but after that I will stop"), naively thinking that one more act of violence would terminate the chain reaction of violence. While we are told no details, Samson stopped acting indirectly, and simply **attacked** the Philistines **viciously and slaughtered many of them.** Afterward, he hid **in a cave in the rock of Etam** (an unknown location). However, Samson was wrong. This chain reaction was far from exhausted.

15:9. *Philistine Revenge.* Although Samson was a Danite (13:2), the place where he sought refuge was in the country of Judah. The Philistines had tracked Samson down and **camped in Judah, spreading out near Lehi**, a place-name that meant "jawbone." The conflict was escalating from the local level to the tribal level, from a private vendetta to a national crisis.

BOY MEETS GIRL

Another way to view the "Samson Stories" would be through a geographical lens: First, the Timnah Tales (Judg. 14–15), which end with a time indicator (twenty years, 15:20); second, the Gaza Sagas (Judg. 16), which end by repeating the same time indicator (twenty years, 16:31). One might speculate that during the Timnah Tales, Samson was about twenty-five years of age, which would make him about forty-five during the Gaza Sagas.

Changing our lens to the next power of magnification, the Timnah Tales could be viewed as the classic "Boy Meets Girl" story (the name of a 1938 romantic comedy starring James Cagney, Pat O'Brien, and a young actor named Ronald Reagan). Samson's take on "boy meets girl" was a little different from a charming comedy, however. Here is his screenplay, spread over two chapters:

A. Boy Sees Girl (14:1)—*Samson was in the Philistine stronghold of Timnah to "party" (drinking, gambling, women) when he saw a girl.*

B. Boy Wants Girl (14:2)—*According to Samson, he liked her looks and desired her.*

BOY MEETS GIRL

C. Boy Demands Girl (14:3–10)—*Samson did not listen to his parents; he wanted the unbelieving Philistine girl anyway.*

D. Boy Gets Girl (14:11–19)—*The marriage was arranged; at the bachelor party Samson gambled and lost (and was a sore loser).*

E. Boy Loses Girl (14:20–15:5)—*The girl's father married her off to someone else.*

F. Boy Really Loses Girl (15:6)—*She and her family were murdered in retaliation for Samson's revenge.*

G. Boy Avenges Girl (15:7–20)—*Furious, Samson took on the Philistines; he would show them!*

D Confrontation (15:10–13)

SUPPORTING IDEA: *Samson's fellow Israelites had no intention of being drawn into armed conflict with their Philistine masters. They preferred to leave their "status" as "quo." The story unfolds by means of dialogue in two confrontations. In the first, Judah was compliant; in the second, Judah was cowardly.*

15:10. *Dialogue #1: Philistines and Judah.* Spokesmen from Judah asked the Philistines, **Why have you come to fight us?** The Philistines explained that they had had enough of Samson, and they planned to take him prisoner **to do to him as he did to us** (while their meaning is vague, at least part of their intention may be inferred from 16:21). Presumably the Philistines expected to have to conquer Judah in order to subdue their supposed champion.

15:11–13. *Dialogue #2: Judah and Samson.* After making promises (one would assume) to the Philistines, **three thousand men** of Judah went to Samson and berated him with the petulant challenge, **Don't you realize that the Philistines are rulers over us?** We are struck by the contented assumption that this was the desired order of things (cp. 8:23). Their rebuke then became a whine: **What have you done to us?** Although Samson had done nothing directly to the Israelites, his actions shattered the status quo of their sham serenity. His reply was not unlike the Philistines' complaint against him: **I merely did to them what they did to me** (see 15:10, where they planned "to do to him as he did to us").

Thankfully, one redeeming aspect of this exchange is that Samson did not retaliate against his countrymen. He did exact a promise from them (because he did not entirely trust them): **Swear to me that you won't kill me yourselves.** They agreed, and Samson permitted them to bind **him with two new ropes**; then they **led him up from the rock**.

At this point one must back away from the story in amazement. Did Judah rally around God's choice of a judge and decide it was high time to obey God's command and take the land God told them to take? No. Judah was not interested in fighting at all. It is suspicious that Judah could not rally an army to challenge the Philistines, but they certainly did rally an army to extradite one man—one of their own!

🄴 Self-Commemoration (15:14–17)

SUPPORTING IDEA: *Samson prided himself in the fact that he humbled the Philistines, again ignoring the role of God's empowerment.*

15:14. *Samson Empowered by Spirit.* One might well suppose that Samson left his Israelite escort at a rendezvous point and walked toward **the Philistines** at **Lehi.** They **came toward him shouting** in celebration and anticipation of finally getting their revenge. But they got more than they bargained for. Two things happened to Samson, both of which were due to the direct intervention of God. First, miraculously the new **ropes on his arms** crumbled and fell apart **like charred flax, and the bindings dropped from his hands** (he did not snap the new ropes with his great strength, as some people misunderstand the passage). Second (but first chronologically), **the Spirit of the LORD came** (Heb., "rushed") **upon him in power.** He was now enabled to fight the Philistines.

15:15. *Samson Eradicated the Philistines.* His choice of weapons was strange, and his victory was solitary (as with Shamgar, 3:31). He did not kill a Philistine warrior and confiscate his weapons for this battle. Instead, he picked up the **jawbone of a donkey** (the condition of the bone was qualified with the adjective **fresh** to point out that again Samson violated his Nazirite vow). With the jawbone Samson **struck down a thousand men**, at odds even more miraculous than the four hundred and fifty-to-one odds Gideon faced against the Midianites (ch. 7). Here, however, the army did not turn against itself. The fierce conflict was face to face. Was Samson in a narrow pass that permitted Philistine warriors only limited access to him? We do not know. If there is a God who can intervene in human history, then no miracle is impossible or unreasonable.

15:16. *Samson Eloquent in Self-Praise.* Samson fancied himself as a man with a gift for words (see 14:14,18b) and tried to immortalize his achievement, not with a paean of praise such as that from Deborah in Judges 5. His poem was brief: **With a donkey's jawbone I have made donkeys of them.**

With a donkey's jawbone I have killed a thousand men. The couplet said nothing about divine help, much less did it praise the covenant Lord. Rather, Samson celebrated himself!

15:17. Samson Entitled "Jawbone Hill." He renamed the place **Ramath Lehi**, or "Jawbone Hill," which probably referred more to the mound of bodies than to any nearby topographical feature.

F Humiliation (15:18–19)

> **SUPPORTING IDEA:** *The God who rendered Samson victorious reminded Samson of his frailty; God ministered to Samson from grace, not merit.*

15:18–19. Samson's self-commemoration was immediately followed by an episode of humiliation. In an astonishing sequel to an astonishing story, Samson became acutely dehydrated! The record of his weakened condition is a reminder to us that God is the ultimate source of all things: military victory, empowerment, and even basic sustenance. Samson (who was dried out) **cried out to the LORD** (who is mentioned for the first time since the birth of Samson): **You have given your servant this great victory. Must I now die of thirst and fall into the hands of the uncircumcised?**

This complaint was disingenuous at several levels. First, he referred to himself as God's "servant," yet this was the first time in this story that he had spoken of God or to God. Second, the occasion for his prayer was a need he could not fill for himself—he called on God only when it was impossible to be self-reliant (not exactly the picture of intimacy desired by the Lord). Third, it was clear in the couplet in which he named "Jawbone Hill" that Samson intended to absorb all the glory for the victory to himself. Fourth, he lamented that surely God would not want him to fall into the contaminated hands of "the uncircumcised Philistines." Yet Samson was the rebel who lived and partied among them and then tried his best to marry into the Philistine community!

Despite the hypocrisy of the plea, God was gracious, and **opened up the hollow place in Lehi, and water came out of it**, meeting his physical need. He named the spring **En Hakkore**, which means "The Spring of the Caller"—not "The Spring of the Provider"—again calling attention to himself as the one who manipulated God! Even though Samson's vision was clouded, we see clearly that God is the Creator, the provider, the sustainer, and the one to whom all glory belongs.

G Jurisdiction (15:20)

SUPPORTING IDEA: *Before Samson's downfall he judged Israel for twenty years of relative peace.*

15:20. The Timnah Tales draw to a close with the statement that **Samson led Israel for twenty years in the days of the Philistines.** There is no reference to "rest" because, as the story of Samson began, we learned that he would only "begin" to deliver Israel (13:5). The next chapter leaps from the Timnah Tales (chs. 14–15) to the Gaza Sagas, twenty years later.

MAIN IDEA REVIEW: *Samson steers a course of vengeance as violence escalates from individual retribution to national revenge. In this chapter he is exposed as manipulative and self-centered.*

III. CONCLUSION

Walking the Walk That We Talk

They say that if you put a frog into a pot of boiling water, it will leap out right away to escape the immediate danger. But if you put a frog in a kettle that is filled with water that is cool and pleasant, and then you *gradually* heat the kettle until it starts boiling, the frog will not become aware of the threat until it is too late. The frog's survival instincts are geared toward detecting sudden changes.

Samson sank deeper and deeper into self-absorption, until he looked indistinguishable from all other pagans (if ever he was distinguishable!). A friend of mine tried repeatedly to get an unbeliever to go to church with him to consider what Christ was like. The unbeliever suggested that they attend their church league basketball tournament instead—he said he wanted to see if Christianity made any difference in the way the men behaved at play. After the game, the Christian was embarrassed, and the unbeliever was smug: "Just as I thought. There's no difference."

Somehow it seems unfair to God, doesn't it? After all, if you heard a seven-year-old butcher Bach on an accordion, it would be wrong to conclude that Bach was a horrible composer. We should not measure the composer by the performer or the playwright by the actor. Yet for some reason God has decided to use us and has subjected himself to this unfairness. He decreed that people come to Jesus through us and that we are to be ambassadors for Jesus Christ (2 Cor. 5:17–21; Eph. 6:20). Our lives are the only Bible most unbelievers will ever read. But if the print is too smudged, the right message does not get across. We need some revised versions. Our lives are to look like our Lord.

PRINCIPLES

- Several times as we near the end of the Book of Judges, we are exposed to this truth: these people are not *worth* saving. But God saves anyway, not because of the *people*, but because of his *promises*.
- Vigilante vengeance is a lose-lose proposition. Civil authorities are to dispense justice, but no one, except God, dispenses perfect justice. This he has promised to do (Rom. 12:17–21).
- Regardless of our conceits and illusions, we are not in control of our lives. Only God is, in whom we "live and move and have our being" (Acts 17:28).
- Our poor behavior reflects on the work of God in our lives. We honor him most when we represent him well (Eph. 4:1–32; 2 Cor. 5:17–21).

APPLICATIONS

- Don't take your own revenge; trust God to handle all inequities.
- Forgive those who have hurt you; your acceptance of them will speak more eloquently than a dozen sermons.
- Be a doer, not just a hearer, of God's commands (Jas. 1:22–25). "Walk your talk!"
- Praise God when victories—large and small—come your way. Even though you may have worked for some of them also, he is the only one "from whom all blessings flow."

IV. LIFE APPLICATION

Vengeance Is . . . Whose?

When Abraham Lincoln was an attorney, he was approached by a man who insisted on bringing a lawsuit for two dollars and fifty cents against an impoverished debtor whom he hated. Lincoln tried to discourage him, but the man was bent on revenge. Lincoln agreed to take the case and asked for a legal fee of ten dollars, which the man willingly paid. Lincoln then gave half the money to the defendant, who then settled and paid the two dollars and fifty cents! But even more amazing to Lincoln was the fact that his client was smugly satisfied. He had gotten revenge! (*Daily Walk,* May 22, 1992).

Revenge absorbs and consumes people, so that they don't think clearly. Let's assume someone has been unkind or even vicious to you, at work, or maybe at school. You know that you could plot to destroy him in creative ways: maybe sabotage results, maybe start a rumor that makes fun of him or ridicules his competency, his family life, or his character. Maybe he has sabotaged you! And so you say, to paraphrase Judith Viorst, "I'll fix him!" But is it *worth* it? And where does it *stop?*

If you retaliate, then your enemy has won in a sense; he has succeeded in bringing you down to his own level, in making you less than God wants you to be. Claire Boothe Luce said at the end of her life, "I don't have a warm personal enemy left. They've all died off. I miss them terribly because they helped define me." Some people live their lives with greater awareness of their enemies and who have hurt them than they have thoughts of their friends and family who love them. Samson was defined by his enemies. You can choose to behave like Samson or like the Savior. It's your choice.

V. PRAYER

"Lord, where we are wrong, make us willing to change; where we are right, make us easy to live with" (Peter Marshall, chaplain to the United States Senate, 1904–1949). We are more than willing to impute malicious motives to our enemies without giving a thought to our own motives. Preserve us from the spiritual myopia that hinders our vision of the larger picture of your grand will being done on earth, as it is in heaven. Through Christ our Lord. Amen.

VI. DEEPER DISCOVERIES

A. Foxes or Jackals?

The same Hebrew word is used for both "fox" and "jackal"; but foxes are solitary, whereas jackals run in packs; foxes are rare in Palestine, whereas jackals are plentiful. Thus we assume that Samson caught jackals, which have the reputation of being the "underworld" of the animal kingdom. They are vicious predators who kill and eat anything. Most people are glad to learn that Samson did not gather puppies or foxes; even so, Samson would hardly be a candidate for membership in his local chapter of the Society for the Prevention of Cruelty to Animals!

B. Donkey (15:16)

Verse 16 is difficult, and there is very likely a pun here. The Hebrew words for "donkey" and "heap" are spelled the same; the pun refers to the mounds of dead bodies piled in a heap. Samson added insult to injury, demeaning the prowess of the enemy Philistines.

VII. TEACHING OUTLINE

A. INTRODUCTION

1. Lead Story: I'll Fix Anthony
2. Context: Judges 14 and 15 take place mostly in Timnah, a Philistine stronghold. The Timnah Tales conclude with a time indicator (twenty years, 15:20); the Gaza Sagas (Judg. 16) also conclude with the repetition of the same time indicator (twenty years, 16:31). Although it is clear that Samson ignored God, God did not ignore Samson; he clearly intended to become the focus of his life (ch. 16).
3. Transition: Samson had left his wedding day enraged; months later he returned for his wedding night, only to be enraged again. As this chapter unfolds, the events that began in a house escalated to the events of a town, to the events of a countryside, and finally to the events of a nation.

B. COMMENTARY

1. Visitation (15:1–3)
2. Retribution (15:4–5)
3. Escalation (15:6–9)
   a. Philistine revenge (15:6)

b.   Samson's revenge (15:7–8)

c.   Philistine revenge (15:9)

4.   Confrontation (15:10–13)

a.   Dialogue #1: Philistines and Judah (15:10)

b.   Dialogue #2: Judah and Samson (15:11–13)

5.   Self-Commemoration (15:14–17)

a.   Samson empowered by Spirit (15:14)

b.   Samson eradicated the Philistines (15:15)

c.   Samson eloquent in self-praise (15:16)

d.   Samson entitled "Jawbone Hill" (15:17)

6.   Humiliation (15:18–19)

7.   Jurisdiction (15:20)

C. CONCLUSION: WALKING THE WALK THAT WE TALK

VIII. ISSUES FOR DISCUSSION

1. Reflect on the role of four women in the Samson story: a savvy, godly mother (ch. 13), a frazzled fiancée (ch. 14), a prostitute (ch. 16), and an enemy agent (ch. 16). What do you think motivated each one?

2. Discuss the following challenge by G. K. Chesterton in light of the Conclusion and the Life Application sections above: "Christianity has not been tried and found wanting, it has been found difficult and not tried."

3. In light of Samson's twenty-year judgeship without any evident spiritual growth on his part, reflect on this brief challenge: Would your level of spiritual maturity suggest that you have been a Christian for twenty years or a Christian for one year twenty times?

4. How would Samson have responded to the following statement by John Newton, composer of *Amazing Grace:* "I make it a rule of Christian duty never to go to a place where there is no room for my Master as well as myself."

Judges 16

A Fairy Tale—in Reverse!

"*I* have found within myself all I need and all I ever shall need. I am a man of great faith, but my faith is in George Gordon Liddy. I have never failed me."

George   Gordon   Liddy

Judges 16

IN A NUTSHELL

*B*etrayed and broken, Samson brought final revenge upon his enemies. His sad life comes to an end, redeemed only by his self-conscious brokenness.

A Fairy Tale—in Reverse!

I. INTRODUCTION

Famous Last Words

*H*umorists have enjoyed telling us about "famous last words" for decades, such as the following:

"No, really—these are the good kind of mushrooms."

"I'll hold it, and you light the fuse."

(Man looking up at much bigger man) "Gee, that's a precious tattoo."

(Man peering into a cave and poking at something) "He's probably just hibernating."

"And what happens if I push this button?"

"So, you're a cannibal."

(Man stretching head upwards) "What duck? What duck?"

If we put the jokes aside, some of the true famous last words of history are not quite so humorous. Reportedly, Winston Churchill's last words (before slipping into a final coma) were, "I'm bored with it all." Louise, Queen of Prussia (d. 1820) said, "I am a queen, but I have not the power to move my arms." Writer Edgar Allan Poe (d. 1849) said, "Lord, help my poor soul." One very poignant statement was from President James K. Polk (d. 1849) to his wife: "I love you Sarah. For all eternity, I love you."

The last words of many prominent Christians were written down for history. At his death John Wesley said, "The best of all is, God is with us!" John Calvin uttered these words: "Thou, Lord, bruisest me; but I am abundantly satisfied, since it is from Thy hand." Catherine Booth, the wife of the general of the Salvation Army, said, "The waters are rising, but so am I. I am not going under, but over. Do not be concerned about dying; go on living well, the dying will be right." Sir David Brewster, the inventor of the kaleidoscope, said, "I will see Jesus: I shall see him as he is. I have had the light for many years. Oh, how bright it is! I feel so safe and satisfied!"

Over the centuries, for many martyrs their sweetest times with their Lord were just before their deaths, even when all others had forsaken them because the Lord was still with them (Ps. 116:15; see Paul's statement in 2 Tim. 4:6–8). Thomas Becket, archbishop of Canterbury (murdered 1170) said, "I am ready to die for my Lord, that in my blood the Church may obtain liberty and peace." Joan of Arc was abandoned and said this just before her death: "It is better to be alone with God. His friendship will not fail me, nor His counsel, nor His love. In His strength, I will dare and dare and dare until I die."

The reformer John Huss was burned at the stake in 1415 with these words: "In the truth of the gospel which I preached, I die willingly and joyfully today." As the flames reached him, Huss was singing, "Jesus Christ, the Son of the living God, have mercy on me."

By contrast, these are Samson's famous last words: "O Sovereign LORD, remember me, O God, please strengthen me just once more, and let me with one blow get revenge on the Philistines for my two eyes. . . . Let me die with the Philistines!" (Judg. 16:28,30). These words do not exactly express the most noble sentiment one may hear, as "famous last words" go. But then, Samson himself was not all that impressive. We have said in the last chapters that Samson was equipped by God to do marvelous things for his Lord, but he squandered his potential. He invested his life in pursuing "little" goals. In this study we close the door on Samson's sad life.

II. COMMENTARY

A Fairy Tale—in Reverse!

MAIN IDEA: *Samson assumed he was accountable to no one for his life. But instead of living happily ever after, he became a broken man. At the end he was redeemed only by his self-conscious brokenness in the last act of his life, when tragedy became triumph and self-gratification became self-sacrifice.*

A From Grace to Disgrace, Case #1: The Philistine Prostitute (16:1–3)

SUPPORTING IDEA: *These three verses record "the thrill of victory" as Samson exposed the Philistine inhabitants of Gaza to public shame and ridicule.*

16:1–3. Samson assumed that the good things in his life—his gifts, his looks, his abilities—were his by right and not by grace, and that their purpose was to make him happy; he was wrong (read Rom. 2:4; Luke 12:48). If the pattern of other cycles were followed, we would now expect to read, "And the land had rest for twenty years," followed by Samson's obituary notice, and then, if true to pattern, a statement cataloging the descent of Israel into sin yet again. However, the story of Samson is not over, and his rebellious beginning is matched by his rebellious ending.

Gaza was the southernmost city among the Philistine Pentapolis (3:3), about forty-five miles away from his home. Samson had no business going again among his avowed enemies; he went simply to satisfy his appetites. Sure enough, at Gaza Samson **saw a prostitute**, and based on his previous patterns of yielding to his lusts (1 John 2:16), we are not surprised that Samson **went in to spend the night with her**.

Over the last two decades Samson had become notorious among the Philistines (beginning with the episodes of chs. 14 and 15). While in Gaza, he was recognized by his Philistine enemies. When word spread that Samson was in town, the men of the city decided to take action. Samson's last recorded victory over them was in an open battleground, but here he was confined within a Philistine stronghold. Surely, they reasoned, the odds and the gods were with them now! **They surrounded the place** ("buzzed around," as in Ps. 118:12a, "they swarmed around me like bees"). The verb probably does not describe a military action but a mob intention.

Their timetable was set: **At dawn we'll kill him**. Samson had a different timetable: he **lay there only until the middle of the night**, and then somehow (the means and method are uncertain—"cloak and dagger" under the cloak of darkness) made it undetected to **the city gate**, which he ripped from its frame with violent force (**together with the two posts**, he **tore them loose, bar and all**). With what must have been screeching noise, there may have been armed opposition, although none was recorded. We are told that in an astonishing feat of strength Samson **lifted them to his shoulders and carried them to the top of the hill that faces Hebron**. Probably he took the gates to the top of a nearby hill in Gaza, and there placed them on the Hebron side.

There is much we do not know about this event because the coverage is intentionally brief. The story illustrates what may be a "representative" encounter between Samson and the Philistines. Two factors emerge as dominant: Samson's appetites and the Philistine's animosity. Samson had not changed, and in fact he had gotten worse (this time he had no intention of marrying the woman). From the Philistine's standpoint, Samson remained—with good reason—at the top of their "Most Wanted" list.

B From Grace to Disgrace, Case #2: Delilah and Dagon (16:4–31)

SUPPORTING IDEA: *The rest of the chapter records, in detailed dialogue, the "agony of defeat." The "champ" became the "chump," a blind P.O.W. used as forced labor in the service of the Philistine god Dagon. Even so, God did not abandon Samson.*

16:4. *The Bait.* The story of Samson and Delilah is the longest vignette in the Samson cycle and is infamous in literature with its classic themes of lust, greed, betrayal, tragedy, vengeance, and restoration. It is easy to categorize Samson as a "he-man with a she-weakness" an idiot with a *femme fatal* flaw—and thus dismiss him from serious consideration other than a warning to men about temptations of the flesh. But this is far too easy, and it doesn't cut deeply enough. Samson's lust was a symptom of a greater problem: Samson was the center of Samson's world.

We recognize similarities from earlier in the Samson saga (ch. 14), only writ large. Samson has gained no wisdom from his past experiences. Initially the only good news was that his parents apparently had died (16:31) and were unable to witness these events. After the episode with the Gaza prostitute (but within perhaps a few months), Samson **fell in love with a woman.** For the first time, it is recorded that Samson developed a deep emotional attachment to a woman. In all of the Samson Saga, while women played critical roles, they were unnamed. His mother was unnamed, his betrothed was unnamed, and the prostitute was unnamed. Here, however, a woman was named: **Delilah.** The actual meaning of her name is uncertain, but probably means "flirtatious one," which would not be lost on the original readers (Prov. 5:3; 7:21). She lived not in the southernmost region of Philistia (the Gaza region) but in one of the northern Philistine cities.

16:5. *The Bribe.* The five **rulers** of the Philistine Pentapolis approached Delilah with a bribe: **Each one of us will give you eleven hundred shekels of silver.** The last time a woman betrayed Samson, she was motivated by self-preservation (14:15); this time Delilah would betray him because of self-indulgence (motivated by greed, she preferred silver to Samson). This amount was exorbitant, totaling 5,500 shekels, or 700 pounds by weight—over three times the amount Gideon received (1,700 shekels of gold, 8:26). The measure of the treasure reveals the Philistines' desperation to seize Samson.

These rulers were clear about their requirements of her and their intentions toward Samson. They wanted to know **the secret of his great strength**, and further **how we can overpower him so we may tie him up and subdue** [afflict or torture] **him**. Delilah was not uninformed about what would happen to Samson once she sold him out. His fate would be worse than death. It would be a life of captivity and torture. Twenty years before (ch. 14), Samson had regarded his betrothed as somewhat disposable; likewise he gave no thought to the fate of the prostitute in the early part of this chapter. Ironically, Delilah had exactly the same uncaring attitude toward Samson, despite his love for her.

16:6–27. *The Blowout.* After the Philistine rulers put their proposition to Delilah, there is no record of negotiations, debate, or even discussion. She embarked on a quest to uncover the source of Samson's strength. Verses 6–20 as a segment consists of four "rounds" of sparring between the two lovers comprised of (a) four attempts by Delilah to wheedle information from Samson, (b) four responses by Samson, each time explaining the source of his strength, (c) Samson's closing assertion each time that he would then be like any other man (notice his recognition that he was different from all other men, a uniqueness that would soon change), and (d) four actions by Delilah to test the information Samson gave her.

16:6–9. *Round 1: The Winner Is . . . Samson.* The first attempt Delilah made was overt; she asked him, **Tell me the secret of your great strength and how you can be tied up and subdued** (see "Samson's 'Blindness' to Delilah" below).

Samson's first response to Delilah was a creative "throwaway." His strength would evaporate **if anyone ties me with seven fresh thongs**. The meaning is either leather strips or "tendons"—either would be from a recently slaughtered animal (see Ps. 11:2, where the term refers to bowstrings). In either case, they were not to be dried, and their freshness again violated God's laws of uncleanness in general, and Samson's Nazirite vow in particular. Samson claimed that he would then **become as weak as any other man**.

After he was asleep, the Philistines brought Delilah **seven fresh thongs** with which she bound him. Presumably she (or the Philistines) felt that his readily forthcoming answer was a major secret just too easily divulged. So rather than bind him and have the Philistines arrive to pick him up, the **men were hidden in the room.** Then Delilah raised the alarm, **Samson, the Philistines are upon you!** Samson **snapped the thongs as easily as a piece of string snaps when it comes close to a flame.** So, at least in "round 1," the secret of his strength was not discovered.

16:10–12. *Round 2: The Winner Is . . . Samson.* No one likes to be ridiculed or taken lightly, and thus Delilah's wheedling complaint (**you have made a fool of me; you lied to me**) was probably not a surprise to Samson. This time when she asked for the truth about his strength, he offered a more reasonable answer (but one that had a twenty-year-old history with the Philistines). His reason for answering at all is illusive. However, the answer of **new ropes that have never been used** sounds quite reasonable to a superstitious group of Philistines (even as it had seemed reasonable to the men of Judah in 15:13). **So Delilah took new ropes and tied him with them. Then, with men hidden in the room, she called to him, "Samson, the Philistines are upon you!"**

Had there been any survivors from "Jawbone Hill" twenty years before, they might have forewarned their comrades that new ropes were not effective against Samson, who **snapped the ropes off his arms as if they were threads.**

16:13–14. *Round 3: The Winner Is . . . a "Tie."* Again the same appeal from Delilah evoked a response. Presumably (because of the simple logistics of the sleep cycles required) we are expected to assume that these episodes took place over a period of several days (or weeks; see v. 16, day after day). Finally, in this third round, Samson got closer to the truth (although Delilah did not know it at the time). He told her that **if you weave the seven braids of my head into the fabric on the loom and tighten it with the pin,** his strength would evaporate. The logistics of this are uncertain: perhaps his eyes cast about the room and rested on a nearby loom that Delilah used, and then later as he slept she interwove the braided locks of his hair with the fabric he saw on the loom. Certainly it did not work: He **awoke from his sleep and pulled up the pin and the loom, with the fabric.**

This round, however, may be considered a "tie" (with apologies for the pun). While in the previous two rounds, thongs and new ropes were not even close to the truth, mentioning his hair as a part of his response was too close for comfort. Samson was playing with fire, setting himself up for a "close shave."

Samson's "Blindness" to Delilah

Within this chapter, it is appropriate to pause and ask some obvious questions: How could Samson not see this coming, particularly in the face of mounting evidence? How could he not be suspicious? Was he, as several commentators suggest, simply an extraordinarily stupid man?

If a banker's girlfriend were to ask him, "Please tell me the code to disarm the security system and the combination to the vault," surely it would cause him to ask, "Exactly why do you want to know?" While Samson has long been characterized as "a he-man with a she-weakness" (and this is revealed with crystal clarity here), his problem was probably due to his "me-weakness."

The term *hubris* captures the idea; it refers to "wanton insolence or arrogance resulting from excessive pride." This was the pattern of Samson's life throughout the Timnah Tales (chs. 14–15). One factor contributing to his downfall was that Samson came to consider himself invulnerable. For all of his life no one was able to afflict him in any way. Apparently Samson saw no personal threat, and he chose to regard Delilah's interrogations as foreplay, a game with the prize of his own self-gratification. In his mind he was not just any man. He was Superman, living in denial that he was playing with his own form of "Kryptonite."

Scripture indicates that rebellious hearts willingly suppress truth. In Samson's case, it may be that the consequences of not suppressing those suspicions were simply too painful for Samson to face. It would have meant this: although he loved Delilah, not only did she not *love* him, not only did she not *like* him, but she *loathed* him—enough to sell him into slavery and torture! One definition of "male" is "an ego wrapped in skin." While this is simplistic and possibly silly, the truth is that when one's self-worth and one's self-identity rest squarely on one's ego and on nothing else, then forcing oneself to face mounting evidence that destroys one's ego becomes almost impossible. The problem is not with the evidence but resides in a prior commitment that has too much at stake to be wrong. Samson's hubris rendered him unable to admit the truth.

16:15–20. *Round 4: The Winner Is . . . Delilah! Samson Is Out!* Finally, Delilah nagged Samson to the point of no return. She pretended to long for intimacy, for the sharing of his deepest secret self, which she defined as disclosure of the secret of Samson's great strength. If he did not open himself to her, she said, she would assume he did not love her (the first mention of love by Delilah). It may be that she withheld her favors from him during this time as well. Samson's reason for sharing was not to achieve intimacy (his attitude toward marital intimacy was established twenty years before in 14:16) but because he was **tired to death** of her **nagging**. She prodded him **day after day** (see 14:16–17). Never a "strong" man (of character), Samson finally relented to her cajoling (see Prov. 21:9,19; 27:15) and **told her everything**. The enemy agent finally achieved her goal!

Samson told her that **no razor** had **ever been used on** his **head**. In order to enfeeble Samson, surely that should have been sufficient information. Nothing more need be said. But Samson bared his soul and traveled far beyond a "need to know" basis; he explained the rationale for his barberless condition—he was an agent of **God since birth**. He did not use the covenant name for the Lord but rather the generic name for a supreme being, an indication of his lack of intimacy with God. Being familiar with his lifestyle, Delilah may have wondered in what sense (other than volume of hair) Samson was **set apart to** his God, as he claimed! Regardless, she knew the ring of truth when she heard it. She now knew that if his head was shaved, his strength would leave him.

So certain was Delilah that **she sent word to the rulers of the Philistines, "Come back once more; he has told me everything."** So the rulers of the **Philistines returned with the silver in their hands**. Meanwhile, she procured the services of someone **to shave off the seven braids of his hair** after she had soothed **him to sleep on her lap**. Although the spiritual condition of Samson is deplorable, the character of Delilah is pointedly vicious.

The sad denouement to this portion of the story played out inevitably; Delilah called, **Samson, the Philistines are upon you**, and on awakening he assumed that he was, as always, in control, independent, and autonomous. This ultimate in "rude awakenings" climaxed with one of the saddest statements in the Samson Saga: **He did not know that the LORD had left him**, the trough of Samson's life. It's one thing to be bereft of God's presence; it's quite another to be so spiritually insensitive that you assume that such a thing has not, and could not, happen to you. It's one thing to lack fellowship with God; it's quite another to be so at variance with God that you don't *know* that you don't know that you lack that eternal relationship.

By confiding his Nazirite vow, he had moved from ignoring God to abandoning God. Now for the first time in his life he would know what it was like to be abandoned by God. When people stubbornly and persistently suppress truth, God may give them over to their own self-generated lies (Rom. 1:24,26,28).

16:21–27. *From Champ to Chump: Samson's Tragic Destiny.* Samson had not realized how close he had come and that his strength "hung by a hair." Of course, the cutting of the hair was not magical. It was simply the last of a three-strand link to God that had been systematically severed, one strand at a time. Ecclesiastes 4:12 refers to the progression of strength found among brothers: "Though one may be overpowered, two can defend themselves. A cord of three strands is not quickly broken."

Samson chose to reverse that process, strand by strand. His link to God was his Nazirite vow, a cord of three strands. As Samson cut them one by one, he did not realize his accruing peril. Perhaps, had his strength diminished proportionately each time he yielded to his appetites, he would have been more vigilant. But he drank wine (repeatedly), he had contact with the dead (carcass of lion, carcasses of men from whom he had taken clothing, fresh jawbone, fresh thongs), and finally divulged the secret of his hair. Others might object that here at least Samson was a victim. But Samson chose love for Delilah over loyalty to the Lord and in effect placed himself in the barber's chair.

The horror of verse 21 is stated with economy: **the Philistines seized him, gouged out his eyes and took him down to Gaza. Binding him with bronze shackles, they set him to grinding in the prison.** One may only wonder at the terror in Samson's mind at the fact that he was now vulnerable to capture and torture, the victim of the most horrible punishments imaginable. It is one thing to lose a limb; it is quite another to lose a sense, particularly the sense of sight that Samson valued and yet abused (recall from 14:1, he "saw" the Timnah woman). For the first time in his life Samson realized that he was no longer in control.

The rest of the story played itself out in Gaza—a suitable place in the minds of the Philistines perhaps because it was here that Samson humiliated an entire Philistine city (16:3). He was given a new role. Rather than serving as God's pro tem deliverer, he was bound with bronze shackles and became the Philistine's grinder of grain in a prison, but for how long we do not know. The debasement of this role was poignant and filled with contrasts. First, "Sunny-boy" was now in permanent darkness. Second, he was given a task for a beast of burden, functioning much like a donkey (the irony of his prior prowess when he used the jawbone of a donkey). Third, he had destroyed the grain crop of the Philistines, so they set him to work as a grinder of their new grain. Finally, the Philistine god Dagon was the god of grain, and the humiliation of Samson's forced labor was a statement by the Philistines of the superiority of their god, who had exacted revenge upon Samson, who had burned much of Dagon's harvest. He was demeaned, debased, disgraced, and degraded.

Still, **the hair on** Samson's **head began to grow again**. The careful reader will take note of the significance of this detail: even in prison God had not abandoned Samson.

The city leaders of the Philistine Pentapolis held a celebration in which they praised their god and offered **sacrifice to Dagon**. The praise was amplified in relation to Samson: **Our god has delivered our enemy into our hands, the one who laid waste our land and multiplied our slain**. In their view, Dagon had finally vindicated himself and humbled the one who had humiliated them. The only thing that would make the celebration better was a collective gloating with Samson as the primary object lesson of the superiority of Dagon. Their shout, **Bring out Samson to entertain us**, was met with action. **They called Samson out of the prison, and he performed for them**, in the sense that his condition was itself a source of their perverse entertainment.

We have no way of knowing if Samson had deliberated what he might do if he were given the chance or if he simply took advantage of an opportunity. When he discovered where he was and what he was there for, he asked the attendant who had brought him up from prison to place him where he could **feel the pillars that support the temple**, so he could **lean against them**. As far as the Philistines were concerned, they would not have let mighty Samson the warrior near those pillars, but blind, weak Samson was no threat.

While Samson may not have known how many people were enjoying his misery, we are told that **the temple was crowded**, and the balcony roof held **about three thousand** people. Very likely between five and ten thousand people, including the rulers of the Philistine Pentapolis, were enjoying the view of what Samson could not see. Samson, however, did not plan to be their entertainer; he planned to be their executioner.

16:28–31. *The Comeback: Samson's Final, Fatal Feat of Faith.* Although Samson was in the temple of Dagon, he was aware of the reality of the covenant Lord and the deceitfulness of the Philistine god. For the second time we are privy to a prayer of Samson. This time he prayed to the Lord, asking God to **remember** him. The concept of remembering encapsulates a common concept in Scripture: "God remembered Noah" (Gen. 8:1). Of course, the omniscient Lord had not *forgotten* Noah, but the verb can bring the connotation, "to act in behalf of." Samson's request was specifically that God would **strengthen me just once more**. Samson's motive may have been less than worthy (**let me with one blow get revenge on the Philistines for my two eyes**), but it is clear that

(a) he trusted the Lord, (b) he knew no other God was true or real, (c) he knew that God was the source of his strength, and (d) he knew that he had to depend upon the Lord to salvage anything from his life.

God answered Samson's prayer, including the plea to **let me die with the Philistines**. After placing his hands on **the two central pillars on which the temple stood**, with **his right hand on the one and his left hand on the other**, he **pushed with all his might**, and the temple collapsed **on the rulers** of the Philistines and **all the people** who were there. Block remarks, "Ever the entertainer, Samson literally brings the house down" (Block, 469). The beginning of his story contained an episode over which he had no control: his *miraculous birth* and Nazirite dedication, instigated by God. The ending of his story reveals Samson as a man who is now aware that he has no control, and the Samson saga closes with a *miraculous death*—empowered by God.

This grisly episode is followed by a poignant statement. Even though in his life Samson had turned away from his own people, in his death his own people did not turn away from him. **His brothers and his father's whole family went down to get him** (retrieving his body from the rubble of a collapsed structure is something that Americans are familiar with since September 11, 2001). If these were biological brothers (as they seem to be), then Manoah and his wife had been granted other children by the Lord. From Gaza **they brought him back and buried him . . . in the tomb of Manoah his father.**

Scripture offers three epilogues to the story of Samson, two of which are obituary statements in this passage. First, Samson **killed many more when he died than while he lived**. Almost like the man who committed suicide because his insurance made him more valuable dead than alive, Samson had little to live for; when measured against his potential, this was a poor victory. Second, there is an echo of the statement in 15:20, **he had led Israel twenty years**. These two statements together comprise the "epitaph" to be carved over the span of Samson's life.

The last statement is found in Hebrews 11:32–34, "And what more shall I say? I do not have time to tell about Gideon, Barak, Samson, Jephthah, David, and Samuel and the prophets, who through faith conquered kingdoms, administered justice, and gained what was promised; who shut the mouths of lions, quenched the fury of the flames, and escaped the edge of the sword; whose weakness was turned to strength; and who became powerful in battle and routed foreign armies." Some of the heroes in Hebrews 11 lived lives of faith and faithfulness; some of them, however, had only great moments of faith, such as Samson's last moments. In a significant way Hebrews 11 is both a "Hall of Faith" as well as a "Hall of Salvage"—every person in the chapter had times of significant failure. Samson, at the pivotal moment at the end of his life, "from weakness was made strong"—by faith!

> **MAIN IDEA REVIEW:** *Samson assumed he was accountable to no one for his life. But instead of living happily ever after, he became a broken man. At the end he was redeemed only by his self-conscious brokenness in the last act of his life, when tragedy became triumph and self-gratification became self-sacrifice.*

III. CONCLUSION

The Illusion of Independence

Samson thought he was in control of his strength and of his destiny. But absolute self-determination is an illusion! When Timothy McVeigh was executed on June 11, 2001, for the Oklahoma City bombing of the Alfred P. Murrah building (killing 168 people), he made no statement except to issue the well-known poem "Invictus" published in 1875 by fellow agnostic William E. Henley (1849–1903):

> Out of the night that covers me,
> Black as the Pit from pole to pole,
> I thank whatever gods may be
> For my unconquerable soul.
> In the fell clutch of circumstance
> I have not winced nor cried aloud.
> Under the bludgeonings of chance
> My head is bloody, but unbowed.
> Beyond this place of wrath and tears
> Looms but the horror of the shade,
> And yet the menace of the years
> Finds, and shall find me, unafraid.
> It matters not how strait the gate,
> How charged with punishments the scrolls,
> I am the master of my fate:
> I am the captain of my soul.

This is a classic statement of self-dependence, of defiance, and of self-reliance against all that the world can do to you! But Henley found out when his five-year-old daughter became sick and died that the meaning of his poem was empty. Every person reading this knows that all it takes is one telephone call for your world to fall apart. We are not in control; God is. We are not the infallible judge of what is good and right; God is. We are not the architect of our destiny; God is. And we are not the captain of our soul; God is.

PRINCIPLES

- Every talent and ability you possess is yours as a gift from God; you are accountable to him for the stewardship of the gifts entrusted to you.
- To the extent that one's focus is fixed on oneself, to that extent self-deception exists.
- God is in control of our lives, and his gracious love will not let us go; he is faithful to his promises (2 Tim. 2:13).
- Even though there is always hope for repentance and renewal, the consequences (or scars) of sin may remain.

APPLICATIONS

- Give your body to God as a living sacrifice (Rom. 12:1–2).
- Avoid placing yourself in situations or circumstances that will tempt you (1 Cor. 9:27; Phil. 4:8).
- When temptation is before you, rely on God's strength to withstand; you do not have to yield (1 Cor. 10:13).
- Examine how you are investing your life. Are your goals big enough?

IV. LIFE APPLICATION

In Pursuit of Little Goals

A few years ago three hundred whales were marooned in shallow water because they were chasing schools of sardines when the tide went out. For most of his life, Samson was like a whale chasing a sardine—a great power chasing little goals. What are little goals? Goals that are self-serving. Like Esau, Samson surrendered his birthright for little goals. John Piper says that sin "gets its power by persuading me to believe that I will be more happy if I follow it. The power of all temptation is the prospect that *it will make me happier*" (cited in *Putting Your Past Behind You* by E. Lutzer, San Bernadino, CA: Here's Life, 1990, p. 54). This is the same pattern of temptation that we see in Eden: "You will be like God" (Gen. 3:5).

Samson had power without purity, and he pursued little goals—his own private sensual fulfillment. Samson never got the woman he wanted, but the tragedy was that he never became the man God wanted. True, God forgives (1 John 1:9). But forgiveness does not necessarily erase consequences. David repented, but Uriah the Hittite was still dead. Samson did grow new hair, but he didn't grow new eyes.

V. PRAYER

Lord, this story is all too real. We are surrounded by temptations to invest our lives in trivial goals. You have given each one of us abilities to use for your glory. May we exercise good stewardship of what you have entrusted to us. We ask that the goals in which we invest our lives would be worthy of eternity. Lord, we have seen that Samson died for what he lived for. May we live for what we say we would die for. Through Christ our Lord, Amen.

VI. DEEPER DISCOVERIES

A. City Gate (16:3)

The city gates were important to any town in the Old Testament world. They were the focus of security and defense. Further, they served as the location where the people gathered for adjudication and for community events (see Ruth 4:1; Prov. 31:31; Neh. 2:3). Often they were attached on either side to tall gate-houses; the norm would be that multiple guard stations would be positioned just inside the gates themselves. It is likely that they were covered with metal sheets to make them fireproof against attack; they were massive, studded with nails, and incredibly heavy.

B. Dagon (16:23)

Dagon was the god of grain, but artifacts found at Ugarit (a city-state destroyed by the Philistines around 1200 B.C.) suggests that Dagon was also regarded as the father of Baal. The Philistines adopted the worship of Dagon after their territorial expansion had begun. This indicates that the religious system of the Canaanites beguiled more people than just the Israelites. The worship of Dagon was most extensive soon after the beginning of the United Kingdom under Saul (2 Sam. 5:1–7).

C. The Architecture of Dagon's Temple

"Although no Philistine temple to Dagon has been discovered in Gaza, excavations at Tell Qasile have revealed a building in Stratum X that illuminates the impressions left by this text. The roof and upper story of this large temple were supported by two cedar pillars slightly less than three meters apart set on round stone bases" (Block, 466).

D. Suicide

Samson's death may be categorized as suicide by some, but the term requires definition. Selfish suicide occurs when a person is so absorbed in his own pain that he takes his life. Selfless or "beneficent" suicide occurs when one chooses to give one's life for the benefit of another (Rom. 5:7). A third and different kind of suicide is that of Samson, in which one chooses to give one's life for the detriment of another; this is good or bad depending on whether one is engaged in a context akin to a "just war." A final and unprecedented kind of suicide took place on the cross, in which the unique Son of God chose (Mark 10:45; John 10:18) to give his life for the benefit of his enemies (Rom. 5:8–10)!

VII. TEACHING OUTLINE

A. INTRODUCTION

1. Lead Story: Famous Last Words
2. Context: After the story of Jephthah (Judg. 11–12), we are hard-pressed to imagine anything worse that could happen in the unfold-

ing story of Israel. Almost everything that can go wrong has gone wrong. Even so, the closure of the story of Samson reaches even greater depths of compromise as God's deliverer ignored his Lord. What follows next are the final episodes of depravity (chs. 17–18; 19–21) that cause us to ask whether this people is worth God's effort. Why does he continue to preserve them? The answer, of course, resides not in the redeemed but in the character of the Redeemer!

3. Transition: Judges 16 concludes the "Samson Saga." In Judges 14 and 15 Samson's life of selfishness was exposed, but after twenty years of influence (and of annoying the Philistines), chapter 16 reveals that Samson was still as self-absorbed as ever. Only through the tragedy of separation from God did he come to appreciate the possibility of closeness to God.

B. COMMENTARY

1. From Grace to Disgrace, Case #1: The Philistine Prostitute (16:1–3)
2. From Grace to Disgrace, Case #2: Delilah and Dagon (16:4–31)
   a. The bait (16:4)
   b. The bribe (16:5)
   c. The blowout (16:6–27)
      (1) Round 1: The winner is . . . Samson (16:6–9)
      (2) Round 2: The winner is . . . Samson (16:10–12)
      (3) Round 3: The winner is . . . a "tie" (16:13–14)
      (4) Round 4: The winner is . . . Delilah! Samson is out! (16:15–20)
      (5) From champ to chump: Samson's tragic destiny (16:21–27)
   d. The comeback: Samson's final, fatal feat of faith (16:28–31)

C. CONCLUSION: THE ILLUSION OF INDEPENDENCE

VIII. ISSUES FOR DISCUSSION

1. Go through the three chapters that contain Samson's saga and make two lists. First, list his opportunities to be used by God that were ignored. Second, list the ways he violated his Nazirite vow.

2. Other people have observed that God does not dry dock failures; he refits them (even when they are to be used for only one final journey). Think your way through some cases in Scripture in which God took wounded warriors, scars and all, and allowed them to become instruments of his glory.

3. Consider the goals that we set for our lives. Are they big enough? Are they worthy of the time and talent that God has entrusted to us? What are some of the goals Samson could have set for his life but failed to do?

4. God has equipped all believers with his Word and with spiritual gifts. Study the word *equip* in 2 Timothy 3:16–17 and Hebrews 13:20–21. While our gifts are different from those of Samson, consider ways in which we are to be good stewards of what God has entrusted to us.

5. Reflect on this proposition: There are two lies Satan wants us to believe. First, that "just once won't hurt," and second, "Now that you have crossed the threshold and have ruined your life, you might as well give up the struggle and enjoy sinning."

6. Often people speak of "brokenness." Charles Spurgeon got it right when he said, "We are but men, frail, feeble, and apt to faint." Why is it that when we are broken by suffering, God's power shines through? Study 2 Timothy 2:20–26 and 2 Corinthians 11:16–12:10.

Judges 17–18

Creating God in Our Own Image

Judges 17–18

I N   A   N U T S H E L L

The story of "religion for hire" illustrates what happened when everyone was doing what was right in their eyes rather than in God's eyes. God's people who choose to ignore God's commands and refuse to worship God's way are in peril of God's wrath.

Creating God in Our Own Image

I. INTRODUCTION

A Fanciful Tale of a Flat Tire

*T*ommy is fifty-eight years old. Forty years ago, he was trying to decide between colleges; should he go to Virginia Tech or the University of Tennessee? It was a toss-up. Well, Tommy's tire had a blowout as he began a trip to visit Virginia Tech. He couldn't get it fixed in time to arrive for his appointment, and it was getting late. He just decided not to go. At all. Since he had already visited and been accepted at Tennesee, he took his blowout as a kind of cosmic confirmation that he should go there.

What he did not know was that if he had gone to visit Virginia Tech, he would have loved it and attended there instead. Janet was a student there from Grand Rapids, Michigan, and she would have become his wife. They would have had a home of laughter and grace and four children: Tommy Jr., Bill, Ethan, and Gail. Ethan grew up and became a research doctor, who invented and patented a new kind of heart valve that saved thousands of lives (including a woman named Frances who lived in Chattanooga). Tommy invested heavily in his son's invention, which would see him into a comfortable retirement.

But Tommy didn't go to Virginia Tech; he went to Tennessee and met a girl named Carol. They married, and it was rough going. They had their ups and downs and separated a couple of times. Finally, she left him for another man. No children. He got a job in Chattanooga and later met and married a divorcee named Frances, who had three children, two of whom were very troubled and rebellious. There was no harmony in the home, no laughter, no joy. Six years after marrying Frances, doctors discovered that she had a heart condition, and in time all insurance companies dropped them. Tommy finally found a way to pay for an operation to implant a heart valve; unfortunately, the valve was not very effective, and after post-operative care drained all of their finances, Frances died. Tommy was left penniless with three miserable step-children. If only, forty years before, Tommy hadn't had a flat tire!

Is that the way life is? Is the course of your life dependent upon this or that chance circumstance, with your entire life's happiness resting on whether or not you have a flat tire? In Judges 17 and 18 a relatively small choice set in motion a chain of events that resulted in the destruction of a family, the degradation of a priesthood, and the decimation of a tribe. But not by chance—by God's design.

II. COMMENTARY

Creating God in Our Own Image

MAIN IDEA: *Judges 17–18 contains the story of people who had the right words but insisted that it was okay with God if they worshiped him on their terms, not his. This cause became the catalyst that set in motion an array of devastating effects. These events were not simply the result of chance but of choices. The little choices we make can have big consequences. Even so, God "works out everything in conformity with the purpose of his will" (Eph. 1:11).*

A The Failure of a Family (17:1–6)

SUPPORTING IDEA: *Family disintegration is illustrated in the family of Micah—who was guilty of stealing, lying, and idolatry.*

17:1–6. The story begins with an introduction to **a man named Micah**, a shortened form of "Micayahu," or "Who is like the Lord?" Two significant events have already taken place: first, Micah had stolen **eleven hundred pieces of silver** from **his mother**, almost a fortune (cp. 8:26 and 16:5). Second, he heard his mother **utter a curse** against the life of the thief. We enter the story almost in mid-confession: **I took it** (he avoided using the stronger verb "stole"). Instead of the promised malediction, his mother blessed him: **The LORD bless you, my son.** In their minds, the benediction canceled the curse. This was nothing more than Hebrew "voodoo," an attempt to manipulate spiritual forces through formulae.

Further, she consecrated her **silver to the LORD** for her **son to make a carved image and a cast idol.** Hebraists rightly suggest that we understand the two terms to describe the carving of an idol, which was then overlaid with silver plate. Then she pledged to her son, **I will give it back to you.**

Before continuing in this story, it is appropriate to pause and observe that this is not a sweet story of a child who felt guilty, confessed a minor crime, and then received his doting mother's gracious forgiveness. While Micah and his mother employed pious words, this was just a veneer. Micah was an older man who stole from his mother, thus violating the fifth commandment (honoring parents) and the eighth commandment (stealing). He confessed only when he heard his mother utter a curse, and he was motivated by superstition and self-preservation.

Micah **returned the eleven hundred shekels of silver to his mother,** who then uttered words of consecration over the fortune "to the Lord for my son to make . . . a cast idol." Thus Micah was to blend the worship of the one true God with the superstitious worship of the Canaanites, using the ephod and teraphim together (teraphim were small household idols; see 17:5; 18:14,17,20). The dedication of one's wealth to the covenant Lord in order to make an idol was utterly incongruous (like a "square circle" or a "bigamous bachelor"), a bizarre contradiction in terms!

Micah's mother **took two hundred shekels** (not the promised eleven hundred; she kept over four-fifths for herself after all!) and **gave them to a silversmith, who made them into the image and the idol,** which were **put in Micah's house**. Micah did not worship God at the place God commanded (in Shiloh; see Deut. 12:4–27) but made worship a matter of convenience (at home). Thus **Micah had a shrine, and he made an ephod and some** Canaanite **idols.** He compounded his offense by ignoring the means of true worship, the Levitical priesthood. Instead, he installed one of his own sons as his priest.

The episode concludes with a transitional and paradigmatic statement: **In those days Israel had no king; everyone did as he saw fit** (or "what was right in his own eyes," NASB). These people were not making idols of Baal but of the Lord. They were sincere in their worship, but they were absolutely wrong—self-deceived, self-deluded, and under the wrath of God.

🅑 The Perversion of the Priesthood (17:7–13)

SUPPORTING IDEA: *The degradation of the priesthood is exposed when a Levite is willing to be bribed into becoming a "priest for hire."*

17:7–13. The segment begins by introducing **a young Levite** (we are not told his name or background at this point) **from Bethlehem in Judah** (a phrase which occurs three times in verses 7–9 in Hebrew, two times in NIV), **who had been living within** the territory **of Judah**. Modern readers need to understand what ancient readers knew: Levites were given no territory of their own but were assigned to live in cities among other tribes. However, Bethlehem was not one of the Judean cities assigned to Levites. This particular young man was on the prowl, looking for a way to better his life (according to his definition), **in search of some other place to stay.**

He came to Micah's house, and his host asked him where he was from. The young man responded that he was **a Levite from Bethlehem in Judah**, and that he was **looking for a place to stay**. Levites were dedicated to priestly service, but only those descendants of the house of Aaron were permitted to serve as priests. This young man was unqualified for two reasons: First, he was not of the house of Aaron; second, it was likely that he was under the prescribed age for priestly service (Num. 4:3,30).

Micah recognized an opportunity to move a bit further toward priestly legitimacy, so he offered a proposition: **Live with me and be my father** (see 5:7) **and priest**. Of course this meant that Micah would displace his own son (who was too young and not qualified) with another man (who was too young and not qualified but of the tribe of Levi). Micah offered him a salary and benefits: **I'll give you ten shekels of silver a year, your clothes and your food** (a far cry from the priestly stipend mandated in Deut. 18:3–4,8). So Micah, who had originally stolen eleven hundred shekels from his mother, "bought" a priest, a young opportunist who was willing to become a "mercenary minister."

Micah treated the young man **like one of his sons**. Micah thought God could be bribed and that the Levite was a "good luck charm" that brought his sanctuary legitimacy: **Now I know that the LORD will be good to me**. As we shall see, Micah's optimism was premature.

ⓒ The Corruption of the Clan of Dan (18:1–31)

SUPPORTING IDEA: *The sins of Israel multiply as the tribe of Dan bribe the Levite and butcher the people of Laish.*

18:1–3a. *Introduction of Dan.* The next chapter continues the story of Micah and the Levite, repeating the phrase **in those days Israel had no king**. But the chapter introduces new characters, and the cast enlarges segment by segment. The **Danites** (exemplars of tribal apostasy) had disobeyed God;

they had not yet come into an inheritance among the tribes of Israel because they had not secured their inheritance as God commanded (Josh. 19:40–48; cp. Judg. 1:34–36). Now they sought a land whose inhabitants were less intimidating. The Danite leaders **sent** a scouting party of **five warriors from Zorah and Eshtaol to spy out the land and explore it** (we are not yet told which land).

En route, they **came to the house of Micah, where they spent the night.** During their visit **they recognized the voice of the young Levite.** This referred to the tonal inflections of this specific young man, rather than a regional dialect (as in 12:6). He had been a wanderer (17:8) and had passed through the towns of Zorah or Eshtaol in his travels (18:2). The reason why this young Levite would be known by prominent Danites (as opposed to any other anonymous traveling Levite) will be revealed at the end of the chapter (18:30).

18:3b–6. *Interrogation of the Levite.* The Danites interrogated the young Levite to find out how he got to Micah's house and what he was doing there. His response was not that the Lord had brought him or that he was on a divine mission. He told the truth: **what Micah had done for him** and how he had **hired** him to be **his priest,** fully acknowledging that he was engaged in "religion for hire." They asked him to **inquire of God to learn whether** their **journey** would **be successful.** The young man responded, **Go in peace. Your journey has the** LORD's **approval.**

Both parties bear significant guilt here. The Danites knew God gave them a different land and told them to occupy it; they failed through lack of faith. Clearly this journey was not God's will, and so they did not ask the Levite to inquire of the covenant Lord but rather used the generic term *God.* On the other hand, the Levite responded in generic ("fortune cookie slogan") terms about their journey. He did not commit himself about their success; it was a non-falsifiable blessing. But he did invoke the covenant name of the Lord—in this case, "in vain." In addition, the Levite apparently used the accoutrements of the priesthood (which the superstitious Danites will steal later in the story) to "divine" his answer. The Urim and Thummim were regarded with no greater sanctity than inverting an "answer eight-ball."

18:7–10. *Investigation of a Land.* The scouts continued their journey, and arrived at **Laish** ("lion"), identifying the land mentioned in verse 2. It was a lush land with good farm potential at the northern end of Israel. It existed in peace under the protection of the coastal Sidonians. Danite reconnaissance revealed that the land was desirable (**lacked nothing**) and the people were wealthy (**prosperous**), unwary (**unsuspecting** and **secure**), and isolated. Upon their return, they reported to **their brothers** (with impatient enthusiasm), **Come on, let's attack them!** They even invoked God's name to create an aura of divine commission to sanctify their aggression.

18:11–13. *Migration of an Army.* The clan of Dan (or at least a representation of them; see the numbers recorded in 4:14 and 7:3) set out. There were **six hundred men**, which (since their families were with them, 18:21) meant there were at least three thousand people altogether. This was not a peaceful migration, since they were **armed for battle**. They **set up camp near Kiriath Jearim in Judah**, which at the time was still **called Mahaneh Dan** ("Dan's Camp"). From there they made their way **to the hill country of Ephraim**, specifically **to Micah's house**.

18:14–18. *Robbery of Religious Relics.* The five spies told their brothers that Micah's house contained **an ephod, other household gods**, as well as the idol plated with silver, all theirs for the taking. Micah was not around, and **the young Levite** gaped in astonishment as he watched the looting of the shrine—which would of course take away his livelihood. Obviously he could do nothing but protest, since **six hundred** Danites, armed for battle, **stood at the entrance to the gate**.

18:19–21. *Purchase of a Priest.* They invited the young Levite to leave Micah, accompany his relics, and be their **father and priest**. After all, they argued, wouldn't it be **better** to **serve a tribe and clan . . . than just one man's household?** Having received a larger bribe (a much larger congregation, the instant respect not just of one family but of a clan), **the priest was glad**—a statement that exposed his character. He was disloyal to Micah, a man who had treated him as a son, and left without a backward glance. The Danite soldiers were cautious. In case of pursuit from the rear, they put **their little children, their livestock and their possessions in front of them** and left.

18:22. *The Chase.* Micah called his neighbors and gave chase. Unhampered by possessions or families, he quickly **overtook the Danites**, only to discover that he would have no opportunity to gain hostages and negotiate; the fighting men were at the rear. Still, his pursuit gives evidence of some measure of boldness. After all, the religious relics had sentimental value, being the result of his stealing from his mother and her lying to him!

18:23–24. *The Challenge.* The **Danites turned** and for a second time became the aggressors. They challenged Micah before he could challenge them: **What's the matter with you that you called out your men to fight?** Their arrogance was astonishing—as though Micah had no right to be offended. Micah assumed they would listen to reason, but he was wrong. He blustered: **You took the gods I made, and my priest**—an acknowledgment that he had invented his own religious system. He complained, **What else do I have?**

18:25–26. *The Coercion.* The Danites threatened to unleash their most ruthless fighters against Micah: **Don't argue with us, or some hot-tempered men will attack you, and you and your family will lose your lives.** Exasperated, Micah knew that he was impotent. What he originally stole from his mother had now ironically been stolen from him.

18:27–29. *Assault (Dan Bullying).* The Danites proceeded **on to Laish, against a peaceful and unsuspecting people.** With no record of warnings or negotiations, **they attacked them . . . and burned down their city.** Because they were in a remote valley, as the Danites had anticipated, **there was no one to rescue them.** Then **the Danites rebuilt the city and settled there,** renaming it **Dan** (no surprise here).

18:30–31. *Apostasy (Dan Blaspheming).* At this point the young Levite set up (religious) shop. But we are in for a shock that should horrify and dismay. Sometimes in Judges main characters remain nameless. For the first time, a character is named at the end of a story, and for dramatic effect. The identity of the young Levite was now revealed. His name was **Jonathan, the son of Gershom, the son of Moses!** This twist in the plot is like a tentacle pulling us back through the story again; his identity gives the story added significance (e.g., the reason why the Danites both recognized and valued him, etc.). The one through whom God gave the Ten Commandments (including commandment number one against false worship) had a grandson who became the exemplar of violating the first commandment! Godliness is not genetic!

It is important to mention two implications from this revelation. First, the identity of the Levite ties the story chronologically to within a hundred years of Israel's arrival in the promised land (perhaps shortly after chapter 3), which reinforces, second, what students of this book already knew—that the placement of these two "Bethlehem" stories at the end was not chronological but theological. Third, since the text indicates that Jonathan's **sons were priests for the tribe of Dan until the time of the captivity** (which is well beyond the time of the judges), this also means that throughout the period of the judges there was a competing site for worship over against God's altar at Shiloh.

Apostate Israelites **continued to use the idols Micah had made, all the time the house of God was in Shiloh** (Dan also became a competing site for worship during the time of the divided kingdom; see 1 Kgs. 12:28–30). Tragically, this case study illustrates that the corruption in Israel extended to the tribe of God's priesthood and affected the highest levels of family commitment.

> **MAIN IDEA REVIEW:** *Judges 17–18 contains the story of people who had the right words but insisted that it was okay with God if they worshiped him on their terms, not his. This cause became the catalyst that set in motion an array of devastating effects. These events were not simply the result of chance but of choices. The little choices we make can have big consequences. Even so, God "works out everything in conformity with the purpose of his will" (Eph. 1:11).*

III. CONCLUSION

The Old Man and the Sea

An old sailor repeatedly got lost at sea, so his friends gave him a nice compass. The next time he went out, he took the compass with him. But as usual he became hopelessly confused and was unable to find land. Finally he was again rescued by his friends. Disgruntled with him, they asked, "Why didn't you use that compass we gave you? You could have saved us a lot of trouble!" The sailor responded, "I couldn't! I wanted to go north, but as hard as I tried to make the needle aim in that direction, it just kept on pointing southeast."

The old man was so certain he knew where he should be going that he stubbornly forced his personal orientation on his compass. Since he couldn't do that, he ignored its guidance and put it aside. In other words, he knew what was right in his own eyes. To extend the fable a bit further, let us assume that the compass was very nice, perhaps bound in leather, with gold letters embossed with the directions N, S, E, W. Let us say that the maker of the oceans also made compasses and decreed, "This compass is your guide; if you follow it your paths will be straight. Do not turn from it to the right or to the left. Then you will always be on course and your journey will have success" (paraphrase of Josh. 1:7–8; Prov. 3:6). What if we were to proclaim "It's not true for me; I know better"? We ignore such guidance at our peril.

PRINCIPLES

- The cost of obedience is nothing compared with the cost of disobedience.
- By forceful negative example, this story contains a warning lest anyone should enter ministry for money or move from place to place for more money, rather than being led by God.
- When faith degenerates into nothing more than ritual or tradition, it loses its vitality, genuineness, and power.
- Faith is objective, not subjective only. When someone places faith in the wrong object (i.e., believes what is false), the intensity or sincerity of faith does not suddenly make the object of faith true.

APPLICATIONS

- Make your decisions wisely; small decisions can have huge consequences!
- Follow the guidance of the Bible. It is God's blueprint for living!
- Avoid cults. Unlike false religions, their proximity to truth can be enticing, particularly when their sense of community is strong.
- Remember: "There is a way that seems right to a man, but in the end it leads to death" (Prov. 14:12).

IV. LIFE APPLICATION

Hearers and Doers

Imagine, if you will, that you work for a company whose president found it necessary to travel out of the country and spend an extended period of time abroad. So he says to you and the other trusted employees, "Look, I'm going to leave. And while I'm gone, I want you to pay close attention to the business. You manage things while I'm away. I will write you regularly. When I do, I will instruct you in what you should do from now until I return from this trip."

Everyone agrees. He leaves and stays gone for a couple of years. During that time he writes often, communicating his desires and concerns. Finally he returns. He walks up to the front door of the company and immediately discovers everything is in a mess—weeds flourishing in the flower beds, windows broken across the front of the building, the woman at the front desk dozing, loud music roaring from several offices, two or three people engaged in horseplay in the back room. Instead of making a profit, the business has suffered a great loss.

Without hesitation he calls everyone together and with a frown asks, "What happened? Didn't you get my letters?" You say, "Oh, yeah, sure. We got all your letters. We've even bound them in a book. And some of us have memorized them. In fact, we have 'letter study' every Sunday. You know, those were really great letters."

I think the president would then ask, "But what did you do about my instructions?" And, no doubt the employees would respond, "Do? Well, nothing. But we read every one!" (cited from Charles Swindoll, *Living Above the Level of Mediocrity*, 242). God's will for our lives is expressed in God's Word; but God expects us to do more than read it; he expects us to live it (see Jas. 1:21–25).

V. PRAYER

O Lord, preserve us from those times when we think we know better than you. At times we are a stubborn people, and our culture invites us to a radical individualism in which truth is private. But your commands are true for everyone, and Jesus' sacrifice on the cross was a public statement for all (Rom. 3:25–26). May we never lose our focus on loving truth and living truth. Through Christ our Lord. Amen.

VI. DEEPER DISCOVERIES

A. "In Those Days There Was No King in Israel" (17:6)

This statement is often misunderstood. The point is not that Israel needed a king in order to be morally upright. The point is that Israel descended into sin with or without a king (e.g., 1 Kgs. 12:25–33). Even within Judges, the only attempt to establish a monarchy led to bloodshed and anarchy instead (Judg. 9, Abimelech). Block notes that "variations of this phrase ["everyone did what was right in his own eyes"], which appears seven times in Judges, recur more than twenty times in Samuel-Kings, usually with reference to the conduct of kings." He continues, "During the monarchy kings led the way in abominable acts; in pre-monarchic times the people did it on their own" (Block, 484).

B. The Danites

The people of Dan wanted the best possible situation for the least amount of effort. They bullied Micah, and then they slaughtered the inhabitants of Laish. The city they called "Dan" later became a center for idolatry (1 Kgs. 12:29). In the end, however, Dan as a tribe virtually disappeared. It was not included among the tribes catalogued in 1 Chronicles nor is it listed among the tribes from which the prophesied 144,000 witnesses will come (Rev. 7:4–8).

C. Manasseh and Moses

If Micah majored in "do-it-yourself" religion, then Jonathan ben Gershom ben Moses majored in "gratify-yourself" religion. He became a free agent and signed with the highest bidder. He went from carrying wood (since he was not of the family of Aaron) to being a priest over a settlement, to being priest over an entire tribe! The unveiling of his name was such a shock that some scribes felt it necessary to add the Hebrew consonant "nun" (pronounced "noon") to Moses' name in order to change it to Manasseh (as was mistakenly transcribed in the KJV). The purpose of such emendation was to protect and preserve the reputation of Moses' family. But truth is truth, whether we believe it or not. Godliness is not genetic.

VII. TEACHING OUTLINE

A. INTRODUCTION

1. Lead Story: A Fanciful Tale of a Flat Tire

2. Context: Judges 3–16 unveiled a descending spiral in which attention shifted from a degenerating nation to defective deliverers. At the beginning of the cycles, at least the leaders (though not the people) were admirable. At the close of the cycles, the leaders had become abominable. The two episodes chronicled in chapters 17–21 offer case studies on the decay of a nation; chapters 17–18 illustrate idolatry (spiritual decay), whereas chapters 19–21 illustrate anarchy (moral decay).

3. Transition: Although the cycles are completed, the story of Israel's degradation has not been fully told. The story of "religion for hire" illustrates that Israel has adopted wholesale the operating principle of moral relativism: "Everyone did as he saw fit" (Judg. 17:6; 21:25).

B. COMMENTARY

1. The Failure of a Family (17:1–6)
2. The Perversion of the Priesthood (17:7–13)
3. The Corruption of the Clan of Dan (18:1–31)
   a. Introduction of Dan (18:1–3a)
   b. Interrogation of the Levite (18:3b–6)
   c. Investigation of a land (18:7–10)
   d. Migration of an army (18:11–13)
   e. Robbery of religious relics (18:14–18)
   f. Purchase of a priest (18:19–21)
   g. The chase (18:22)
   h. The challenge (18:23–24)
   i. The coercion (18:25–26)
   j. Assault (Dan bullying) (18:27–29)
   k. Apostasy (Dan blaspheming) (18:30–31)

C. CONCLUSION: THE OLD MAN AND THE SEA

VIII. ISSUES FOR DISCUSSION

1. We made comments about Micah, but also consider Micah's mother: First, she did not confront her son in order to evoke repentance. Second, she initiated the blending of worship of the Lord with idolatry,

in direct contradiction to the commandment of God (Exod. 20:4–5). Third, rather than take the consecrated silver to Shiloh or some other center of worship, she kept it close by. Fourth, like Ananias and Sapphira (Acts 5) she lied about the amount that she actually dedicated to the Lord (not "I surrender all," but "I surrender 18 percent"). Micah and his mother used religious words as tokens to play religious games; the reality of the living Lord was absent from their lives. Read about the proper biblical roles of children and parents (e.g., Deut. 6:4–9; Eph. 6:1–4; 2 Tim. 1:5), and discuss where you think Micah's home fell short.

2. God is not limited; he may use human instruments to accomplish his will whether those individuals choose to obey or disobey him. The Danites were used to punish the family of Micah, and later the Chaldeans were used to punish Israel (Hab. 1). Read Genesis 50:20 (in its surrounding context) and discuss this proposition: "God may use even the evil choices of human beings to bring about his will."

3. This story provides us with a case study of false worship. Do not misunderstand: They thought they were worshiping the true God. These were not idols of Baal but relics of the Lord. However, they placed hope in man-made representations of God rather than in the person of God. Similarly, modern cults seem "so close" even though they may deny only one or two of orthodoxy's doctrines (like the Trinity, or the sufficiency of canonical Scripture). What should our response be to this challenge? (Hint: consider particularly the challenges of false teaching found in Galatians, Colossians, 2 Peter, Jude, 1 John, and 2 John.) But wait—it is also true that their communities are so inviting and so sincere. What should be our response to the collective warmth often found in a cult community? (Hint: consider the challenge of Eph. 4 and the exhortations in 1 Cor. 1–4.)

Judges 19–21

An X-Ray of an XXX-Rated Culture

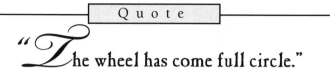

Q u o t e

"*T*he wheel has come full circle."

E d m u n d , i n W i l l i a m
S h a k e s p e a r e ' s *K i n g L e a r*

HISTORICAL PROFILE: TWO TALES
(JUDGES 17–18; 19–21)

Judges 17–18	Judges 19–21
Sin: Idolatry	Sin: Anarchy
Focus: Spiritual Decay	Focus: Moral Decay
Main Tribe: Danites	Main Tribe: Benjamites
Issue: Homelessness	Issue: Extinction
Cause: sinful choices	Cause: sinful choices
Army of 600 (18:11,16,17)	Army of 600 (20:47)
Levite (eight times)	Levite (two times)
Grandson of Moses	Grandson of Aaron
Mt. Ephraim (17:1)	Mt. Ephraim (19:1)
Bethlehem (17:7,8,9)	Bethlehem (19:1,2,18[two times])
Concludes with Shiloh (18:31)	Concludes with Shiloh (21:19–24)
Relative ethics (17:6)	Relative ethics (21:25)

Judges 19–21

I N   A   N U T S H E L L

*T*he climax of Israel's moral depravity is exposed through a litany of unspeakable sins—everyone does what is right in his own eyes.

An X-Ray of an XXX-Rated Culture

I. INTRODUCTION

Spiraling Toward Sodom

"I have spent the best years of my life giving people the lighter pleasures, and all I get is abuse and the existence of a hunted man." Who was this persecuted paragon? Alphonse ("Al") Capone. Serial killer Jeffrey Dahmer was interviewed in February 1994 by Stone Phillips for *Dateline* (NBC). He said he had believed that humanity was on earth by purely natural causes and that death ended everything. He said that if there was no God, then why should he modify his behavior? Why shouldn't he kill and cannibalize his victims? So he killed seventeen people.

While these cases are extreme, it is true that in Western culture the suppression of God and denial of moral absolutes has gradually changed our moral climate. In 1957 the Everly Brothers sang the hit song, "Wake up, Little Suzie," which contains the line, "Our reputation is shot." Why? Because they stayed out too late together without a chaperone. This is a far cry from the explicit sexuality bombarding us from today's entertainment media. One wag observed that years ago young women blushed when they were embarrassed, but these days it seems that they are embarrassed if they blush.

Moral absolutes are considered a relic of the past. Belief in the truth of the Bible is often met with ridicule and derision. Not long ago my father, who is a Gideon, was replacing a worn Bible in a local hotel. He noticed that someone had glued a label inside the Bible, printed by a well-known atheistic organization. It said: "Warning: Thinking people have determined that this book is dangerous to the mental and physical health of everyone."

As we begin our study of the last story in Judges, notice that there is only one person named in this entire three-chapter episode: Phinehas, the grandson of Aaron. In the previous story (Judg. 17–18) the only person named was Jonathan, the grandson of Moses! These two stories together make the point that within three generations the nation had degenerated and turned away from God. What was stated at the beginning of the book as almost a "throwaway" statement (Judg. 2:7,10) is now unveiled as a fitting bookend, enclosing the book from beginning to end as a masterpiece of internal coherence.

Further, although Phinehas makes a cameo appearance in our story, everyone else is anonymous! This is not accidental. In a time when everyone did what was right in his own eyes, the characters portrayed in this story could be just about anyone in Israel; the names might change, but the rebellion against the covenant Lord remained constant. *When God's commands are ignored, we are all potential Sodomites!*

II. COMMENTARY

An X-Ray of an XXX-Rated Culture

MAIN IDEA: *A personal sin escalates into the sinful behavior of a city (ch. 19), which escalates into the sinful behavior of a tribe (ch. 20), which escalates into the sinful behavior of a nation (ch. 21)! On the individual level, a woman will be dismembered, and on the corporate level a nation will almost amputate one of its own tribes.*

A Rape: Benjamin's Perversion (19:1–30)

SUPPORTING IDEA: *The virtue of hospitality, turned inside out, becomes the horrific lens through which we view the decadence of a culture.*

19:1–10. *Excessive Hospitality.* The story begins with the formula, **in those days Israel had no king** (see 17:6; 18:1; 21:25). This story (like Judg. 17–18) does not follow chronologically after the tale of Samson but took place earlier in the period of the judges—as the presence of the grandson of Aaron indicates (20:28). Its placement here is due to its nature as a moral finale—or trough!—of the Book of Judges.

The main character of this chapter is **a Levite who lived in a remote area in the hill country of Ephraim.** He married, as a "second-class" wife (**concubine**), a girl **from Bethlehem in Judah.** This geographical note introduces us to the second of three "Bethlehem" stories (see "Introduction to Judges and Ruth: 3. Bethlehem: A City of Two Tales"). The woman proved adulterous, and **she left** her husband to return **to her father's house in Bethlehem.** Four months later her husband pursued her and begged her to return to him, which apparently she agreed to do.

Her father, who was delighted at this turn of events, insisted that they accept his hospitality. The Levite agreed and, after a three-day celebration, prepared again to leave. The father prevailed on them to stay for yet another meal and then for yet another night. **On the morning of the fifth day,** the father persuaded them to stay until the afternoon and then tried to get them to stay yet another night. At this point the Levite realized that if he did not leave now, he might never return home! Foolishly, as it turned out due to perilous travel conditions, he set out in the early evening and went toward **Jerusalem.**

19:11–15. *Deficient Hospitality.* After having traveled only about five miles, they arrived at Jerusalem, where the servant suggested they **spend the night.** The Levite rejected this idea because Jerusalem (**Jebus**) was not an Israelite city but **an alien city.** Instead, they would try to reach **Gibeah or Ramah,** about five miles farther. At this point we are unsure if his motive was safety or prejudice, or a mixture of both; whatever his motive, his plan backfired.

They arrived at **Gibeah** as the sun was setting, so they **stopped to spend the night.** Even though they had passed from the territory of the tribe of Judah (Bethlehem and Jerusalem) into the territory of the tribe of **Benjamin** (Gibeah), there was still the expectation that a traveling Levite would be graciously received. But in contrast to the effusive hospitality of his father-in-law, there was a curious absence of hospitality among the Gibeanites. Even though they presented themselves as visible travelers **in the city square, . . . no one took them into his home for the night.** This breach will shortly be explained by a shocking display of depravity, but at the moment it must have been puzzling for the Levite and his entourage.

19:16–23. *Protective Hospitality.* The only person to show concern for them was **an old man** who was not from Gibeah or from the tribe of Benjamin but was from the tribe of **Ephraim.** He was currently **living in Gibeah.** He asked the strangers where they were from and where they were going. The Levite replied that he lived **in the hill country of Ephraim** but was on his way from an errand in Jerusalem (which he did not explain). He made three points clear: First, he was returning **to the house of the LORD**; second, in the meantime **no one has taken me into his house**; and third, he had his own supplies with him (**straw and fodder for our donkeys and bread and wine for ourselves**) and needed only shelter.

The old man invited them to his house and offered them his own hospitality. They accepted his offer and went home with him; the animals were fed, the guests were refreshed (**washed their feet**) and fed, and **they were enjoying themselves**.

However, **some of the wicked men** (Heb., "sons of Belial"; see 2 Cor. 6:15) **of the city** were aware that the Ephraimite had shown hospitality to the stranger who had been in the town square. They **surrounded the house** and demanded that the Ephraimite surrender **the man** (they did not know he was a Levite nor would it have mattered) so that they could **have sex with him**. The Ephraimite begged them, **don't be so vile** and appealed to them as **friends**; his reason was not that their demand was an abomination to God but was explained in terms of a hospitality code: **This man is my guest**.

19:24–28. *Perverted Hospitality.* At this point the story takes an astonishing detour, as the value of hospitality trumps the value of chivalry (the protection of the vulnerable). The Ephraimite offered heterosexual rape as an alternative to homosexual rape! Even more astonishing, he offered his very own **virgin daughter**, along with the Levite's **concubine**. The proposal was that the Gibeanite men would be permitted to **use them and do to them** what was "good in your eyes" (literally), a thematic reminder of the climax of this book: "Everyone did as he saw fit" (Judg. 17:5; 21:25).

The Ephraimite's cowardly proposal was matched and exceeded only by the Levite's self-serving action of thrusting his **concubine . . . outside to them** (while the Hebrew is unclear, contextually it seems that this was done by the Levite, not the Ephraimite). The horror of this young woman's night is briefly told: **They raped her and abused her throughout the night.** Evidently her "husband" wrote her off and was glad to have saved his own skin. Later she made her way back to the Ephraimite's threshold, where she spent the remainder of the night. The next morning **her master** (not "husband") . . . **opened the door** not to search for her but **to continue** his journey, evidently without her. To his surprise there she lay, unable to respond to him when he callously commanded, **Get up; let's go.** She was dead. He placed her body **on his donkey and set out for home**.

19:29–30. *Distorted Honor.* The Levite's distorted sense of honor was offended, and when he arrived at his home, he took her body and **cut it into twelve parts and sent them into all the areas of Israel**, apparently accompanied with an explanatory message and a plan for meeting. The reaction to this gruesome show-and-tell object lesson was immediate: the recipients exclaimed that **such a thing** had **never been seen or done** since they left **Egypt**. The national cry was, **Consider it!** Clear action must be taken! But again, the nation would act precipitously and not think of seeking guidance from the Lord until they were rashly committed to a plan.

B Revenge: Benjamin's Purge (20:1–48)

SUPPORTING IDEA: *A local sin became a catalyst for national confrontation which erupted into a civil war in Israel; all the tribes waged war against Benjamin.*

20:1–7. *Levite's Grievance (Distorted).* The Israelites gathered from north to south, including some from the Transjordan area, **before the LORD in Mizpah**. The degree of collective outrage may be seen in the gathering of **four hundred thousand soldiers**. The **Levite** was invited by the tribal leaders to tell his story. His shortened version told the basic facts: **The men of Gibeah came after me and surrounded the house, intending to kill me. They raped my concubine, and she died.** But students of Scripture will notice glaring distortions and omissions.

First, he omitted any reference to his family problems without which none of this would have happened in the first place. Second, he made it sound as though Gibeah was his intended destination, omitting any mention of his ignoring advice to stay in Jerusalem. Third, he inflated his personal danger by claiming that the men of Gibeah intended to kill him; technically, they intended to ravish him, not kill him. Fourth, he omitted the fact that he traded his concubine's skin for his and that he was the criminal (or, at best, the coward) who thrust her out the door.

Additionally, careful readers will note that the focus of this abridged version is entirely on himself as the aggrieved victim (**I . . . my . . . me . . . me . . . my . . . my**). He concluded with a challenge to the Israelites to **speak up and give your verdict**. From this point, the Levite disappears from the story.

20:8–11. *Israel's Reaction (Outraged).* Others have observed that this was the first time in this period of Israel's history that the nation was unified (**as one man**, a phrase that recurs three times)—unfortunately, they were "united" in an alliance to destroy one of their own! They planned the order of their waves of attack based on the casting of lots. They also planned the logistics of supply lines for provisions (manned by 10 percent of their army).

Their plan, in brief, was to attack the city of Gibeah in order to **give them what they deserve**. They were bent on revenge!

20:12–16. *Benjamin's Response (Obstinate).* One serious issue remained: What about the relationship of Gibeah to the host tribe, **Benjamin**? Unfortunately for the rest of Israel, the Benjamites refused to surrender their tribal brothers and instead chose tribal unity over national unity. They **mobilized twenty-six thousand swordsmen** in addition to **seven hundred chosen men** from **Gibeah**. The Benjamite army included deadly marksmen: **seven hundred** left-handed men, **each of whom could sling a stone at a hair and not miss** (see comments on the Benjamite judge Ehud in Judg. 3:15–30). Without doubt, victory would be costly.

20:17–19. *Battle Plans.* No generals or prominent leaders are identified by name in this story (with one exception, v. 28). It is as though throughout the story the tribes simply act in unison, although not in unity. The army amassed against Gibeah, with Israel mustering **four hundred thousand swordsmen**. They went to Bethel, the temporary location of the tabernacle (see "Deeper Discoveries") and cast lots to discern the order of battle (**who of us shall go first?**). Note that they did not inquire of the covenant Lord but rather used the divine generic name (**God**). Their question was not whether they should attack their covenant partner or whether the Lord would suggest some other way of dealing with the problem apart from civil war. Their minds were made up, and God "gave them over" to their plan (Rom. 1:24,26,28).

The text states that **the LORD replied, "Judah shall go first."** This response made sense because the victim (not the Levite but the concubine!) was from Bethlehem in Judah. The Book of Judges began with the query from the Lord as to who should go first against the Canaanites in order to possess the land. At that time they inquired of the covenant Lord, who responded that Judah should go first (Judg. 1:1–2; this similarity of beginning and ending reflects favorably on the internal coherence of the book). They **pitched camp near Gibeah** and were ready to attack.

20:20–22. *Battle #1.* After receiving confirmation from the Lord, the Israelites may have expected a rout or a reasonably painless victory. This was not to be the case. Instead, the Benjamites killed some **twenty-two thousand Israelites** in the first battle. The number of casualties suffered by Benjamin was not reported but must have been small (since their army originally consisted of about twenty-seven thousand men, v. 15, and about twenty-five thousand were struck down in the third battle, vv. 26–48).

20:23–25. *Battle #2.* The Israelites were emotionally demoralized (they **wept before the LORD**—this time using God's covenant name) and asked the Lord if they should attack again. Probably by means of the use of lots, the Lord confirmed, **Go up against them.** In this second battle, the Israelites lost **eighteen thousand** men. For a second time, we are not told of Benjamite casualties, but the rest of Israel had now lost a total of forty thousand soldiers.

20:26–48. *Battle #3.* For the third time the Israelites came before God in **Bethel.** This time they presented themselves differently before the Lord; they wept and **fasted that day until evening and presented burnt offerings and fellowship offerings to the LORD.** For the first time in the Book of Judges the **ark of the covenant** is mentioned, as well as **Phinehas** the aggressive grandson of **Aaron.** The mention of Phinehas as still alive is one of the key reasons why this climactic episode is actually dated early in the cycles of the judges and is placed here thematically, not chronologically (see "Deeper Discoveries"). Again they inquired from the Lord, and this time the word from the Lord contained an affirmation of victory: **Go, for tomorrow I will give them into your hands.**

The Israelites planned **an ambush.** After what appeared to be a halfhearted attack, they quickly retreated, and the Benjamites pursued them, thinking they were **defeating them as before.** After drawing the Benjamites away from the city, the Israelites attacked from the flanks, and **struck down 25,100 Benjamites,** so that **on that day twenty-five thousand Benjamite swordsmen fell** (see "Deeper Discoveries"). Then the Israelites razed the Benjamite towns, destroying everything in sight. The only survivors were **six hundred men** who escaped **into the desert to the rock of Rimmon** (about four miles east of Bethel), **where they stayed four months.**

🄲 Regret: Benjamin's Preservation (21:1–25)

> **SUPPORTING IDEA:** *The aftermath of the civil war included guilt and remorse; rather than allow Benjamin to become extinct, the Israelites contrived to preserve the tribe through murder and kidnapping.*

21:1–7. *Problem #1: Extinction of a Tribe.* Now that they had won the war, the Israelites were faced with a problem of "winning the peace." The thoroughness of their victory had created a dilemma. Few Benjamites were left alive, and all were male. At the same time, the Israelites had **taken an oath at Mizpah** (presumably at Judg. 20:1) prohibiting any of their tribes to give their daughters in **marriage to a Benjamite**. Further, all Israelites were prohibited from marrying outside Israel (Exod. 34:11,16; Deut. 7:3). For the original readers of this book, where would Saul the king—and later, for today's readers, Saul of Tarsus—come from (both were Benjamites)?

So there was another meeting at **Bethel**, where they wept **bitterly** and **cried** out to the LORD. Their complaint was directed away from themselves, and was almost against God: **Why has this happened to Israel? Why should one tribe be missing from Israel today?** The answer, of course, was obvious. They *themselves* were responsible for their precipitous action and its results for Benjamin.

The solution to their problem is a case study in immoral machination. They looked back through the "minutes" of their Mizpah meeting and took note of another **oath** they had taken: also at Mizpah they had vowed to execute any Israelite who did not join them in the Benjamite battle. A contrived solution was forming: Could they "kill two birds with one stone"? Rather than break their first foolish vow, could they solve the problem by activating their second foolish vow? If they killed some other Israelites, would that free up enough women to serve as wives for the surviving Benjamites?

21:8–11. *Problem #2: Exacting Punishment on Non-Combatants.* They went through the attendance roster of those who had reported for combat duty, searching for omissions. They found that **none of the people of Jabesh Gilead** (a town about two miles east of the Jordan River) had reported. A detachment of **twelve thousand** warriors was dispatched with the mandate to kill every person in the town, men, women, and children, with one exception: virgin women.

21:12–15. *Contrived Solution #1: Killing Their Brother Israelites.* We are spared the details of this horrific fratricide and simply given the result: they found **four hundred young women who had never slept with a man**, and brought them to the **Shiloh** encampment. Biblically, men are to be protectors, not abusers, of women—but biblical priorities were turned on their head in the days of the judges. The question of how these young women might feel about being orphaned from their families and "harvested" for enforced marriages is ignored.

The next step was for **an offer of peace** to be sent to the **Benjamites** who remained in retreat at their refuge, **the rock of Rimmon**. The offer of pardon was embraced, as were **the women of Jabesh Gilead who had been spared**. However, there were four hundred women for six hundred men, a ratio which further grieved the Israelites, because **there were not enough for all of them** (doubtless if the genders were reversed—six hundred women for four hundred men—their consciences would have been assuaged). The Israelites **grieved for Benjamin** because in their strange view **the LORD had made a gap in the tribes of Israel**. The tone of the language suggests that they assumed no responsibility for the situation.

21:16–25. *Contrived Solution #2: Kidnapping Their Sister Israelites.* Not only did the Israelites not embrace accountability for their own actions; they did not think logically. The operating principle of the Israelite leaders was that **the Benjamite survivors must have heirs**, and that unless there were women for the remaining two hundred men, the tribe would become extinct. (But how likely was it for a tribe of four hundred families to become extinct?)

They cast about for another contrived solution. It was again repeated that **we can't give them our daughters as wives**. So what would be a second source for gathering available females? Their solution was shocking and audacious. At **the annual festival of the LORD in Shiloh** the daughters of the citizens of Shiloh danced before the Lord. The scheme was laid out: The bachelor Benjamites were to **hide in the vineyards**, and then at the appropriate time were to rush forth and **seize a wife from the girls of Shiloh and go to the land of Benjamin**. The kidnapping was somehow authorized and the subsequent marriages sanctioned without reprisal against the fathers of Shiloh because technically these fathers were not "giving" their daughters to the Benjamites (in violation of the oath cited in 21:1,18); their daughters were "taken."

When the aggrieved fathers of Shiloh complained, they would be told, **You are innocent, since you did not give your daughters to them.** Like the New Testament Pharisees, the tribal leaders had laid down their own *ad hoc* rules and now were concocting their own loopholes; like children, they changed the rules of the game they were making up as they went along.

We must remember that many events recorded in Scripture are *descriptive*, not *prescriptive*. The tribal leaders were not obeying God; they were doing what was "true for them." Even further, this episode is symptomatic of the larger societal problem, or as Block puts it, "Wickedness is democratized" (Block, 583). The vulnerable are abused. Justice is gone from Israel. The Book of Judges fittingly concludes: **In those days Israel had no king; everyone did as he saw fit.** Literally, they were doing what was right in their own eyes. It is important to note that they were doing what they thought was right, not what they thought was wrong! The nation had lost its moral moorings and had adapted and adopted their morality from the Canaanites.

> **MAIN IDEA REVIEW:** *A personal sin escalates into the sinful behavior of a city (ch. 19), which escalates into the sinful behavior of a tribe (ch. 20), which escalates into the sinful behavior of a nation (ch. 21)! On the individual level, a woman will be dismembered, and on the corporate level a nation will almost amputate one of its own tribes.*

III. CONCLUSION

God's Solution

God offers a solution to the moral failures described in these chapters. Strangely it is illustrated by arguably the most notorious criminal in the last century: No, not Alphonse Capone. His greed and murder are things we understand because we all experience greed, and we can understand the anger that motivates murder.

I am referring to Jeffrey Dahmer, whom I mentioned at the beginning of this chapter. Dahmer had told interviewer Stone Phillips in February 1994 that he had no reason to change his behavior because if there was no God, there were no universal morals, and there was no accountability in an afterlife. In that same interview Dahmer then added these words: "I have since come to believe that the Lord Jesus Christ is God, and that one day I, and everyone else, will be held accountable to Him." (Jeffrey Dahmer was murdered on November 29, 1994, by another prison inmate.) The only solution to the kinds of social, political, and moral ills that plague humanity is to embrace the gospel of Jesus Christ, the King of kings, the Lord of lords, the ultimate Judge (John 5:22–27).

PRINCIPLES

- The reason God bears with his people has nothing to do with their merit but everything to do with his character and glory. He has made covenant promises, and "if we are faithless, he will remain faithful, for he cannot disown himself" (2 Tim. 2:13).
- God desires that husbands love their wives as Christ loved the church (Eph. 5:25). Any violation of this role of love and protection (e.g., the Levite) constitutes a breach of the pattern of Christ's protective love (Eph. 5:27–29).
- The distorted values of a culture gone awry are often manifested in the distorted values of individuals.
- The story of the Levite sounds a sober warning: "These things occurred as examples to keep us from setting our hearts on evil things as they did" (1 Cor. 10:6).
- The only solution to cultural and individual depravity is the gospel of Christ (Rom. 1:16–17; 1 Cor. 1:18,24).

APPLICATIONS

- Be careful what you demand from God; you may get it!
- Resist the lure of the values of the culture; they lead down the path of destruction (Matt. 7:13–14).
- Do what is right in God's eyes, not what is right in your own eyes!

IV. LIFE APPLICATION

Lessons from a "Snuff Film"

I have never heard a sermon on this portion of Scripture. It's hard to read; it's even harder to study. Yet Judges 19–21 is God's inspired Word, and there are things here for us. "These things happened to them as examples and were written down as warnings for us, on whom the fulfillment of the ages has come" (1 Cor. 10:11).

Why are all the main characters anonymous in this story? To have a name is to have identity, to have significance. In a day when everyone did what was right in his own eyes, as others have observed, the Levite could be every

Levite, the woman could be every woman, every host could commit atrocities against women, every husband could abandon his wife, every man could be callous toward women, every woman was a potential victim of rape and murder, every town was a potential hell-hole, every tribe was a potential gang.

We have watched sin grow through the cycles of the Book of Judges. Now at the end, we see the chaos of a culture gone callous: every person does what is right in his own eyes. Judges 19–21 is a "snuff film" that makes this point: As people began to ignore God's commands, the moral lines became blurred and eventually obliterated. As people become de-*sensitized* to evil, they then become de-*sanitized* in their lifestyles.

Focus	Sins
Rape (Chapter 19)	Adultery (19:2)
	Inhospitality (19:15)
	Homosexuality (19:22)
	Vicious Cowardice (19:24)
	Rape (19:25)
	Murder (19:26)
	Callousness (19:27–29)
Revenge (Chapter 20)	Lying (20:5)
	Rash Vows (20:8)
	Ungodly Priorities (20:13)
	Disobedience (20:27)
	Slaughter (20:48)
Regret (Chapter 21)	Rash Vow (21:1)
	Incrimination (21:8)
	Massacre (21:10–11)
	Subjugation (21:12)
	Bullying (21:22)
	Kidnapping (21:19–23)

V. PRAYER

O Lord, this story exhausts our souls. We sometimes forget that in our hearts resides the potential for great wickedness (Jer. 17:9). We acknowledge that we are saved by grace, not by any merit of our own. We confess that at times we are apathetic to your commands and more attuned to the lure of the culture than to the love of the cross. Our confession of Christ is not always matched by authentic obedience. May we be warned, may we be aware, may we be alert, may we be authentic. Through Christ our Lord. Amen.

VI. DEEPER DISCOVERIES

A. Battle Details

Three factors made the outcome of these battles so bloody. First, Benjamin was embedded within a hilly country. It was hard to attack and easy to defend. Second, Benjamin was tenaciously defending its own home territory, with which they were familiar. Third, the soldiers of Benjamin were good fighters. They were able to pick off the opposition by flinging stones at over ninety miles per hour with slings (Judg. 20:16) before the Israelites could get close enough for hand-to-hand combat.

B. Sodom and Gibeah

After a verbal and grammatical analysis of Judges 19:22–24 compared with Genesis 19:4–8, Block concludes, "Of the words found in Genesis almost one-fourth (sixteen) occur in the same form in Judges. An additional twenty-four expressions from Genesis find a close counterpart" (Block, 532–534). The point is that there is a literary analogy drawn between the behavior of the Israelites and the moral anarchy of Sodom and Gomorrah that is quite intentional. Any relationship the Israelites enjoyed with God was by grace, not by merit.

C. Two Civil Wars: A Comparison

In America's Civil War 530,000 men died, more than the total number of men who died in two subsequent world wars. The North lost 365,000 men while the South lost 165,000. Of those 530,000 casualties, 215,000 were lost to disease (for the North, 140,000; for the South 75,000). Bacteria were more deadly than bullets! In this Israelite civil war, there were a total of 65,000 casualties. Almost all were lost in the first few days of battle. But even more tragic, there were 450,000 moral casualties!

D. The Tabernacle

The tabernacle was located at Bethel during this episode (Judg. 20:27). This is surprising because it had been at Shiloh (Judg. 18:31) both before (Josh. 18:1) and after (1 Sam. 1:9). It may have been brought to nearby Bethel solely for the purpose of this conflict, a sort of tribal "good luck charm."

E. Phinehas

Phinehas stands out as the only person named in this entire three-chapter episode. He was the son of Eleazar and grandson of Aaron, known as an uncompromising defender of the true Lord (e.g., Num. 25:7–13; 31:6; and Josh. 22:9–34, where Phinehas held together a fragile tribal coalition). Ezra was descended from Phinehas (Ezra 7:5).

F. Battlefield Report

The summary description of the final battle is given in Judges 20:29–36a. In true Ancient Near Eastern fashion, after a summary description is given, the same story is told again in elaborate detail (particularly focusing on the ambush details) in Judges 20:36b–46. (For a discussion of this form of story-telling, see Kenneth A. Kitchen, *Ancient Orient and the Old Testament*, 116–127.)

VII. TEACHING OUTLINE

A. INTRODUCTION

1. Lead Story: Spiraling Toward Sodom
2. Context: The cancer of disobedience spreads from a family (17:1–6) to a religious system (17:7–13) and finally to an entire tribe

(18:1–31). Judges 17–18 illustrates the principle that spiritual decay leads inevitably to moral decay, which is the theme of Judges 19–21.

3. Transition: At this point not only are the cycles of the judges complete, but the family and religious systems are in disarray (Judg. 17–18). This last story reinforces the discouraging verdict and further demonstrates that all tribal and social structures are in disarray.

B. COMMENTARY

1. Rape: Benjamin's Perversion (19:1–30)
   a. Excessive hospitality (19:1–10)
   b. Deficient hospitality (19:11–15)
   c. Protective hospitality (19:16–23)
   d. Perverted hospitality (19:24–28)
   e. Distorted honor (19:29–30)
2. Revenge: Benjamin's Purge (20:1–48)
   a. Levite's grievance (distorted) (20:1–7)
   b. Israel's reaction (outraged) (20:8–11)
   c. Benjamin's response (obstinate) (20:12–16)
   d. Battle plans (20:17–19)
   e. Battle #1 (20:20–22)
   f. Battle #2 (20:23–25)
   g. Battle #3 (20:26–48)
3. Regret: Benjamin's Preservation (21:1–25)
   a. Problem #1: Extinction of a tribe (21:1–7)
   b. Problem #2: Exacting punishment on non-combatants (21:8–11)
   c. Contrived solution #1: Killing their brother Israelites (21:12–15)
   d. Contrived solution #2: Kidnapping their sister Israelites (21:16–25)

C. CONCLUSION: GOD'S SOLUTION

VIII. ISSUES FOR DISCUSSION

1. Read Matthew 5:46–47, Matthew 7:20, and James 1:25–27. How does God measure the genuineness of our faith?

2. If you survey Judges 19–21, it is not hard to pick out those who were vulnerable and regarded as expendable—those who became the chief victims of crimes and greed in all three chapters. Who are the vulnerable in *our* society? How do you think God would evaluate us? (Note: The depravity "on display" in the Book of Judges is set in direct contrast to godliness "on display" in the Book of Ruth.)

3. What do Judges 17:6 and 21:25 have to say about the days in which *you* live? How does the truth of these verses become evident in your daily life? What do you think God wants you to do about it?

4. What is the only remedy to the kind of sin described in these chapters?

Ruth 1

"'Til Death Do Us Part"

I. INTRODUCTION
When God Is Out to Get Us

II. COMMENTARY
A verse-by-verse explanation of the chapter.

III. CONCLUSION
Changing Attitude by Changing Altitude

An overview of the principles and applications from the chapter.

IV. LIFE APPLICATION
Here, or Home?

Melding the chapter to life.

V. PRAYER
Tying the chapter to life with God.

VI. DEEPER DISCOVERIES
Historical, geographical, and grammatical enrichment of the commentary.

VII. TEACHING OUTLINE
Suggested step-by-step group study of the chapter.

VIII. ISSUES FOR DISCUSSION
Zeroing the chapter in on daily life.

BOOK PROFILE: RUTH

- One of two books in the Bible named after Gentiles (other book is Luke)
- Told through speeches (of eighty-five verses, fifty-nine contain dialogue)
- No miracles in this book (contrast the Book of Judges: many miracles, angelic visitors, etc.)
- No villains in this book
- Everyone is *named* in Ruth (exception: "what's-his-name" in 3:12; 4:1–8)
- All of the main characters face a crisis of some sort, and their decisions reflect their priorities
- A love story, even though the word *love* only appears once (4:15)
- Several prayers and blessings are uttered, but everyone prays for and blesses someone else
- Two key concepts: *chesed* (God's loyal love, close to the idea of grace) and *go'el* ("kinsman-redeemer")

IN A NUTSHELL

*D*espite the darkness of the days of the judges and the despair of personal loss, individuals are always welcomed back into God's loving arms.

"'Til Death Do Us Part"

I. INTRODUCTION

When God Is Out to Get Us

She came from one of the older established families in town. Old money. Social status. Her family went to the "first church." She and her husband had two sons. He decided to relocate the family to greener pastures in a different town, where he thought life would be more pleasant. But he died of a sudden heart attack at age forty-eight. The business venture into which he had put all their money went bankrupt, and the family was left penniless. The two boys had to quit high school and go to work. In order to make ends meet the boys took a second job at a factory, late shift. They also married girls outside their race and religion, which was hard for their mother to adjust to. One night returning home at 2:00 a.m., the older brother fell asleep at the wheel and ran off the road. Both sons were killed. The woman who had previously had it all now had nothing! She felt that God was against her. She told the girls to go home to their parents. One did, one did not.

Okay, so it sounds kind of familiar. This made-up story is found in the first chapter of Ruth—just change a few details and transport the people back about three thousand years. There are times when God's people suffer greatly. When bad things happen to good people, how do we hold on to our view of a loving God? Like Job, Naomi became embittered against God, yet she still believed! She gave up on God's goodness, but she did not give up on God.

II. COMMENTARY

"'Til Death Do Us Part"

> **MAIN IDEA:** Life's tragic circumstances often lead to despair and depression; sometimes we have no sense of the immediate presence of God. Even so, he may bring others alongside to encourage and strengthen in time of need—whether or not we are receptive.

🅰 Loss of Family (1:1–5)

SUPPORTING IDEA: *Sometimes people who belong to God compromise their faith, with disastrous consequences.*

1:1–2. *Migration to Moab.* The Book of Ruth begins by "putting us in our place," **the days when the judges ruled** (see "Introduction to Judges and Ruth"). Within this period six details are specified that sharpen the focus of this story. First, **there was a famine in the land**. Second, the famine affected **a man from Bethlehem in Judah, together with his wife and two sons**. While we are unsure of the specific time period involved, the freedom of travel and the lack of mention of Moabite oppression may put the events shortly after the Moabite oppression of Eglon was quelled by Ehud—close to the days of Gideon.

Third, the man took his family **to live for a while** ("sojourned," a temporary relocation) **in the country of Moab**. Two wrongs were involved here; he abandoned God's promised land, and he went to the land of God's enemies. Fourth, all four family members were identified by name. The patriarch was **Elimelech** ("my God is king"), his wife **Naomi** ("pleasant"), and their sons were **Mahlon** ("frail") and **Kilion** ("weak"—the meanings given for the names of both sons are not certain). Fifth, they were **from Bethlehem, Judah**. The name "Bethlehem" means "house of bread," which is ironic in light of the famine from which they fled, and the abundance to which only one of them would return (v. 22). Sixth, they were **Ephrathites**, an old name for the region which may indicate "old" residents (Gen. 35:19; 48:7)—almost conveying the idea of a moneyed aristocracy (which fits both the notoriety accompanying Naomi's return and the statement that she went out "full" but returned destitute, v. 21).

1:3–5. *Misfortune in Moab.* Of the four people we have just met, we immediately read the obituaries of three. First **Elimelech, Naomi's husband, died**, leaving her only **with her two sons**. The boys married two **Moabite women**, in direct violation of God's law (Deut. 7:3–4). Their names were **Orpah** ("firmness of neck," possibly a reference to stately beauty and poise) and the other was named **Ruth**, whose name may possibly refer to "friendship" or "refreshment." We are told nothing about their home life or about their worship rendered either to the Lord of Israel or to Chemosh, the god of Moab. Both **Mahlon and Kilion** (alongside their father) died, but no causes of their death are given.

Certainly these marriages took place within the total of **ten years** that the family lived in Moab—and possibly not long before the young men died, since both couples were childless. **Naomi was left without her two sons and her husband.** This is the only place in the Old Testament where this particular word *sons* was used of married men; often it means small children (as in 4:17). The meaning was that Naomi "lost her boys," and the term speaks of her closeness with her sons. Ironically, the very reason they left Bethlehem was to escape death, yet death overtook 75 percent of the family.

ⓑ Loss of Friend (1:6–18)

> **SUPPORTING IDEA:** *Even in despair, a weak believer (Naomi) may behave benevolently and choose the hard path, while a new believer (Ruth) may behave nobly and refuse to take the easy path.*

1:6–10. *Naomi's Preparations.* The future looked desolate for Naomi and her two daughters-in-law. They could not remain where they were and survive. Naomi **heard in Moab that the LORD** (who is sovereign over *feast* or *famine*, Deut. 28:23–24,38–40) **had come to the aid** of Israel and had provided **food** (literally, "bread") **for them**—a play on the name "Bethlehem." "The 'house of bread' is being restocked" (Block, 631). Consequently **Naomi and her daughters-in-law prepared to return . . . to the land of Judah.** En route Naomi possibly reflected on the last journey she had taken, one that left her empty in an alien land. Rather than visit the same fate on these young women (who would be aliens in Israel), she came to a decision. Her genuine and sacrificial affection for them was evident in the first dialogue in the book: **Go back, each of you.** Naomi felt it would be in their best interests for them to stay with their families of origin. In that context they could more easily remarry.

Unexpectedly (considering her present distorted view of God), Naomi invoked a double benediction, blessing them in the covenant name of the Lord. First, she declared, **May the LORD show kindness** (see "Deeper Discoveries"). Second, **May the LORD grant . . . rest** (security) **in the home of another husband.** While her sons were alive, Ruth and Orpah were good wives; Naomi knew it, acknowledged it, and thanked them for it. (No mother-in-law jokes could arise from this book!) Her intention at this point was both to *return them* geographically and to *release them* emotionally. **Then she kissed them.**

The daughters-in-law responded with similar emotion and together **wept aloud**, a phrase denoting loud wailing. Together they protested, **We will go back with you to your people**.

1:11-13. *Naomi's Deductions.* Naomi responded with a lesson in logic aimed at their best interests. Any one of these points should have been sufficient to send them back; but like an avalanche, if you dodge one stone, there are others! (One wonders if, when alive, Elimelech ever won any disputes with his wife!)

First, she said, **I am too old to have another husband**. A second implication arose from this point: Even if she were not too old to have a husband, she was too old to bear sons. Third, even if she weren't too old to have sons, **Would you wait until they grew up?** (Possibly this was a nice way of saying that Orpah and Ruth would be too old when the sons came of age!) Finally, she delivered the most acrimonious argument: **It is more bitter for me than for you, because the LORD's hand has gone out against me!** Naomi regarded herself as divinely "jinxed" by the specific and intentional judgment of God. Orpah and Ruth could remarry and have the security of a family, whereas Naomi anticipated a lonely and impoverished old age. She did not want to "rub off" on these young women.

The entire argument revolved around what would be best for them (v. 11, "return home"; v. 12, "return home"; v. 15, "go back"; twice calling them **my daughters**), without a consideration of what these alternatives would mean for Naomi herself. She truly loved her daughters-in-law and was willing to give them up for their good! If they were reasonable about future prospects, they would listen to her logic.

1:14-18. *Ruth's Declarations.* **At this they wept again. Then Orpah kissed her mother-in-law good-by, but Ruth clung to her.** Orpah wanted to be a wife again; Ruth chose to remain a daughter. Orpah made the natural choice, but Ruth made the supernatural choice. Using Orpah's example as leverage, Naomi persisted, **Your sister-in-law is going back to her people and her gods** (see "Deeper Discoveries"). **Go back with her.** Ruth's response was a classic statement of commitment, a watershed decision that would change her life. Even though she knew of the covenant Lord imperfectly through the lens of Naomi's troubled life, it was compelling enough to motivate her to hold fast to Naomi and the Lord, as she turned her back on Chemosh and Moab. She affirmed a three-part declaration of commitment: (1) **Where you**

go I will go, and where you stay I will stay. (2) **Your people will be my people and your God my God.** (3) **Where you die I will die, and there I will be buried.**

The first declaration was a pledge of constant *companionship* with Naomi. The second was a pledge of *commitment:* The relationships that give significance to one's life would also be adopted by Ruth (Naomi's people, her God—at this point Ruth used the more generic name for God). Third, Ruth pledged to *commemorate* Naomi: To cherish her memory to such an extent that after Naomi's death she would live in the same location (possibly for decades) and then at her own death be buried in the same place. Ruth gave up her culture, language, her family (both of her parents were still alive, 2:11), and any prospects of a future family (see Luke 14:33).

She concluded the speech by invoking the witness of the covenant Lord of Israel in an oath: **May the LORD deal with me, be it ever so severely, if anything but death separates you and me.** The Hebrew was more expressive, "Thus may the Lord do," probably accompanied by a universally significant gesture of judgment, perhaps akin to drawing one's finger across one's neck (1 Sam. 3:17). If she should be unfaithful to her commitment to Naomi, she asked *now* with a binding oath that the Lord would judge her severely *then.*

The last phrase admits several variations. It makes sense contextually to understand the phrase to read, "If *even* death parts you and me," not excluding death but including death (see Rom. 8:38–39; 1 Cor. 15:55–57). Having seen Ruth's determination, Naomi **stopped urging her** to return home. Ruth the Moabitess, the former worshiper of Chemosh, displayed levels of trust and love that should be found among the people of the Lord.

C Loss of Face (1:19–22)

SUPPORTING IDEA: *Sometimes believers allow their personal pain to disable their ability to see God's providential care in the circumstances of their lives.*

1:19. *Rumor from the Women.* The journey progressed; **the two women went on until they came to Bethlehem,** about fifty miles from Moabite territory.

Given her state of mind, Naomi probably hoped for an unnoticed arrival and absorption into the life of the town. This was not to be. As they entered, **the whole town was stirred because of them**. Naomi was now impoverished, and her young companion was not Naomi's daughter but a Moabitess! Naomi was from a prominent family and was recognized by people who had known her before. The uncertainty of identification behind the collective question that buzzed around (**Can this be Naomi?**) was not calculated to boost one's ego.

1:20–22. *Retort from Naomi.* Naomi, whose logic against her daughters-in-law had been impeccable, threw logic to the wind in an emotional outburst! Intensely aware of her drastic change in fortune, in visage, and in family, Naomi responded angrily, **Don't call me Naomi** ("pleasant"). **Call me Mara** ("bitter"). The reason was clear in her mind, put into four propositions: **The Almighty has made my life very bitter . . . has brought me back empty . . . has afflicted me . . . has brought misfortune upon me**. The first and fourth phrases use a title for God (*Shaddai*) that is probably derived from an ancient word for "mountain," denoting strength and stability; significantly it occurs in the establishment of the covenant in Genesis (17:1). The second and third phrases use the covenant name for the Lord found in Exodus (e.g., 3:14).

Naomi got one thing absolutely right: God is sovereign. Her view of sovereignty was skewed, however, because (as others have observed) she saw only God's power without his pity, she saw sovereignty without sympathy, she saw justice without grace. She saw herself as the bull's-eye at the center of God's cosmic target. But the majestic sovereignty of God is also found within a transitional detail that closes this chapter: they arrived **in Bethlehem as the barley harvest** (the first of several periods of harvest) **was beginning**. This fact will frame the picture that follows.

MAIN IDEA REVIEW: *Life's tragic circumstances often lead to despair and depression; sometimes we have no sense of the immediate presence of God. Even so, he may bring others alongside to encourage and strengthen in time of need—whether or not we are receptive.*

III. CONCLUSION

Changing Attitude by Changing Altitude

Have you ever experienced disappointment with God? It happens when you do what you think the Lord wants, but then things don't turn out the way you expect. God doesn't come through—like when you stick your neck out and do the ethical thing at work, but instead of getting praise, you get fired. Naomi had experienced disappointment with God. She lost her husband, her two sons, her wealth, her position, and her looks. It's interesting . . . she gave up on God's goodness, but she did not give up on God. She became an embittered believer who interpreted God in a "worst case" scenario whenever possible. "Why don't you show yourself loving to me? Show yourself kind to me? Or just show yourself?" Sometimes it seems easier to identify the hand of Satan than the fingerprints of the Savior, doesn't it?

Naomi felt God was out to get her. John Piper observed, "I would take Naomi's theology any day over the sentimental views of God which dominate evangelical magazines and books today. Naomi is unshaken and sure about three things: God exists. God is sovereign. God has afflicted her." I agree. But Naomi forgot that God can turn tragedy into triumph (Gen. 50:20). As the story unfolds in the next chapters, Naomi's *attitude* will be transformed when she gains *altitude*—seeing the circumstances of life from God's viewpoint. Significantly, God did not send a prophet to correct her or a judge to punish her; he sent barley, Boaz, and a baby!

At this point, however, she interpreted God's love for her by her circumstances rather than interpret her circumstances by God's love. Naomi said, "God is out to get me!" Ruth took her hand and said, "Come, let's go together. Your God will be my God."

PRINCIPLES

- The choices we make in this world have consequences.
- We misunderstand God's plan when we interpret God's love for us by our circumstances (Jesus said we would experience suffering in this world, John 16:33).
- When we demand resolution of all problems our way, we forget that this world is not the arena for final justice.

- Even when we feel abandoned by God, he is giving us his most microscopic attention.

APPLICATIONS

- Revel in the impossibility. God has been faithful in the *past;* he will supply your needs (not your "greeds") in the *present!*
- Don't be spiritually myopic; allow others to minister to you when you are hurting.
- Do the noble thing, even when it hurts. Remember: this world is not your home or your hope.
- Trust the Lord in the inequities of life; your attitude is determined by your altitude.

IV. LIFE APPLICATION

Here, or Home?

Consider Ruth. She was a young working woman whose life was hard: single, married, and then single again, living in a multicultural society, and responsible for the care of an older relative who always looked at life as a glass half empty. What if nothing good happened in the next chapter? What if she and Naomi simply eeked out a miserly living, year after year, with Ruth always being tired after a day of manual labor, with Naomi always surly and in poor health until she died. What if Ruth stayed in Bethlehem, known all her life as "the alien," until she also finally died? In other words, if there had been no Boaz—is God still good?

There is an old story of a missionary who was returning home after a lifetime of service, and all of the loved ones he had left behind had gone to be with the Lord. As the ship docked, there were crowds and bands waiting to greet governmental dignitaries who were on board. There was no one waiting to greet him, however, and he began to feel bitter about his current plight. He said, "Lord, I have sacrificed my life for you, committed myself to your service, and now that I arrive home I am all alone." As soon as he had uttered the words, he had a sense of God's presence reminding him of the eternal view, "My child, you're not home yet."

Dr. Jean Staker Garton made this statement: "Many Christians say glibly, 'Lord, I'll gladly bear the cross and follow you.' But in our hearts we add, 'If it's lightweight, collapsible, transferable, and with a money-back guarantee.' If you are a Christian, make sure you look good on wood." Think about it: sometimes life is not fair. But this life . . . is not life. It's the foyer to the future with the Father.

V. PRAYER

O Lord, it is so much easier to live by sight than by faith. Yet we know that you are the Sovereign of the universe and that nothing comes into our lives that has not first passed through your hands. We embrace the truth that all things are working together for the good of those who love you. At times this is clear; at other times we "see through a glass darkly." We ask that you give us the ability to see the big picture through your eyes, that we gain your perspective, that our attitude gain your altitude. Through Christ our Lord. Amen.

VI. DEEPER DISCOVERIES

A. One-Fifth of a Megilloth

The Book of Ruth was one of the five Megilloth, the small "scrolls" that were read annually at Jewish festivals: the Song of Songs at Passover, Ruth at Feast of Weeks (our Pentecost, fifty days after Passover; Exod. 23:16), Lamentations on ninth Ab (commemorating the fall of Jerusalem in 596 B.C.), Ecclesiastes at the Feast of Tabernacles (Tishri), and Esther at the Feast of Purim (Adar). It is likely that Ruth was read at the Feast of Weeks because her betrothal took place during this festival (Ruth 1:22; 3:2).

B. Moab

Moabite territory was about fifty miles southeast of Bethlehem, and its different terrain meant that its climatology was not always the same as in Bethlehem. The relationship between the Jews and the Moabites was strained due to their origins (the incest of Lot with his daughter, Gen. 19:30–38), their rejection of Israel (Num. 22–24), their seduction of Israel (Num. 25), and their recent oppression of Israel (Judg. 3:15–30; see Block, 627). *Reli-*

giously, they worshiped Chemosh, the savage war god. *Politically*, they had been ruled by Eglon, the fat king who placed the Israelites in servitude for eighteen years and was killed by Ehud. This was a strange place for a supposed worshiper of the true God to sojourn.

C. Naomi the Heretic?

One questions the orthodoxy or at the least the maturity of Naomi's theology—first in blaming all her woes on the Lord (vv. 13,21); second in encouraging her daughters-in-law to return to the idolatry of Chemosh (v. 15). One might add her bitter eruption at God when the Bethlehemites were acknowledging her return (vv. 19–20). Critics should keep in mind that Naomi's knowledge was imperfect, that she lived during the conflicted days of the judges, and that we are all saved by redemptive grace, not by theological consistency.

D. "The Moabitess"

Ruth is named twelve times in the book, and five references add "the Moabitess" (1:22; 2:2,21; 4:5,10; cp. 2:6). She is named only once outside the book (Matt. 1:5), embedded within the genealogy of Jesus Christ.

E. "Chesed"

This important Hebrew word contains several rich nuances: loyal love, kindness, grace, mercy, and other similar qualities anchored in the moral attributes of the Lord himself. Since Ruth and Orpah had shown *chesed* to Israelites (the family of Elimelech, 1:8), she asked that the Lord might show *chesed* to them (Gen. 12:3).

F. Ruth's Conversion (1:16)

There is some question as to when Ruth became a believer in the Lord. Her statement in 1:16 is not the prototypical "Roman Road," but it is not unreasonable to understand from the oath made to the covenant Lord of Israel in the next verse (1:17) that at this point her commitment was genuine. Boaz understood (from others, who also had understood) that she had made a decision of commitment to the covenant God of Israel (2:11–12). She had been a daughter-in-law of Naomi presumably for sufficient time to know enough of the Lord in whom she was placing her faith.

G. "If Anything but Death Separates You and Me" (1:17)

Different translations render Ruth's statement with alternative understandings. Block suggests that Ruth is saying that nothing but death will separate her from Naomi (for his reasons, see Block, 643). Still, this does not preclude the meaning "even death," because Ruth then declared that she would die and be buried where Naomi was buried. In other words, her commitment to Naomi extended through Naomi's life, and even through the rest of Ruth's life to Ruth's death.

VII. TEACHING OUTLINE

A. INTRODUCTION

1. Lead Story: When God Is Out to Get Us
2. Context: The Book of Ruth begins with a Hebrew phrase connecting Ruth with the Book of Judges: "In the days when the judges ruled." This chapter continues the story of the days of the judges, with a twist: it reminds us that it is possible for people who live in difficult times, and who have difficult lives, to be faithful to the Lord.
3. Transition: Before there is any good news (Ruth 2–4), there is the bad news that we live in a world with suffering, difficulty, and relationships that change over time (ch. 1). How are those people who choose to remain true to the Lord supposed to live in such times?

B. COMMENTARY

1. Loss of Family (1:1–5)
   a. Migration to Moab (1:1–2)
   b. Misfortune in Moab (1:3–5)
2. Loss of Friend (1:6–18)
   a. Naomi's preparations (1:6–10)
   b. Naomi's deductions (1:11–13)
   c. Ruth's declarations (1:14–18)

3. Loss of Face (1:19–22)
   a. Rumor from the women (1:19)
   b. Retort from Naomi (1:20–22)

C. CHANGING ATTITUDE BY CHANGING ALTITUDE

VIII. ISSUES FOR DISCUSSION

1. Reflect on Ruth 1:1–5. Does the fact that you are a believer mean that your life will be free of suffering?
2. Would you consider the first part of this story uplifting? Does it offer any hope that this story will be any different from those found in the Book of Judges? (I suggest not.) So why is the rest of the story (Ruth 2–4) so different from the Book of Judges?
3. Make two columns, and label them "the mind of the world" and "the mind of Christ." Think of as many practical, daily-life kinds of topics as you can, and contrast the two ways of thinking and living.
4. Looking ahead, what was it that enabled the characters of the Book of Ruth to live *above* the influences of their surrounding culture? Now reflect on this question more personally: How do I live above the influences of my culture? (You may want to read Rom. 6; 12; Eph. 4:17–5:2,15–21; Phil. 2:1–11; 4:4–9.)

Ruth 2

Boy Meets Girl

I. INTRODUCTION
Best of Times, Worst of Times

II. COMMENTARY
A verse-by-verse explanation of the chapter.

III. CONCLUSION
Let's Play "What Am I Thinking?"

An overview of the principles and applications from the chapter.

IV. LIFE APPLICATION
From Desolation and Depression to Delight

Melding the chapter to life.

V. PRAYER
Tying the chapter to life with God.

VI. DEEPER DISCOVERIES
Historical, geographical, and grammatical enrichment of the commentary.

VII. TEACHING OUTLINE
Suggested step-by-step group study of the chapter.

VIII. ISSUES FOR DISCUSSION
Zeroing the chapter in on daily life.

"*God* is not an employer looking for employees;
he is an eagle looking for people who will take
refuge under his wings."

J o h n   P i p e r

Ruth 2

I N   A   N U T S H E L L

God *is at work providentially arranging the details of our lives to
accomplish his purposes.*

Boy Meets Girl

I. INTRODUCTION

Best of Times, Worst of Times

Charles Dickens's 1859 novel *A Tale of Two Cities* began with the famous statement, "It was the best of times, it was the worst of times." Sound familiar? Most people stop there. Dickens continued, "It was the age of wisdom, it was the age of foolishness, it was the epoch of belief, it was the epoch of incredulity, it was the season of Light, it was the season of Darkness, it was the spring of hope, it was the winter of despair, we had everything before us, we had nothing before us, we were all going direct to Heaven, we were all going direct the other way." This description sounds like the days of the judges—a time of spiritual schizophrenia! We have seen this "good news/bad news" story replayed over and over. The Book of Ruth shows us that in the worst of times, God is planning for the best of times (4:13–22).

This did not happen by accident. God was "behind the seen," working all things together (including the sinful choices of sinful people) for good to those who love him. Chapter 1 of Ruth was a speed bump on that journey. It concluded with two widows who had no observable hope living in Bethlehem. But as chapter 2 begins, we are poised at the top of a roller-coaster ride, ready to take off.

It is tempting to cast this chapter in a romantic mode, although that was not foremost in the minds of the key characters. But as with many good romances, the readers know more than the players. The shy interest Boaz displayed, coupled with his kindness (*chesed*), placed alongside his charming hesitation because he regarded himself as an unworthy suitor, invite us to root for him in a pursuit that he does not yet acknowledge. Ruth is unaware of the significance of his interest. Her unassuming innocence, attributing his interest to nothing more than God's blessing (which it surely is), likewise invites us to regard her as a winsome maiden. The roller-coaster track will have twists and turns, ups and downs, a surprise ending, and it will be over before we know it. So let's jump on board and disengage the brakes.

II. COMMENTARY

Boy Meets Girl

> **MAIN IDEA:** *Even in discouraging times, God was unfolding his plan to bring about the redemption of the world through his Messiah. The details of the daily discussions of people like Ruth and Boaz, and their budding romance, seem to have little to do with God's cosmic purposes, but even so, God is the master conductor orchestrating the plan of redemption.*

A Boy Sees Girl (2:1–7)

> **SUPPORTING IDEA:** *Ruth determined to support herself and Naomi through the hard work of gleaning; those who noticed her— including Boaz—were impressed.*

2:1–7. Two critical facts set the stage for the events in this chapter. First, Ruth and Naomi arrived in Bethlehem at the beginning of the barley harvest (1:22). Second, **Naomi had a relative** who was **a man of standing** (probably meaning "wealth, social status, respect") in Bethlehem. (The same term is used in Proverbs 31:10 to describe the nobility of character of Lemuel's ideal woman.) His name was **Boaz**. The meaning of his name is uncertain, although it may mean "in him is strength" or "in the strength of the Lord [I trust]."

Ruth knew enough about Israelite religion to realize that the Lord places value on acts of benevolence done for the vulnerable: the alien, the widow, and the orphan (see "Deeper Discoveries"). Since Ruth was an alien, and since both Ruth and Naomi were widows, they qualified on two of the three standards. However, Ruth asked permission twice (vv. 2,7) because it was indeed the days of the judges (1:1), and nothing could be taken for granted. Ruth initiated the proposal: **Let me go to the fields and pick up the leftover grain behind anyone in whose eyes I find favor.** Naomi approved the plan, and responded with affection, **Go ahead, my daughter**.

Naomi's absence from such a basic life-sustaining effort merits some speculation. It is doubtful that her absence was due to depression and disinterest in life; after all, she had made the effort to return to Bethlehem. Later when encouragement came (2:20), she still did not join Ruth in the fields. While it is possible that her focus was on domestic chores while Ruth ventured out to gather the grain, it is more likely that she was simply too old or physically frail to do the back-breaking work required of gleaners. But Ruth embraced her new life fully, yet was aware that she risked harassment because she was an alien, and worse, a Moabite.

The NIV is too tame in describing what happened by the phrase, **as it turned out**; the Hebrew says (literally), "her chance chanced upon," making it clear that such "chance" is under the providential direction of God, as the rest of the story clearly shows (see Prov. 16:33). On her very first day of work Ruth "chanced upon" a particular section of the outlying fields of Bethlehem, and then "chanced upon" some property within that section, and then "chanced upon" a field within that property (2:8), **belonging to Boaz, who was from the clan of Elimelech**. The God who brought bread to Bethlehem (1:6) and who governed the timing of their return (1:22) was not now uninvolved! He had plans for their future, of which they were unaware.

The human author of the Book of Ruth also stands outside the story in amazement, driven by the truth of the tale whose privilege is his to tell. The Hebrew makes it clear by the word *behold* (translated **just then** by the NIV)— a word which occurs first in the text in order to draw our attention to the event and its providential timing. The first words we hear this "nobleman" utter are gracious words of benediction: [May] **the LORD be with you**, to which his workers responded, **The LORD bless you!**

While the second greeting is uttered by people whose motives may be mixed and whose commitment to the Lord may be questionable (indeed, note the warnings about them in vv. 9,15,16,22), the first greeting is offered by a man deeply committed to the Lord. His relationship with the Lord is the first thing of which he speaks to his employees and later will be the first thing brought into his conversation with a member of the opposite sex (v. 12).

After greeting the workers, **Boaz asked the foreman of his harvesters**, not "Who is that young woman?" but **Whose young woman is that?** Two points are worthy of note: First, the presence of the adjective "young" points to his awareness of the disparity in their ages. Second, at the same time the possessive pronoun indicates Boaz was asking for her family relationship. Was she attached to a husband? It is difficult to evict all romantic interest on Boaz's part from this chapter; it is much more likely that he viewed her with benevolent interest on which he would not presume to act, because of the disparity in their ages.

The **foreman** may not have known her name, but he knew Naomi and identified Ruth as **the Moabitess who came back from Moab with Naomi**. This racial identification was not made in disparagement, however, because he then volunteered more than Boaz had asked: First, she had not presumed but had asked politely if she would be permitted to glean, and second, she had a good work ethic—she had **worked steadily from morning till now, except for a short rest in the shelter** (although the phrase is difficult in Hebrew, the gist is clear).

Ⓑ Boy Meets Girl (2:8–13)

SUPPORTING IDEA: *Ruth was surprised to receive the unexpected personal attention of Boaz, which he explained was a result of his respect for her character.*

2:8–13. Before Boaz spoke to Ruth, we infer from his conversation with Ruth that first he rode over to the men who were doing the lions' share of harvesting and gave them strict orders not to harass the Moabitess: "Hands off!" Then he approached Ruth, and a fascinating conversation ensued. Just as Boaz's first words to his workers were words of benediction, his first words to Ruth were cordial words of respect and distance (**My daughter**, see 1:11,12,13; 2:2) and of protection. He requested that she not stray to another field but rather stay in his field **with my servant girls**. Then she learned that Boaz had told the men not to touch her. (Block notes, "Boaz is hereby instituting the first anti-sexual-harassment policy in the workplace recorded in the Bible," Block, 660).

Further, not only was he her protector; he was her provider. When she was thirsty, she was authorized to do what other gleaners could not do: **get a drink from the water jars the men have filled**.

This went far beyond rote compliance with the letter of the law for gleaners. Such kindness was overwhelming to Ruth, who responded in action and in words: First, **she bowed down with her face to the ground** in a gesture of deference and thankfulness. Second, she exclaimed, **Why have I found such favor in your eyes that you notice me—a foreigner?** The truth is that a man of *chesed* does not treat people as objects (to be used) but as subjects (to be valued; on *chesed* see comments, p. 315). Ruth probably understood from the treatment of Naomi as an alien in Moab the kind of rejection that she could expect in Bethlehem. This was what she had prepared herself for. But instead she received kindness that she never expected, and she did not understand why.

Boaz's response removed at least part of the mystery: **I've been told all about what you have done for your mother-in-law since the death of your husband**, which he then rehearsed: She left her family (**father and mother**), she left her **homeland** (Moab), she was willing to live among people she **did not know** in a land she did not know. Apparently people in the town (1:19–21) had talked, and it is possible that Naomi was known to be difficult at times. This Moabitess gained the deep respect of Boaz, even before he saw her. She had shown *chesed* to Naomi (1:8; 3:1).

Then Boaz pronounced a benediction: **May the LORD repay you for what you have done. May you be richly rewarded by the LORD, the God of Israel, under whose wings you have come to take refuge.** The Lord does indeed balance justice and mercy in the cosmos, whether in this life or in the next. Boaz's prayer was that Ruth would received wholeness within this life. What he did not know is that he was going to become the catalyst that would fulfill his own benediction. The picture Boaz had of Ruth was a person who, like a small chick, alone and untended and unprotected, had run to the open arms (wings) of safety with the Lord, seeking protection and asylum (Matt. 23:37).

Ruth responded, deeply touched, and in vulnerability told Boaz that he had given her **comfort** (the Hebrew has the idea of allowing someone to breathe deeply again) **and have spoken kindly** (literally, "spoken to my heart") **to your servant**. Her amazement was compounded because in her mind she did not even **have the standing of one of** [Boaz's] **servant girls**.

Boy Feeds Girl (2:14–17)

SUPPORTING IDEA: *Ruth was surprised to receive the unexpected personal hospitality of Boaz, which he did not explain.*

2:14–17. At mealtime (and it is unlikely that Ruth had any food with her since she did not know where she was going that morning) **Boaz** again surprised Ruth. First, he apparently took his meals with his employees. Second, he invited her (and no other gleaner) to **come over** and dine with him, going far beyond the boundary of kindness that any gleaner had a right to expect. He invited her to **have some bread and dip it in the wine vinegar**, probably a sauce concoction to make eating hard bread more pleasurable. The other harvesters probably felt that they were too good to eat with Ruth, since she was a destitute alien woman. Third, Boaz shocked everyone by serving Ruth himself with **roasted grain**, removing any doubt in anyone's mind that she fell under his protection. His generous portion (**she ate all she wanted and had some left over**) permitted her to take some home to Naomi.

After she returned to work, Boaz ordered his harvesters to pull out stalks in her path from grain already cut and gathered into bundles. (Children understand that "gleaning" from the bowl of cake icing is a treat; but if their mother were to remove icing from the cake to put back into the bowl for them to glean, that would be super-abounding grace!) Further, he warned them not to **embarrass her** or **rebuke her**. Before, Boaz had taken steps to protect her from physical abuse ("told the men not to touch you," v. 9); here he protected her from verbal abuse.

Ruth continued to work non-stop **until evening**. After threshing what **she had gathered**, its volume was **about an ephah** (see "Deeper Discoveries"). Thus Boaz's workers obeyed him, but at the same time Ruth worked hard. If he had simply given her the grain, it might not have been valued as much.

Ⓓ Girl Reports to "Mother" (2:18–23)

SUPPORTING IDEA: *For the first time Naomi began to recognize the providential hand of God caring for her and Ruth.*

2:18–23. Ruth returned home to Naomi and showed her **how much she had gathered** and fed her with the leftovers from the meal. Naomi responded with enthusiastic rapid-fire questions about their blessed benefactor. We are not told the detail in which Ruth responded, but she finally said **the name** of the land-owner: **Boaz** (either he introduced himself in a part of a dialogue which was not recorded, or she heard it from other workers who talked about him). This gave rise to three statements from Naomi, the first being yet another expostulation of excitement: **The LORD bless him!** Second, she affirmed that the Lord had **not stopped showing his kindness** (*chesed*, see 1:8, where Naomi was thinking of a Moabite husband for Ruth) **to the living** (meaning Ruth and Naomi) **and the dead** (meaning Mahlon; Ruth may have wondered what she meant by this last phrase).

Naomi explained, **That man is our close relative** (which I'm sure Ruth thought was nice), and not only that, **he is one of our kinsman-redeemers**. The term (*go'el*) may have carried little or no significance for Ruth. Still, she added what she hoped would be helpful information: **He even said to me, "Stay with my workers until they finish harvesting all my grain."** Naomi enthusiastically agreed to this as a worthy plan in order for Ruth to be protected—and in her mind, this would assure ongoing contact between Boaz and Ruth. **So Ruth stayed close to the servant girls of Boaz to glean until the barley and wheat harvests were finished**, a period of about seven weeks.

> **MAIN IDEA REVIEW:** *Even in discouraging times, God was unfolding his plan to bring about the redemption of the world through his Messiah. The details of the daily discussions of people like Ruth and Boaz, and their budding romance, seem to have little to do with God's cosmic purposes, but even so, God is the master conductor orchestrating the plan of redemption.*

III. CONCLUSION

Let's Play "What Am I Thinking?"

It is possible to speculate on what our main characters were thinking. As we study their motives, there are lessons to learn about grace, honor, and chivalry. First, consider Ruth. She was not the kind of person who demanded her rights; she was not a "taker" but a "giver." She did not presume on Naomi, on the field supervisor, on Boaz, or even on God. As far as she was concerned, she found a dream job on her first day at work; the working conditions and benefits exceeded her expectations. Her boss was a man of chivalry. She never, even unconsciously, felt that she was *owed* grace; rather, she felt *awed* by grace.

Second, consider Boaz. He was a businessman who lived his faith in the workplace. He did not compartmentalize his life into "sacred" and "secular." Remember, these were the days of the judges, and Boaz had rough people working for him (2:9,15–16,22; Bethlehem was *not* Mayberry!). Furthermore, Boaz was upright and honoring of the opposite sex; there was no hint of impropriety on his part toward Ruth, even though she was even more vulnerable than most women, being a Moabitess, and a widow at that! He was a man of chivalry, in the best sense of the term.

PRINCIPLES

- God calls believers to serve him as "salt and light" in the workplace.
- Believers are not to compartmentalize their lives into categories of "sacred" and "secular"; all of life is sacred (read Col. 3:23–24 for our motives at work).
- We are never owed grace, but we should always be awed by grace.
- Sometimes receiving God's grace means things do not go the way we want, as when Paul learned his life lesson, "My grace is sufficient for you, for my power is made perfect in weakness" (2 Cor. 12:9).

APPLICATIONS

- Live your faith in the workplace; people will notice.
- Be known as a giver, not as a taker.
- Don't lose hope; God remains on his throne!
- "Always preach the gospel; when necessary, use words" (St. Francis of Assisi).

IV. LIFE APPLICATION

From Desolation and Depression to Delight

In Ruth 1, Naomi was *dismal*. But when we leave chapter 2, Naomi was *delighted*. There was a divine cloud of hope on the horizon, about the size of a man's hand (1 Kgs. 18:44). God was on the move on her behalf. Naomi recognized in Boaz's kind actions more than Ruth did and probably more than Boaz did! For the first time, possibly in more than a decade, Naomi had some measure of hope, anchored in the blessings of the covenant Lord. So while Ruth was thinking "barley," Naomi was thinking "bride." While Ruth was thinking "bread," Naomi was thinking "wedding cake." While Ruth was thinking "grain," Naomi was thinking "Grandma!"

But I want to be clear about this, because one could misunderstand. Do we see circumstances change and then gather hope? Or do we see God's character and then gather hope, despite the circumstances? Jeremiah made it clear that it is careful meditation on the nature of God's faithfulness that brings hope (Lam. 3:21–25). This is hard because we would much rather *look around* and see evidence for hope than *look up* and believe hope. However, for right now faith is not sight, and sometimes our circumstances do not change. Naomi moved from despair to delight. But God had not changed. He was always there, eager for his children to take refuge and rest in him. "Have mercy on me, O God, have mercy on me, for in you my soul takes refuge. I will take refuge in the shadow of your wings until the disaster has passed . . . I will praise you, O Lord, among the nations; I will sing of you among the peoples. For great is your love, reaching to the heavens; your faithfulness reaches to the skies. Be exalted, O God, above the heavens; let your glory be over all the earth" (Ps. 57:1,9–11).

V. PRAYER

O Lord, you have told us that we may be content in our earthly circumstances because our citizenship is in heaven. We confess that it seems easier to us to walk by sight than by faith; we ask forgiveness for those times when we gauge our understanding of your love by our circumstances rather than by your promises. We ask that we would take courage from your grace, be awed by your loving-kindness, and take refuge in your wings. Through Christ our Lord. Amen.

VI. DEEPER DISCOVERIES

A. Women in Ruth and Judges

Examining the first chapters of Ruth canonically, this chapter provides a startling contrast to what one might expect in the days of the judges. The last "Bethlehem" episode (Judg. 19–21) told the tale of a vulnerable woman who was abused, disrespected, betrayed, and raped; in the same tale other women were kidnapped and used as objects of barter. There was no protector. In Ruth, however, rather than endure brutal mistreatment, two very vulnerable women (one an alien!) receive *chesed*.

B. God and the Vulnerable

God made provision for the vulnerable in his economy, particularly the alien, the widow, and the orphan (Lev. 23:22; Deut. 10:18–19; 24:17–21; 27:19). Benevolence to any of these is taken as piety rendered to God himself.

One reason is that by definition none of these can do anything in return for their benefactor, so that our motives for helping them must be pure and not reciprocal (Matt. 5:46–47). That is, we do not give in order to receive; we give because God told us to give, and because he is the greatest of all givers (John 3:16; 2 Cor. 9:15; Jas. 1:27).

C. Ephah

An ephah of grain would be around six U.S. gallons. Block points out that according to 1 Samuel 17:17, "An ephah of grain could feed fifty fighting men" (Block, 670), which would mean several weeks' supply for the two widows.

D. Levirate Marriage (2:11)

Naomi's statement that God had shown his kindness to the dead has as its background the Old Testament practice known as Levirate marriage (Deut. 25:5–10; see Matt. 22:24), in which a (presumably unmarried) brother would marry his brother's childless widow in order to have off-spring. The first child was accounted the son of the dead man so that his name would continue in Israel. The practice formally applied to brothers, but apparently was extended in the time of the judges to the nearest kinsman down the family line. Block observes, "The word 'levirate' derives from the Latin 'levir,' 'brother-in-law.' It has nothing to do with Levi or Levitical" (Block, 636, n. 58).

E. Kinsman-Redeemer

The term for kinsman (go'el, found in 2:20; 3:9,12; 4:1,3,4,6) carries with it more responsibilities than would seem immediately evident. In the Old Testament the go'el had family responsibilities to make restitution, carry out justice, protect family-owned land, and (probably) to continue the family line (see comments on 4:1–6). The participle of the root means "to redeem" (Ps. 19:14; Prov. 23:11; see Job 19:25). Levirate marriage is not tied to the go'el linguistically, but clearly it was so understood by Old Testament Jews. Naomi had this in mind when she combined both ideas in the same breath. God had been kind to the dead (the Levirate marriage) . . . (literally) he is our go'el (Ruth 2:20).

E. Levirate Marriage (2:11)

Naomi's statement that God had shown his kindness to the dead has as its background the Old Testament practice known as Levirate marriage (Deut. 25:5–10; see Matt. 22:24), in which a (presumably unmarried) brother would marry his brother's childless widow in order to have offspring. The first child was accounted the son of the dead man so that his name would continue in Israel. The practice formally applied to brothers, but apparently was extended in the time of the judges to the nearest kinsman down the family line. Block observes, "The word 'levirate' derives from the Latin 'levir,' 'brother-in-law.' It has nothing to do with Levi or Levitical" (Block, 636, n. 58).

VII. TEACHING OUTLINE

A. INTRODUCTION

1. Lead Story: Best of Times, Worst of Times
2. Context: Ruth 1 introduced two vulnerable women who were potentially subject to the same brutal mistreatment described in Judges 19–21. However, Ruth 2 is a watershed in the story, showing that there is a remnant in Israel of people who fear God, even in Bethlehem! Chapters 3 and 4 will demonstrate the genuineness of their faith in the Lord of Israel.
3. Transition: In the last chapter Naomi was despondent and convinced that God had set her as the bull's-eye of his cosmic target. In this chapter Naomi moved from despair to delight. What happened? As it turned out, it was the people Ruth met during her first day on the job. The action of the chapter takes place first in the house (vv. 1–2), then mostly in the field (vv. 3–17), and then in the house again (vv. 18–23).

B. COMMENTARY

1. Boy Sees Girl (2:1–7)
2. Boy Meets Girl (2:8–13)
3. Boy Feeds Girl (2:14–17)
4. Girl Reports to "Mother" (2:18–23)

C. CONCLUSION: LET'S PLAY "WHAT AM I THINKING?"

VIII. ISSUES FOR DISCUSSION

1. As you face "impossibilities" (situations with no easy solution), and as you trust the Lord in them, what might you expect? Here are some options other believers have met:

   - The outcome will be exactly what we expect and hope for, even if we don't know how God will bring it about (Abram's mental dilemma recorded in Heb. 11:17–19).
   - The outcome will be similar to what we expect, but God may adjust the details (Paul's plans to go to Rome, Rom. 15:22–24, though not in chains—however, note the outcome in Phil. 1:12–14).
   - The outcome will be what we feared it would be, but we no longer need to fear it (2 Cor. 4:7,16–18; 12:8–10).
   - The outcome is still unknown—like the way Ruth felt in Ruth 1–2, and the way you may feel right now!

   After reading and meditating on these passages, how does God want us to face the challenges of life?

2. Select two qualities each from Boaz and Ruth that you admire. Reflect first on why you chose them and second on how these qualities can be translated into the way the Lord wants us to live in the midst of *our* "days of the judges" (Judg. 21:25; Ruth 1:1).

Ruth 3

"Some Enchanted Evening"

"*T*o love at all is to be vulnerable.... The only place

outside Heaven where you can be perfectly safe from all the

dangers ... of love is Hell."

C .   S .   L e w i s

Ruth 3

I N   A   N U T S H E L L

*G*od's people navigate through a delicate situation and risk serious misunderstanding in order to pursue God's will.

"Some Enchanted Evening"

I. INTRODUCTION

Shine On, Shine On, Harvest Moon

*T*he good news is this: Boaz has continued to be both respectful and chivalrous and has kept Ruth under his protection. But for Naomi, the bad news is that Boaz has said and done nothing more than be gracious. If she were to write for counsel from a second millennium B.C. advice column, it might read like this: "Dear Abigail, my widowed daughter-in-law has daily contact with an older man who shows concern about her and respect for her. In fact, from the moment he saw her, he was deeply interested and has treated her like a princess. But fast-forward two months, and he still has not said one word to take their relationship to the next level. She likes him, but he's not getting any younger! How do we get him to ignite his inertia, to light his lethargy, to cancel his coma? Signed, Befuddled in Bethlehem."

Naomi was befuddled, baffled, and bewildered! Boaz clearly had no immediate plans to change his bachelor status. Worse still, tonight was the last night of the harvest celebration, and the regular contact between Ruth and Boaz would come to an end. It was time for some initiative. The time had come to take a risk!

II. COMMENTARY

"Some Enchanted Evening"

> **MAIN IDEA:** *There is a time for God's people to wait passively for God to remove obstacles, and there comes a time for God's people to engage those obstacles. Both are done in faith that God works all things together for good for those who love him, and that God is concerned about the details of our lives. All three characters in this chapter took risks that rendered them vulnerable; all three trusted God; all three were motivated by love.*

🅰 Naomi Plots: The Mate (3:1–5)

> **SUPPORTING IDEA:** *Naomi devised a plan whereby Boaz was informed of Ruth's interest, but in a way that he could say "no" with minimal embarrassment for everyone involved.*

3:1–5. Two months have passed by quickly. Naomi was certain that Boaz's interest in Ruth went beyond being a kind-hearted benefactor. So **one day Naomi** approached Ruth with the kindness befitting a loving mother, calling her **my daughter** before introducing a very delicate subject. The question was put, **Should I not try to find a home for you, where you will be well provided for?** It was time for Ruth to put aside mourning and to enter other dimensions of family life. After introducing the subject, Naomi identified the object of her plan: **Boaz** [is] **a kinsman of ours** (note the plural possessive, as in 2:20). Naomi had long thought of Ruth as her own daughter, and the extension of "kinsman-redeemer" protection to Ruth was both legal and logical.

Naomi then explained that the plan cannot be delayed: "Behold" (absent in the NIV), **tonight he will be winnowing barley on the threshing floor** (see "Deeper Discoveries"). Then she outlined her strategy: be attractive, be attentive, be assertive, and be available. First, Ruth was to remove all vestiges of mourning and make herself *attractive:* **Wash and perfume yourself, and put on your best clothes.** The term probably referred to an outer covering rather than a special garment from Ruth's wardrobe. As a poor gleaner, it is unlikely that there would have been a selection from which to choose; she had just arrived in Bethlehem from famine conditions, carrying all that she had.

Block offers a convincing parallel that clarifies the meaning: When David's baby son finally died, he then washed himself, put on perfumed oil, put on his garment (using the same Hebrew word translated here by NIV as "best clothes"), and entered the temple to worship (2 Sam. 12:20). The ablutions, preparation, and clothing signified to David's men that his time of mourning was over.

Similarly, Ruth's preparation would indicate that her formal mourning period was over. If she had indeed been wearing mourning garments, this would help explain Boaz's romantic inertia. Now Ruth's appearance would be a visual announcement that she was ready to return to regular life, which included the possibility of marriage.

Second, Ruth was to make herself *attentive* to the place where Boaz rested after the day's work and celebration were complete: **Don't let him know you** are there until he has finished eating and drinking. **When he lies down, note the place where he is lying**. We are not, however, to think of Ruth gingerly stepping over somnolent bodies lest she awaken someone, until she finally identified the sleeping form of Boaz. Apparently Boaz slept somewhat apart from the rest of the workers. This explains why the ensuing conversation and actions went unnoticed.

Third, Ruth was to be *assertive*: **Go and uncover his feet and lie down**, an action that would serve two purposes. It symbolized the humility with which she approached him (to counter any misunderstanding of brazenness), and it also awakened this old warrior, but gradually—not suddenly (lest Boaz get "cold feet").

Fourth, Ruth was to be *available*: **He will tell you what to do.**

Ruth's statement to Naomi (**I will do whatever you say**) was a more forceful statement than simply "I will do this." It was an acknowledgment of several things: First, she trusted Naomi's *commitment* to the Lord to have her do only what was morally right. Second, she trusted Naomi's loving *attachment* to her that she was not being put at undue risk, in terms of safety from seduction (her purity). Third, she trusted Naomi's *judgment* that this was the best way to approach the situation, in terms of safety from slander (her reputation). Finally, she trusted Naomi's *assessment* of Boaz's character and his response, despite the plethora of possible responses that she might envision. She simply trusted Naomi.

Ⓑ Ruth Proposes: The Date (3:6–10)

> **SUPPORTING IDEA:** *Ruth was willing to risk her safety and her reputation based on Naomi's judgment, and willing to trust their common evaluation of Boaz as a man of chivalry.*

3:6–10. The grain had been threshed, winnowed, and prepared for transport back to the town, a task which would have to wait for the morning. As she had promised, Ruth **went down to the threshing floor and did everything her mother-in-law told her to do**. This summary statement is unpacked in the next verses. After the celebration Boaz **was in good spirits**; no pun, I'm sure—he was not drunk but happy and content! When he **went over to lie down at the far end of the grain pile**, Ruth took note of his location and after he was asleep **approached quietly** (the same word used in 1 Sam. 24:4),

uncovered his feet and lay down at his feet. Whether she slept is unknown, but in view of the circumstances it would seem doubtful.

Then **in the middle of the night** (or about midnight), he shivered and groped for his cloak but "behold" (not translated in NIV) he **discovered a woman lying at his feet**. The obvious question was asked (**Who are you?**) and answered (**I am your servant Ruth**). Before, Ruth had placed herself below the status of Boaz's servants (2:13). The term she used here is a different term ("handmaiden"), a term whose connotations diminish their relative difference in status; in one sense he has moved from being a "knight with a scullery wench" to a "knight with a maid-in-waiting."

Ruth did not stop there; she made her desire for marriage perfectly clear: **Spread the corner of your garment over me**. The idiom itself was poignant and recalled an earlier statement of Boaz's respect for Ruth: She had sought protection under the "wing" of the covenant Lord (2:12). Here the same Hebrew word is repeated; the connection with the term from chapter 2 is intentional. There Boaz invoked the blessing of the Lord upon Ruth; here Boaz became the agent through whom the Lord would bless Ruth. There Ruth came under the "wing" of the Lord; here the "wing" of the Lord becomes the "wing" of Boaz (see parallel with Ezek. 16:8, where God was claiming Israel for a wife). Thus Ruth brought the covenant Lord into her request *implicitly*.

Rather than have Boaz think her excessively brazen, Ruth *explicitly* stated the theological rationale for her request by adding immediately an all-important detail: **Since you are a kinsman-redeemer**. At this point we may assume that Ruth was fully aware of the meaning of *go'el* and the attendant responsibilities of that role. Boaz was nothing if not a man of integrity, so to place this responsibility before him would evoke—and rightly so, as it turned out—an honorable and positive response. Ruth may have been unprepared for the enthusiasm of his response, however. Rather than reluctant or hesitant assent, he responded in amazement and excitement. His initial utterance (the benediction **the LORD bless you**) again placed the Lord center-stage in their plan.

The difference in age between the two must have been significant, adduced from two statements. First, he (again) addressed her as **my daughter** (2:8). In his mind he was too old for Ruth, and he had not wanted to make her uncomfortable by displaying interest in her. He continued, **This kindness is greater than that which you showed earlier**, that is, in caring for Naomi (as everyone knew, 2:11–12). His humble perspective was winsome. Actually, Ruth's choice to leave her family and her land and her religion and devote herself to the care of a mother-in-law was a far greater manifestation of *chesed* than her present action, but that was not how Boaz saw it!

Once she removed her mourning garments, as a "free agent" (Block's term) she could have had her pick of any of the available young men! Of this Boaz has no doubt whatsoever (**you have not run after the younger men, whether rich or poor**). In his view, not only had Ruth bestowed *chesed* on Naomi; she had now bestowed *chesed* on him, and he regarded himself as the most blessed of men. He did not have to pray about this, seek counsel about this, or even think about this. Such a blessing was directly from the hand of the Lord, and Boaz sang the doxology!

In sum, we are aware that two obstacles prevented Boaz from making any overtures to Ruth: First, as an older man he did not think she would be interested in him. Ruth removed that obstacle. However, the second obstacle was that another man could come between them—a nearer kinsman. Ruth removed the first obstacle, and so Boaz set about removing the second.

Ⓒ Boaz Promises: The Wait (3:11–18)

> **SUPPORTING IDEA:** *Boaz felt himself the recipient of grace both from God and from Ruth; he treated Ruth with respect and accepted the risk of pursuing the role of go'el in her behalf.*

3:11–18. The setting for moral compromise would not be difficult to imagine. Boaz loved Ruth. The stars were out, he had drunk a lot of wine, they were alone, it was midnight, and she had asked to be taken under his cloak. These were the days of the judges, and all around them there were fertility cults where orgies were considered matters of worship. But Boaz refused to do anything shameful; he was truly a man "above reproach" (1 Tim. 3:2). Boaz, her protector, assuaged any concerns: **Don't be afraid. I will do for you all you ask.** He also assured her (in view of the events of the evening) **all my fellow townsmen know that you are a woman of noble character.** The same term translated "noble character" was used of Boaz in Ruth 2:1 (and is also found in Prov. 12:4; 31:10).

Ruth now knew what Boaz felt about her (we knew, but she did not) and that he would like to spend the rest of his life caring for her. However, there was a kinsman closer to them within the family tree. Boaz intended to challenge the man **in the morning, and if he wants to redeem, good; let him redeem**. Although Boaz himself would be broken-hearted, Ruth (and Naomi) would be cared for. **But if he is not willing, as surely as the LORD lives I will do it**.

The overlapping responsibilities of Levirate marriage and *go'el* (and our lack of understanding of how they were applied at this time) make the strict criteria by which these matters were to be adjudicated somewhat uncertain. Neither Boaz nor the unnamed relative had a legal obligation to marry Ruth (according to a strict interpretation of Levirate responsibility). Naomi's plan hinged on their sense of moral obligation (see discussion, p. 330).

Because of the lateness of the hour, the vulnerability of a woman out by herself in the middle of the night (note that 2:22 refers to an attack during daylight!), and the reputations of both Boaz and Ruth within the town (2:1,4, 11–12; 3:11), the best alternative was for Ruth to remain through the night with Boaz (**stay here for the night . . . lie here until morning**) and then return **before anyone could be recognized**. Indeed, before she left, Boaz gave the order (presumably to a trusted servant), **Don't let it be known that a woman came to the threshing floor**. It is doubtful that Ruth and Boaz did much sleeping; perhaps they talked quietly through the rest of the night.

In the early morning hour, both returned to town. Boaz measured out **six measures of barley** for Ruth to take with her, which would serve two purposes. First, it would be a pledge to Naomi of his intentions (his stated reason); second, it might provide an explanation to curious neighbors why Ruth was out and about at such an hour. Meanwhile, Boaz **went back to town** to lay plans for approaching the nearer kinsman.

It is likely that Naomi also slept little through the night. She literally asked, "Who are you, my daughter?" (NIV, **How did it go, my daughter?**) If we take the question at face value, Naomi was asking her if she was Ruth the widow of Mahlon, or Ruth the engaged bride of Boaz. Ruth responded in excited "show-and-tell" fashion, telling her **everything Boaz had done for her** and added, "**He gave me these six measures of barley, saying, 'Don't go back to your mother-in-law empty-handed.'**" To Ruth, Boaz had given *verbal* assurances. Naomi now received a *visual* assurance that, one way or another, Naomi's "empty" days were over (the same word that was used in 1:21). And one way or another, Ruth would have a husband; who that would be, Boaz did not know.

Naomi received the message and reveled in it: **Wait, my daughter, until you find out what happens. For the man will not rest until the matter is settled today.** Phase 1 of Naomi's plan was complete; now she and Ruth would wait together until they learned the outcome of Phase 2.

> **MAIN IDEA REVIEW:** *There is a time for God's people to wait passively for God to remove obstacles, and there comes a time for God's people to engage those obstacles. Both are done in faith that God works all things together for good for those who love him, and that God is concerned about the details of our lives. All three characters in this chapter took risks that rendered them vulnerable; all three trusted God; all three were motivated by love.*

III. CONCLUSION

Sadie Hawkins Day

In November of 1937 Sadie Hawkins first appeared in Al Capp's comic strip, *Li'l Abner*. Sadie was so ugly that her father, the powerful mayor of Dogpatch, U.S.A., was afraid he'd never marry her off. In desperation, he decreed a Sadie Hawkins Day. All unmarried men in Dogpatch had to line up, and they got a ten-second head start before Sadie and the other unmarried women began running after them. The man each woman caught would end up in front of Marryin' Sam for a shotgun wedding. Apparently Sadie was as quick as she was ugly and caught her man. But the ladies of Dogpatch liked it so much that it became an annual affair cherished by women and dreaded by bachelors.

While we smile at Al Capp's cartoon world, there is no way around the fact that Ruth said to Boaz, "Marry me." Think about it. Ruth was not a brazen woman. Would she have done this if Naomi had said nothing? No. She had a pattern of presuming *nothing* in her own behalf about anything (2:2,7). But here we see "a woman proposing to a man; a young person proposing to an older; a field worker proposing to the field owner, an alien proposing to a native, a poor person making the demand of a rich man" (Block, 687, 692).

Ruth put herself on the line. But this way, she could show her love for God by obeying his Word. She was willing to take part in a levirate custom for the Lord's sake and for the sake of one of his people. As a consequence, by grace she was placed in the genealogical line of her Messiah!

Why take such a risk? There is a difference between giving of yourself and giving yourself! The hen and the hog were discussing their respective contributions to breakfast of eggs and bacon. For the hen it was an offering; for the hog it was total commitment! Everyone in this chapter is a "giver" not a "taker." Naomi sought Ruth's best interest. Ruth sought Naomi's and Boaz's best interests. Boaz sought Ruth's and Naomi's best interest. And sometimes total commitment involves taking risks—by faith!

PRINCIPLES

- Even more than you do, God wants his will done in your life.
- We have seen, over and over, that God is at work behind the so-called "chance" details of the lives of his people.
- God has a way of overcoming obstacles and allowing stumbling blocks to become stepping stones.
- People who love God naturally want to do God's will; his will becomes their will—even when it includes hardships.

APPLICATIONS

- Do you give *of* yourself to Christ, or do you give *yourself* to Christ? Do you want parts of God, or do you want God? Give all of who you are to all of who God is.
- Be aware that faith involves risk!
- Be encouraged that your risks are anchored in God's character and based on God's promises.

IV. LIFE APPLICATION

Love Is a Risk

C. S. Lewis said, "To love at all is to be vulnerable. Love anything, and your heart will certainly be wrung and possibly be broken. If you want to make sure of keeping it intact, you must give your heart to no one, not even to an animal. Wrap it carefully round with hobbies and little luxuries; avoid all entanglements; lock it up safe in the casket or coffin of your selfishness. But in that casket—safe, dark, motionless, airless—it will change. It will not be broken; it will become unbreakable, impenetrable, irredeemable. The alternative to tragedy, or at least to the risk of tragedy, is damnation. The only place outside of Heaven where you can be perfectly safe from all the dangers and perturbations of love is Hell" (Lewis, *The Four Loves*).

All three characters in this chapter took risks. All three were motivated by love. The possibilities for misunderstanding were huge! It was possible for Ruth to misunderstand Naomi's reliance on God's law for the kinsman-redeemer. It was possible for Boaz to misunderstand the offer Ruth made him. It was possible for both Ruth and Naomi to misjudge the kind of man Boaz was.

All three characters reflected the heart of their heavenly father who took the risk of love (John 3:16). God is in love with us (astonishing, isn't it?). He loves us so much that he would rather die than live without us. His love motivated him to become vulnerable—incarnated as a baby, not a king. Atonement was made. His arms are open. How do we respond?

V. PRAYER

"Disturb us, Lord, when we are too well pleased with ourselves, when our dreams have come true because we have dreamed too little, when we arrive safely because we have sailed too close to the shore. Disturb us, Lord, when with the abundance of things we possess, we have lost our thirst for the waters of life; having fallen in love with life, we have ceased to dream of eternity; and in our efforts to build a new earth, we have allowed our vision of the new Heaven to dim. Disturb us, Lord, to dare more boldly, to venture on wider seas where storms will show your mastery; where losing sight of land, we shall find the stars. We ask you to push back the horizons of our hopes; and to push into the future in strength, courage, hope, and love" (reported prayer of Sir Frances Drake).

VI. DEEPER DISCOVERIES

A. Naomi's Plot

How long Naomi had reflected on this particular plan and its timing is unknown, but it is safe to assume that this was not carried out on a moment's whim. Many commentators have speculated on the strange strategy and considerable risk inherent within this unique plan. From everything we know of the integrity of Ruth and Naomi (and also of Boaz), we are not to read any sexual enticement or lurid motives into the strategy. There may be further cultural information that would enhance our perspectives which we do not have right now. But it is safe to grant Naomi a "best case" interpretation about her intentions and about Ruth's submission to her intentions. This interpretation is validated by Boaz's interpretation, which harmonized exactly with what both Naomi and Ruth intended to accomplish.

B. Ruth's Reliance

Ruth's willingness to trust Naomi's plan should not surprise anyone. After all, this was the woman who had said she would look after Naomi for the rest of her life (Ruth 1:16–17). She was fulfilling that promise in a tangible way. The character of submission found here is much like that of another woman in the line of the Savior, Mary. Such submission was predicated upon absolute trust in the sovereign power of a sovereign God: "For nothing is impossible with God" (Luke 1:37). The Book of Ruth, of course, contains no miracles, much less the superlative miracle of the virgin birth. But the same spirit that continued the genealogical line to the Messiah will be expressed in the words of her descendant in years to come: "I am the Lord's servant . . . may it be to me as you have said" (Luke 1:38). Mary's example? Ruth.

C. Grain

Harvested grain was put through a three-step process. In the first step grain was separated from husks by being trodden out by animals. In the second step the mixture was thrown into the air during a stiff breeze; chaff was blown away while the heavier grain fell straight down. In the final step the grain was collected and guarded (which included sleeping on the site, if winnowing was done during a late night breeze) until it would be stored (recall Judg. 6:4, where the Israelites tried to hide their grain so the Midianites would not steal the fruit of the work). Thus threshing floors were in positions favorably exposed to winds, such as open hills (in Judg. 6:11, Gideon's desperation was measured in his willingness to beat out his wheat in an enclosed winepress).

D. The Age of Boaz

In 1960 *The Story of Ruth* hit the big screen. Included in the "trailer" were these words: "A Moabite priestess renounces her gods for the God of Israel. Since she is a foreigner, her dedication is not readily accepted by the villagers." Obviously Hollywood was not exactly true to the story! And in the movie Boaz was—maybe—ten years older than Ruth. Exactly how much older was Boaz than Ruth? We do not know, but certainly he was not senile or even frail. He put in a full day's work alongside his workers and then spent the night with the harvest, protecting it with his weapons. He was old enough to call her "my daughter" three times! He was not a twenty-five-year-old "hunk," but then he was not Grandpa McCoy either. Maybe we are looking at someone about fifty-five marrying someone about twenty-five.

E. Dry Measures (3:15)

While we do not know the exact measure of barley that Boaz gave Ruth, it was heavy enough that he had to place it upon her. The measure that fits best is six seahs, and since there were three seahs to an ephah (about four to five gallons; see Isa. 40:12; Exod. 16:36), she would have been carrying about twice what she had gleaned that first day in the field (approximately eighty to ninety pounds of grain).

VII. TEACHING OUTLINE

A. INTRODUCTION

1. Lead Story: Shine On, Shine On, Harvest Moon

2. Context: In chapter 1 Naomi was in despair and depression; nevertheless, Ruth loved her. In chapter 2 Naomi began to find reasons for hope, even as Ruth continued to support her. In this chapter Naomi planned for a future for Ruth and herself, based upon the provisions of God and the character of Boaz. Ruth was compliant to her wishes. All of those involved in this chapter desired that God's will be done.

3. Transition: For weeks now Boaz had treated Ruth with respect but with personal detachment. Time seemed to be running short. Soon the harvest would be over, and regular contact between Ruth and Boaz would no longer occur. Rather than wait passively, Naomi and Ruth took the initiative and embarked on a course of action.

B. COMMENTARY

1. Naomi Plots: The Mate (3:1–5)
2. Ruth Proposes: The Date (3:6–10)
3. Boaz Promises: The Wait (3:11–18)

C. CONCLUSION: SADIE HAWKINS DAY

VIII. ISSUES FOR DISCUSSION

1. Reflect for a while on both the *actors* and the *actions* in this chapter. Every player faithfully did what he or she was supposed to do. But what if they had not done so? Further, what could have gone wrong? (Remember, these were still the days of the judges!)

2. List the character traits, actions, and attitudes that you see forming in the relationship between Boaz and Ruth that you believe will contribute to a great marriage. Describe how these might translate to today.

3. Where is God in this chapter (besides v. 10)? Was the Lord orchestrating these events? Do you think it was God's will for Naomi to interfere or not? Should she have simply prayed about it and done nothing else? What would *you* have done? While we should not take one case and make it normative for all cases, the question remains: how do we balance the patience of passively waiting on

the Lord (which is biblical) with the faith of actively getting involved in pursuing the answers to our own prayers (which is also biblical)?

Ruth 4

Happily (For)Ever After

I. INTRODUCTION
Reading an Ancient Court Transcript

II. COMMENTARY
A verse-by-verse explanation of the chapter.

III. CONCLUSION
David's Root

An overview of the principles and applications from the chapter.

IV. LIFE APPLICATION
Doing What Comes Next

Melding the chapter to life.

V. PRAYER
Tying the chapter to life with God.

VI. DEEPER DISCOVERIES
Historical, geographical, and grammatical enrichment of the commentary.

VII. TEACHING OUTLINE
Suggested step-by-step group study of the chapter.

VIII. ISSUES FOR DISCUSSION
Zeroing the chapter in on daily life.

"*D*on't waste your time waiting and longing for large opportunities which may never come. But faithfully handle the little things that are always claiming your attention."

F. B. Meyer

Ruth 4

IN A NUTSHELL

*G*od is at work behind the scenes, and "behind the seen," to work all things together "for the good of those who love him" (Rom. 8:28). The story of Naomi, Ruth, and Boaz concludes, happily (for)ever after.

Happily (For)Ever After

I. INTRODUCTION

Reading an Ancient Court Transcript

*P*retend you are an ordinary field worker in Bethlehem during the days of the judges, specifically at the time of Ruth. What events would you have observed?

First, you would have seen two women walk past your fields into town—one of them obviously a foreigner. Naomi was an embittered woman who described herself as someone whom God delighted in tormenting. It was clear to all that she had nothing—except a widowed Moabite daughter-in-law (Ruth 1). Then you would have been surprised by two things: First, you would have been impressed at the hard work undertaken by this young Moabite widow. And second, you would have been surprised because the country squire, Boaz, kept looking in her direction, providing more "supervision" of that part of the field than normal (Ruth 2).

Some weeks later, on your way back to town after the grain was harvested, if your eyes were sharp, you might have noticed Ruth, no longer in her mourning clothes, quietly going in the wrong direction—out from town toward where all the harvested grain was being kept overnight. But if you knew Boaz was there, you would know that she (a young woman alone at night) would be kept safe (Ruth 3).

And now, as you are on your way through the gate to the field to start transporting the grain, you notice a crowd gathered. You look closer, and all the elders are there—very unusual for this time of day—and then you see Boaz with another man in the middle of them, surrounded by a crowd of townspeople pressing against one another, every one of them trying to get close enough to hear what is happening. It turns out to be a fascinating legal mini-drama. This chapter of Ruth records the "court transcript" (Ruth 4).

II. COMMENTARY

Happily (For)Ever After

> **MAIN IDEA:** *In the end God overcomes all obstacles to bring Naomi from emptiness to fullness, to bring Boaz from being a bachelor to being a happily married man, and to bring Ruth from being an alien widow to being the great-grandmother of Israel's greatest king! God's redemptive purposes will not be thwarted.*

A Litigation (4:1–6)

> **SUPPORTING IDEA:** *Boaz carefully maneuvered Naomi's "nearer" kinsman into a position where he had to decide whether to fulfill his responsibilities as go'el.*

4:1–2. *Boaz's Urgency.* Ruth had recently received two confident promises. First, Boaz had told Ruth to be patient because her future was secure and she would be protected (3:13)—one way or another. Second, Naomi had confirmed the resolve of Boaz, certain that he would "not rest" until he had secured the future of Ruth and Naomi, in fact "today" (3:18).

Naomi's confidence in Boaz's determination was not misplaced. He was indeed a man of resolve and action. Boaz **went up to the town gate and sat there**, awaiting the man he sought. This entire mini-drama (vv. 1–12) takes place at the city gate, a place where elders gathered to adjudicate conflicts (see "Deeper Discoveries").

Clearly Boaz had not originally planned to return to town this morning. He had, after all, spent the night with his grain, anticipating the day's work of transporting grain from the fields. At this early hour others of the townspeople were coming *from* the city on their way *to* the fields to begin their day's work. But Boaz now had different priorities; his life was about to change forever. He did not wait until the evening (3:13, "in the morning"), a time when he could easily have accomplished the same objective after his grain had been transported (that is, instead of accosting the man as he was departing, he could have confronted him when he was returning). However, Boaz was not thinking about his business but about his bride; his focus was not on retail but on Ruth.

Boaz took the initiative and gathered the required cast of characters for the drama that would unfold: the **kinsman-redeemer**, and **ten of the elders of** the town—all of whom were willing to trust Boaz that this distraction from the beginning of their workday was worthy of their attention. Other observers, recognizing that something important was taking place, also gathered as the audience ("all those at the gate," v. 11) and became uninvited "witnesses" (v. 10). When the nearer kinsman was passing by, Boaz called to him and asked him to turn aside.

It is ironic that not only is the closer *go'el* the only person unnamed in this book, but he is given a caricature name, "Mr. X" (or "Mr. So-and-So," or "John Doe"—contrary to the NIV translation, **my friend**). The purpose for his anonymity and its caricature is not stated; while it may be to diminish our respect for him (as Block suggests, 707), it may simply be to focus attention on Boaz by contrast.

4:3–4. *Topic 1: Naomi's Land.* What follows has been described as the first millennium B.C. equivalent to our court transcript. Boaz got right to his first point: His concern was the case of **Naomi** and **the piece of land that belonged to our brother Elimelech**. Boaz told "Mr. X" that since he was the closest kinsman-redeemer, he possessed the right of first refusal. However, if he chose not to redeem the property, Boaz had immediate plans to do so, because he was **next in line**. Boaz was not operating on impulse because nothing was said about Ruth. Boaz was following a strategy that he deemed wise for this set of circumstances (and, as it turned out, he was correct).

Still, there is little doubt that Boaz's heart sank when he heard the immediate response from the man, **I will redeem it**. At this point, "Mr. X" was unaware that Boaz was pursuing a strategy whose intent was to displace him as the *go'el*. While the first aspect of the exchange focused on *Naomi's land,* Boaz proceeded to the second issue, *Ruth's hand.* He had been hooked, and Boaz was about to reel him in.

4:5–6. *Topic 2: Ruth's Hand.* Boaz maintained that if the nearer kinsman agreed to "part one," he must also agree to "part two." Boaz presented the obligation to marry Ruth in such a manner that the man could infer that he was being forced into a marriage that he had no time to think about. Boaz told him that in addition to being the *go'el* for one widow (Naomi), he must also serve as the *go'el* for a second widow (Ruth). She was described, if not in unattractive terms, as **the Moabitess . . . the dead man's widow, in order to maintain the name of the dead with his property.** Boaz knew what Ruth was like (as did his people, 3:11), but arguably few others did. Indeed, Boaz was the only male in the town who had had regular contact with Ruth!

Why did Boaz mention the land first, then Ruth? Was he subtly being a chauvinist? No, he was being wise. Sometimes the way something is presented invites a particularly negative response (like estimating the value of a priceless gold frame mounting a painting by Vermeer versus the same frame enshrining a "velvet Elvis"). He manipulated the situation so the kinsman was thinking in terms of profit-and-loss. While the man's mind was in his ledger, Boaz switched categories on him. So now, rather than view a financial responsibility through eyes that were excited about Ruth, he was invited to view Ruth through the lens of finances!

His response was perhaps more of a reaction than the result of careful deliberation—and exactly what Boaz had hoped: **Then I cannot redeem it because I might endanger my own estate**. Probably he was not a rich man, and he discovered that the exchange would not be an *addition* to his property but a *subtraction,* because he would have to support Ruth as well as Naomi (cp. Ruth's vow in 1:16–17). While our understanding of his dilemma is complicated by our lack of knowledge of the exact customs about family and community legal transactions, as well as by our ignorance of this man's family and financial circumstances, one thing is clear. While gaining Naomi's land would be to his advantage (or at least not to his detriment), gaining Ruth's hand would complicate both his life and his bank account. Possibly it could mean that the inheritance he would be passing to his other children would be compromised.

There are unanswered questions here: What children? How much money? Did Ruth's ethnicity matter to him? Was that part of what was behind Boaz's intentional reminder that Ruth was "the Moabitess"? These are questions for which we simply do not have answers (after all, he's "Mr. X"!). But we do know that this was not a risk he was willing to take, which of course is in contrast with Boaz, who was willing to take any honorable risk to gain Ruth.

B Negotiation (4:7–12)

SUPPORTING IDEA: *Boaz willingly and enthusiastically embraced the role of go'el to Naomi and Ruth; the people of Bethlehem witnessed the transaction and blessed their family.*

4:7–8. Abdication by the Nearer Go'el. Verse 7 offers us an explanation for a custom that presumably had been abandoned by the time the book was written. Not only was the letter of the law disobeyed in Israel during the days of the judges; the spirit of the law was also ignored, to the point that *ignoring* truth had evolved into *ignorance* of truth! Hence the explanation: **Now in earlier times in Israel, for the redemption and transfer of property to become final, one party took off his sandal and gave it to the other.**

The practice harkens back to Deuteronomy 25:5–10:

> If brothers are living together and one of them dies without a son, his widow must not marry outside the family. Her husband's brother shall take her and marry her and fulfill the duty of a brother-in-law to her. The first son she bears shall carry on the name of the dead brother so that his name will not be blotted out from Israel. However, if a man does not want to marry his brother's wife, she shall go to the elders at the town gate and say, "My husband's brother refuses to carry on his brother's name in Israel. He will not fulfill the duty of a brother-in-law to me." Then the elders of his town shall summon him and talk to him. If he persists in saying, "I do not want to marry her," his brother's widow shall go up to him in the presence of the elders, take off one of his sandals, spit in his face and say, "This is what is done to the man who will not build up his brother's family line." That man's line shall be known in Israel as The Family of the Unsandaled.

There are significant differences explained by the differing circumstances (see "Deeper Discoveries"). In Ruth 4 we see how the sandal was used when a man passed his rights on to another. The loosing of the sandal signified a **method of legalizing transactions.**

In view of his own situation, and in view of the offer of Boaz to become *go'el*, "Mr. X" yielded his claim with a statement (**buy it yourself**) and a confirming action (**he removed his sandal**). In a day when there were no permanent records of court proceedings or transcripts, witnesses were to recall transactions, and such dramatic visual effects made transactions memorable. The meaning of the sandal originally probably signified sovereignty over property rights—one would be able to "walk" one's property (Ps. 60:8; Deut. 1:36; Josh. 1:3).

4:9–10. *Declaration by Boaz.* Boaz solemnized the moment by proclaiming **to the elders and all the people** (who had gathered to observe what was happening) that **today** they were **witnesses** (mentioned twice) to two important decisions. First, the transfer of **property** rights (**of Elimelech, Kilion and Mahlon**) which now came to Boaz. This did not mean Boaz purchased the property, but rather that the right of oversight and redemption had passed from Mr. X to Boaz. Second, he had **also acquired Ruth the Moabitess, Mahlon's widow, as my wife, in order to maintain the name of the dead with his property.** Thus the name of Mahlon would **not disappear from among his family or from the town records** (incidentally, for the first time in the Book of Ruth we know to which of the two brothers Ruth was married).

4:11–12. *Benediction by Witnesses.* **The elders and all those at the gate said, We are witnesses** (the Hebrew has no verb, simply "Witnesses!"). What followed these legal proceedings was an unexpected *triple benediction* (note the threefold repetition of **may**), probably from a spokesperson among the assembly to which all other witnesses enthusiastically assented.

First, they asked that Ruth be fertile **like Rachel and Leah, who together built up the house of Israel.** Through these two women (and their handmaids) came the twelve tribes of the nation Israel. The focus was not on harmony within the household, nor was it on the characters of the offspring, but simply the idea of fertility. They were asking that the intention of the Levirate marriage would be fulfilled.

Second, the benediction asked that Boaz would **have standing** (see 2:1) **in Ephrathah and be famous in Bethlehem**—a prayer that the patriarch of this new family would prosper, and that the name of Boaz (alongside that of Mahlon, but not displaced by it) would continue in Israel.

Third, the benediction focused (in a sense) on the as-yet-unconceived child Obed, with the request that **through the offspring the Lord gives** (Ps. 127:3) **you by this young woman, may your family be like that of Perez, whom Tamar bore to Judah.** Note that the blessing was not "through all your offspring," which may indicate that Boaz had no previous children (although it is quite possible that he was a widower). In other words, the heir to Mahlon would also be the heir to Boaz. Boaz was from the tribe of Judah, and Tamar bore to Judah both Perez and Zerah. Perez, however, was the direct ancestor of Boaz, and therefore is mentioned here (Gen. 46:12; Num. 26:20).

Since the first part of the benediction did not include family harmony but fertility only, so this aspect of the prayer ignored the unethical behavior of the characters mentioned (Gen. 38) and focused on the success of the Levirate marriage. The patriarchal characters involved in the substance of the blessing at times lived morally questionable lives. Boaz and Ruth lived in moral uprightness. If God blessed their ancestors, hopefully God would all the more (*a fortiori*) bless their descendants. The only person absent from the benediction was Naomi, but that will be rectified in the next verses.

Block observes, "Had they been around long enough to see the fulfillment of their prayer, [these witnesses] would have observed the establishment of a name and a house far greater than Perez, the house of King David, a name commemorated to this day in the flag of the state of Israel" (Block, 724).

 ## Generations (4:13–22)

> **SUPPORTING IDEA:** *God blessed this family both with a child and later with a dynasty; Naomi, who ended her days like a queen, did not know that her great-great-grandson would become Israel's king.*

4:13–17. *Family and Friends of Obed.* Ruth 1:1–5 offered the condensed version of a story that took ten years in the living. And then in 1:6–4:12 we have been taken through a period of time extending no longer than two months. Now verse 13 of chapter 4 compresses the first year of marriage, conception, and the birth of a baby boy. **Boaz took Ruth and she became his wife**. Through the unfolding drama of this book, Ruth "the Moabitess" has gone from being a foreigner (2:10), to being lower than a migrant worker (2:13), to being a "lady-in-waiting" (3:9), to being a "wife" (4:13). Furthermore, **the LORD enabled her to conceive, and she gave birth**. God, who had closed her womb while married to Mahlon, now opened her womb to give Boaz **a son**.

The women of Bethlehem who had heard firsthand of Naomi's emptiness (1:19–21) now offered praise (4:14a), prayer (14b), prediction (15a), and pronouncement (15b). Their *praise* was **to the LORD, who this day has not left you without a kinsman-redeemer** (in contrast to when she returned to Bethlehem a year earlier). The *go'el* in mind was not Boaz, or else the temporal statement would be superfluous; instead, they were thinking of the child as the one who would provide security (or a sense of fulfillment) for his grandmother.

Their *prayer* was that the child would **become famous** (that his name would be well-known) **throughout Israel**. This would indeed be the case, although for reasons greater than any of them would ever live to discover. Ironically, this child was biologically unrelated to Naomi, but he was tied to her heart with cords of love bound more tightly than blood.

Their *prediction* (in the loose sense of offering their best wishes) was that **he will renew your life and sustain you in your old age** (literally, "gray hair"), a safe statement to make to a woman who previously had lost her husband and her two sons. Finally, their *pronouncement* had to do with the one who had borne this child to Naomi, her faithful daughter-in-law Ruth. Ruth demonstrated unconditional love for Naomi and treated her **better . . . than seven sons** (see Job 1:2; 1 Sam. 2:5). The way Ruth cared for Naomi was regarded as a net gain of five sons! Naomi was encouraged never to take this treasure of a daughter for granted.

Naomi took the child to her **lap** ("bosom," although not as a wet-nurse) and became his "nanny" who, alongside his parents, helped raise the boy. **The women living there** referred to him as Naomi's **son** and **named him Obed**—not meaning that they, instead of Boaz and Ruth, chose his name, but rather that this birth was an event in which these women adopted more than a passive interest in Naomi's life. They embraced the characters, the event, the name, and God's providential plan. The name itself (Obed means "servant") is probably a shortened form of Obadiah ("servant of the Lord"). First-time Jewish readers who arrived at this point in the story would have had their breath taken away as they discovered that the baby was none other than **the father of Jesse, the father of David**!

One of the grand themes of Scripture that is reflected in this section is that God desires to move his children from a sense of insecurity and fear to a sense of peace and contentment. Naomi began with emptiness (1:21), and went from the security of this life (being filled) to a sense of purpose in this life (or being fulfilled, 4:14–17). At the end she knew that there had been a plan according to which everything worked together for good (Rom. 8:28). The original readers of this story were able to stand even further back and evaluate the circumstances of her life because they knew even more—that God's plan was unfolding beyond Naomi's lifetime. God took her through emptiness and brought about the line of David. Modern readers are able to stand back with even greater distance than the original readers of Ruth and know that there is something more—from the line of David would come the Messiah (2 Sam. 7:13; Luke 1:32–33)!

4:18–22. *Forebears of David.* The story concludes with the only one of two places in the Old Testament (the other being 1 Chr. 2:1–15) where David is connected with the tribe of Judah—a connection that is repeated in the New Testament (Matt. 1:3–6, where Jesus is tied to the line of Judah). The genealogy begins with a common formula, **This, then, is the family line of** [name, followed by the list of names]. The list begins with **Perez** probably for two reasons: He was the immediate son of Judah (see Gen. 49:8–10, where Judah was given the "right to hold the scepter in Israel," Block, 734), and he was the first in the line who was the offspring of a "Levirate" marriage, connecting the genealogy with the storyline of Ruth.

The genealogy proceeds in descending order (some genealogies ascend; see "Deeper Discoveries") from Perez to David and includes these progenitors: **Perez, Hezron, Ram, Amminadab, Nahshon, Salmon, Boaz, Obed, Jesse,** and **David.** Proximity in biblical genealogies did not always require direct descent; **father** was at times meant to be taken literally but often was meant to be understood as "ancestor" (e.g., Matt. 3:9). Some ancestors were (for one reason or another) omitted from genealogies. This listing is identical to the genealogies in 1 Chronicles 2:5–15 and Matthew 1:3–6 (in the NASB, Luke 3:33 adds the name of Admin between Ram and Amminadab).

The narrator knew something that Boaz, Ruth, and Naomi did not know: That the greatest king in the Old Testament was going to result directly from this story. And you and I know something that the narrator did not know. Eventually the King of kings would also come from this story (although through the prophet Nathan, David knew that God was working through his line—2 Sam. 7:8–17). In the darkest days of Israel, the period of the judges (Ruth 1:1), God was laying a foundation for redemption from sin.

MAIN IDEA REVIEW: *In the end God overcomes all obstacles to bring Naomi from emptiness to fullness, to bring Boaz from being a bachelor to being a happily married man, and to bring Ruth from being an alien widow to being the great-grandmother of Israel's greatest king! God's redemptive purposes will never be thwarted.*

III. CONCLUSION

David's Root

One Christmas I was driving my friend, a visiting scholar from Nigeria (whom I will call Thomas), to an appointment. Since I had been studying the genealogy of Jesus for a Christmas sermon, I casually asked him if genealogies were more appreciated in African culture than they are in America. His face lit up and enthusiastically he told me about the importance of genealogies. Thomas said that when they read the Bible, they *never* skip a genealogy—to them it is the most important part. They call it their "root."

When Thomas was a young man, a person might get a job, or be refused a job, based on his ancestry. At one point the British offered a competition-based teaching position that he desired. Whoever got first on a series of exams got the post. My friend came in first, but the British refused him the position because, even though he was an outspoken Christian, his father had been a well-known Muslim—in other words, because of his root. At African weddings (indeed, at his own wedding) as a part of the ceremony, the genealogies (root) of both groom and bride are recited as far back as can be remembered.

The story of Ruth concludes with a recitation of the "root" of David. One day the Messiah will be "a shoot [that] will come up from the stump of Jesse . . . the Spirit of the LORD will rest on him" (Isa. 11:1–2). David called the Messiah—his own descendant—"My Lord" (Ps. 110:1; Matt. 22:41–46). And there will come a time when eventually "in that day . . . the nations will rally to him [the root of Jesse]" (Isa. 11:10; see Isa. 53:2).

PRINCIPLES

- God sometimes delights in using the frail and the unexpected to accomplish his purposes and show his love.
- God uses people who have the right priorities and who stand for principle in an age of moral relativism.
- God does not always make our paths easy, but he does make them "straight" (Prov. 3:5–6).
- Like Boaz, God wants us to do things properly but shrewdly (Matt. 10:16).

- When believers feel God has abandoned them (Naomi's attitude in Ruth 1), he remains intimately involved in the details of their lives (Naomi's recognition in Ruth 4).

- There are times when God operates in our lives on a "need to know" basis, and we don't always need to know, only to trust and obey.

APPLICATIONS

- Follow the example set throughout the Book of Ruth: "pray continually" (1 Thess. 5:17).

- Be faithful; God is (2 Tim. 2:13)!

- Trust the Lord; he has bigger plans for the investment of your life than you do.

- Be careful of your testimony; you have an audience (Phil. 4:5; 1 Cor. 11:10; Heb. 12:2)!

IV. LIFE APPLICATION

Doing What Comes Next

R. P. Dugan records a particularly dramatic moment from our nation's history. May 19, 1780, was a particularly dismal day in Hartford, Connecticut.

> At noon the skies turned from blue to gray and by mid-afternoon had blackened over so densely that, in that religious age, men fell on their knees and begged a final blessing before the end came. The Connecticut House of Representatives was in session. And as some men fell down and others clamored for an immediate adjournment, the Speaker of the House, one Colonel Davenport, came to his feet. He silenced them and said these words: "The Day of Judgment is either approaching or it is not. If it is not, there is no cause for adjournment. If it is, I choose to be found doing my duty. I wish, therefore, that candles may be brought!" (Dugan, *Winning the New Civil War* [Sisters, OR: Multnomah, 1991], p. 183).

It is widely acknowledged that "90 percent of life is just showing up." Being available and doing our duty as unto the Lord are the essential components of basic faithfulness. In closing these studies in Judges and Ruth, one point is clear: God wants his children to be faithful, to live extraordinary lives in sub-ordinary times.

Boaz and Ruth were ordinary people who lived faithful lives. In contrast to the Book of Judges, this small book contains no miracles. It's "life as usual." But from God's viewpoint, "life as usual" is of eternal value!

V. PRAYER

O Lord, there are times when we beat our drums of self-importance over our grand plans, when in truth we exist at your pleasure, for your glory. We ask that we would invest each day with eternal value and live each hour with awareness that no matter what you have called us to do, it is the Lord Christ whom we serve (Col. 3:23–24). Through Christ our Lord. Amen.

VI. DEEPER DISCOVERIES

A. "The Moabitess"

At times in this book we almost forget that "the Moabitess" is not really Ruth's last name! But the title is a reminder that God was at work in the life of a woman whose background ("root") was outside of God's covenant. The phrase is constantly repeated not as a slur but as an indication of grace (see 1:22; 2:2,21; 4:5,10, altogether five out of the twelve occurrences of the name "Ruth"). The only time when its use is questionable (which is explainable in terms of Boaz's probable strategy) is in Ruth 4:5 (see Commentary comments on Ruth 4:5–6).

B. Genealogies

Biblical genealogies are very diverse. Some misinformed reader might assume that they are all just alike, only with different names corresponding to the period being recorded. Actually, they are alike, but in the same way that a bicycle with training wheels and a Mercedes are alike—both have four wheels and both offer mobility. There are significant differences! Some genealogies are workhorses; their purpose is to convey a large amount of information.

Others have a single point. Some genealogies are like stadium floodlights, exposing everything in view. Most are like theatre spotlights, focusing on one point, one person, or one line. The genealogy of Jesus Christ recorded in Matthew 1 includes four women, all of whom were not Jews but Gentiles— including Ruth (one was a Hittite, two were Canaanite, and one a Moabite). Nor were they paragons of purity; three of the four could have been stoned for adultery. The exception? Ruth.

The purpose of including this genealogy, in light of the coming Davidic covenant (2 Sam. 7), serves to point us again to the Lord behind all covenants. God is moving history in a direction, interweaving strands of your story and mine, working all things together for good to accomplish his purposes.

C. Gates

The entire courtroom drama (Ruth 4:1–12) took place in the gates, the most important place in the community life of any ancient town. In our story it was the place that people passed through on their way to the fields; it was the place of military defense, and it was also the place of gathering for any event of significance in the lives of the townspeople (see Judg. 5:8,11; 16:2–3; Prov. 31:23,31; "Deeper Discoveries" on Judg. 16:3).

D. Levirate Marriage: The Revised Version

There are differences in the application of the Levirate responsibilities between Deuteronomy 25 and what we read in the Book of Ruth. Deuteronomy envisions and describes penalty due to reputation because the brother *can* fulfill the law but obstinately refuses to do so. Thus he is publicly humiliated (the woman removes his sandal, spits upon him, and his name is henceforth associated with scandal). In Ruth the situation is quite different.

First, in Deuteronomy the man is a brother, here he is not Mahlon's brother but is a further kinsman. Second, in Ruth "Mr. X" does not simply refuse, but apparently he cannot bear the financial burden of both responsibilities ("land" and "hand"). Third, in Deuteronomy there is no other kinsman, which means that the name of his brother will indeed die because of his refusal; here there is a willing alternate. Fourth, in Deuteronomy the man is prepared to let the name die for selfish reasons; here Mr. X was motivated by family reasons. Thus Ruth was not present during this legal exchange. She did not remove his sandal (he did it himself), nor was he publicly humiliated by being spat upon or by loss of reputation in the town.

VII. TEACHING OUTLINE

A. INTRODUCTION

1. Lead Story: Reading an Ancient Court Transcript
2. Context: This chapter closes the saga of the family of Elimelech. Ruth proved to be a loyal and loving daughter to Naomi, caring for her and providing for her needs (chs. 1–2). Naomi proved to be a clever advocate for Ruth, planning for her future (ch. 3). In this chapter Boaz is the key player, and he is more than delighted to invest the rest of his life caring for them both.
3. Transition: In the last chapter Ruth became vulnerable before Boaz and let him know that she wanted him to marry her. What would Boaz do? His response was enthusiastic, immediate, and methodical. As the chapter opened, he lay in wait for the nearer kinsman!

B. COMMENTARY

1. Litigation (4:1–6)
   a. Boaz's urgency (4:1–2)
   b. Topic 1: Naomi's land (4:3–4)
   c. Topic 2: Ruth's hand (4:5–6)
2. Negotiation (4:7–12)
   a. Abdication by the nearer *go'el* (4:7–8)
   b. Declaration by Boaz (4:9–10)
   c. Benediction by witnesses (4:11–12)
3. Generations (4:13–22)
   a. Family and friends of Obed (4:13–17)
   b. Forebears of David (4:18–22)

C. CONCLUSION: DAVID'S ROOT

VIII. ISSUES FOR DISCUSSION

1. The Book of Ruth is filled with blessings (1:8–9; 2:4,12,20; 3:10; 4:11–12,14–15). Read each one and reflect on the fact that they ascribe to the Lord all that has happened. God brings his plans to pass!

2. Sometimes we wonder why God allows obstacles to enter our lives. Read John 9:1–2 and 2 Corinthians 11:22–12:10; Paul's response when in misery was to pray (see v. 8). The small Book of Ruth contains several examples of the New Testament admonition to "pray without ceasing." The harvest (our exposition of Ruth) is now over, but it may be useful to "glean" from this book what we may learn about the ongoing attitude of prayer and benediction:

    *   in misery (1:8)
    *   in the market place (2:4)
    *   in meeting (2:12)
    *   in thanksgiving and hope (2:19–20)
    *   in joy (3:10)
    *   in marriage (4:11–12)

3. Much has been said about the concept of the "kinsman-redeemer" (Heb., *go'el*). The grid below includes some specific requirements and their corresponding fulfillments. After studying the passages in Ruth, compare them with the pattern of redemption found in our Lord Jesus Christ.

Requirement	Book of Ruth	Pattern of Christ
Must be *related* (blood)	2:3,20; 3:9	Heb. 2:9,14–16; Gal. 4:4–5
Must be *able* to redeem	3:13; 4:4–10	Heb. 7:23–25; 1 Pet. 1:18–19
Must be *free* to redeem	2:1	Heb. 4:15; 7:26
Must be *willing* to redeem	3:11–13; 4:4–5	Heb. 12:2; John 10:11–18
Result: **Rest!**	1:9; 3:1	Heb. 3–4; Matt. 11:28–29

Glossary

allegory—A means of presenting or interpreting a story by focusing on hidden or symbolic meanings rather than the literal meaning

angel—A messenger from God, either heavenly or human, who delivers God's message of instruction, warning, or hope

atonement—God's way of overcoming sin through Christ's obedience and death to restore believers to a right relationship with God

confession—Admission of personal sin and seeking forgiveness from others

consecration—Setting apart for God's use

conversion—God's act of changing a person's life in response to the person's turning to Christ in repentance and faith from some other belief or from no belief

covenant—A contract or agreement expressing God's gracious promises to his people and their consequent relationship to him

discipline—Instruction or training used by God to train his children in righteous living

ethics—The study of morality and moral decisions that guide human conduct

evil—Anyone or anything that opposes the plan of God

exodus, the—The most important act of national deliverance in the Old Testament when God enabled the Israelites to escape Egypt

faith—Belief in and personal commitment to Jesus Christ for eternal salvation

grace—Undeserved acceptance and love received from another, especially the characteristic attitude of God in providing salvation for sinners

holy—God's distinguishing characteristic that separates him from all creation; the moral ideal for Christians as they seek to reflect the character of God as known in Christ Jesus

idolatry—The worship of that which is not God

Lord—A title for God in the Old Testament; also used for Jesus in the New Testament; means owner or master worthy of obedience

Messiah—the coming king promised by the prophets; Jesus Christ who fulfilled the prophetic promises; *Christ* represents the Greek translation of the Hebrew word *messiah*

Glossary

miracle—An act of God beyond human understanding that inspires wonder, displays God's greatness, and leads people to recognize God at work in the world

obedience—Hearing and following instructions and directions from God; expected of believers

omnipotent—God's unlimited power to do that which is within his holy and righteous character

omnipresence—God's unlimited presence in all places at all times

omniscience—God's unlimited knowing

prophet—One who speaks for God

sin—Actions by which humans rebel against God, miss his purpose for their life, and surrender to the power of evil rather than to God

sovereignty—God's freedom from outward restraint; his unlimited rule of and control over his creation

spirit—The quality, power, or force within persons that makes them open to relationship with God; the Spirit of God

wrath of God—God's consistent response opposing and punishing sin

Yahweh—The Hebrew personal name of God revealed to Moses; this name came to be thought of as too holy to pronounce by Jews; often translated LORD or Jehovah

Bibliography

Any commentator stands on the shoulders of others. The works listed below will be of benefit to any student of the books of Judges and Ruth. Three sources must be mentioned as invaluable: Daniel I. Block, *Judges, Ruth* (Broadman & Holman, 1999); Leon Wood; *The Distressing Days of the Judges* (Zondervan, 1975); and Robert L. Hubbard, *The Book of Ruth* (Eerdmans, 1988). The comprehensive work of Daniel Block, which is the most complete volume on both books available, was of particular benefit. While I did not always adopt Block's conclusions, I am deeply indebted to him for tackling all issues and discussing all options.

Barber, Cyril J. *Judges: A Narrative of God's Power.* Neptune, N.J.: Loizeaux Brothers, 1990.

Block, Daniel I. *Judges, Ruth.* The New American Commentary. Edited by E. Ray Clendenen. Nashville, Tenn.: Broadman & Holman, 1999.

Boling, R. G. *Judges.* Garden City, N.J.: Doubleday, 1975.

Constable, Thomas L. "A Theology of Joshua, Judges, and Ruth." In *A Biblical Theology of the Old Testament.* Edited by Roy B. Zuck. Chicago: Moody Press, 1991.

Cundall, Arthur E. *Judges.* Tyndale Old Testament Commentaries. Edited by D. J. Wiseman. Downers Grove, Ill.: InterVarsity Press, 1968.

Elwell, Walter A., editor. *Evangelical Dictionary of Theology.* 2nd ed. Grand Rapids, Mich.: Baker Book House, 2001.

Gundry, Stanley, editor. *Show Them No Mercy: Four Views on God and Canaanite Genocide.* Grand Rapids, Mich.: Zondervan, 2003.

Harrison, Roland K. *Introduction to the Old Testament.* Grand Rapids, Mich.: Eerdmans, 1969.

Howard, David M. *An Introduction to the Old Testament Historical Books.* Chicago: Moody Press, 1993.

Hubbard, Robert L. *The Book of Ruth.* Grand Rapids, Mich.: Eerdmans, 1988.

Huey, F. B. *Ruth.* In The Expositor's Bible Commentary. Edited by Frank E. Gaebelein. Grand Rapids, Mich.: Zondervan, 1992.

Inrig, Gary. *Hearts of Iron, Feet of Clay.* Chicago: Moody Press, 1979.

Kaiser, Walter C. *Hard Sayings of the Old Testament.* Downers Grove, Ill.: InterVarsity Press, 1988.

_____. *Toward Old Testament Ethics.* Grand Rapids, Mich.: Zondervan, 1983.

Kitchen, Kenneth A. *Ancient Orient and the Old Testament.* Downers Grove, Ill.: InterVarsity Press, 1966.

Lindsey, F. Duane. "Judges." In *The Bible Knowledge Commentary: Old Testament.* Edited by John F. Walvoord and Roy B. Zuck. Wheaton, Ill.: Victor Books, 1985.

Merrill, Eugene H. *An Historical Survey of the Old Testament.* Grand Rapids, Mich.: Baker, 1991.

_____. "The Book of Ruth: Narration and Shared Themes." *Bibliotheca Sacra,* 142:566 (1985).

Moore, G. F. *A Critical and Exegetical Commentary on the Judges.* 2nd ed. International Critical Commentary. Edinburgh: T. & T. Clark, 1908.

Morris, Leon. *Ruth.* Tyndale Old Testament Commentaries. Edited by D. J. Wiseman. Downers Grove, Ill.: InterVarsity Press, 1968.

Slotki, Judah J. *Judges: Introduction and Commentary.* In The Soncino Books of the Bible. Edited by A. Cohen. London: The Soncino Press, 1950.

Tenney, Merrill C., editor. *The Zondervan Pictorial Encyclopedia of the Bible.* Grand Rapids, Mich.: Zondervan, 1975.

Wolf, Herbert. *Judges.* In The Expositor's Bible Commentary. Edited by Frank E. Gaebelein. Grand Rapids, Mich.: Zondervan, 1992.

Wood, Leon. *A Survey of Israel's History.* Grand Rapids, Mich.: Zondervan, 1970.

_____. *The Distressing Days of the Judges.* Grand Rapids, Mich.: Zondervan, 1975.